TALES OF THE HASIDIM

★ ★

THE LATER MASTERS

MARTIN BUBER

TALES OF THE HASIDIM

★ ★

THE LATER MASTERS

SCHOCKEN BOOKS / NEW YORK

Translated by Olga Marx

14 13 12   87

Library of Congress Catalog Card No. 47-2952

Printed in the United States of America
ISBN 0-8052-0002-9

TABLE OF CONTENTS

INTRODUCTION

The period which followed the first three generations of hasidism is usually treated as one of incipient decline. But that is an over-simplification of what really happened. Confronted by such a development, we must always ask what elements of the movement before us exhibit a deterioration which can, nevertheless, go hand in hand with the enrichment, ramification, and even strengthening of other elements.

There is no doubt that the crude power characteristic of the outset of hasidism lessened during this second epoch, which mainly occupies the first half of the nineteenth century, though certain of the exponents of hasidism lived past that time. The main outlines of the first hasidic tidings and struggles become complicated or blurred, and the sacred passion to bring heaven and earth closer to each other often gives place to the kind of organized religiosity we can trace in every great religious movement which persists past the generations of awakening and revolt. But at the same time comes a variety and abundance of new spiritual life which does not, it is true, deepen the basic ideas of hasidism in any essential respect, but does expand the province in which these ideas can be realized and applies them to the problems of everyday life to a far greater extent than before. The form in which these ideas are expressed has less elemental vigor but often more brilliance. Aphorisms, parables, and symbolic fairy tales which up to that time occurred only as the naive, witty, but unfinished improvisations of genius, achieve literary perfection.

The real problems of the second period are not apparent in the sphere of the spirit and teachings of hasidism, but in that of its inner structure. They emerge in three different sets of relationship: that of the zaddik to the congregation, of the zaddikim and their congregations to one another, and that of the zaddik to his school. In this second period of hasidism all three relationships are occasionally affected by noteworthy and serious changes.

It is common to both periods for the zaddik usually to be "hidden" at first, and only subsequently to "reveal" himself, i.e., let it be known that heaven has called him to its service. In addition to this call there generally is a teacher who appoints him to his office and vouches for him. In other words: The community receives its leader from "on high," directly through the manifest grace of heaven that rests upon him, and indirectly through his election and appointment by his teacher, whose own vocation, in turn, provides the basis for this act. It is only when one of the great teachers dies and the question arises who among his disciples is to succeed him, and then only if there is neither agreement nor schism, that the hasidim themselves make the decision. This is not done according to any prescribed formula, but always in a way suggested and determined by the current situation. If we are to believe legend— and the legendary incidents we are told of correspond to similar known incidents in the history of religion—a decision of this kind is always made and accepted as something mysterious. The congregation is fused to an unprecedented entity, and as such, feeling the will of heaven internally as it were, dares to fulfil that will. In the second period the instances of such decisions multiply. They occur both when a zaddik dies sonless, as well as when he leaves behind a son who is considered a candidate for the succession.

A conversation which has been handed down to us is characteristic of this altered situation. It took place between Rabbi Mendel of Kotzk (a great and tragic figure whom it would be more precise to include in the fourth generation though he really belongs to the fifth) and young Mendel of Vorki, the son of his friend Rabbi Yitzhak of Vorki, nine months after Yitzhak's death. The rabbi of Kotzk is trying to discover who will succeed his friend, for Mendel has rather avoided becoming the successor than striven for that honor. The rabbi of Kotzk asks: "What about the 'world'?" [i.e., the congregation]. His disciple replies: "The world stands" [i.e., the question of the succession has not yet been solved]. Then the rabbi continues: "They say that you will take over the world." And young Mendel answers: "If that were so, I should have a feeling." In conclusion the zaddik says: "They say it is the hasidim who make a rabbi." Thereupon Mendel of Vorki replies: "I was never eager to accept alms." By that he meant that he did not wish to receive the gift of heaven from the hands of the congregation and that he did not recognize their authority, but kept to the great hasidic tradition.

What he is resisting in this way is expressed very clearly in a bitter jest uttered by Rabbi Mendel of Rymanov, a zaddik who lived during the time of the transition from the first period to the second. "If a thousand believing hasidim were to gather around a block of wood," said he, "it too would work miracles." It is obvious that he was using the word "believing" to mean superstitious. These hasidim do not believe that heaven has chosen a zaddik and sent him to them, but that the congregation has the right to have a true zaddik and therefore not merely receives but can even "make" him. The natural consequence of such a point of view is that zaddikim whose aptitude for their vocation is dubious multiply. "One ought not to take the chair until one hears Elijah's call." This saying illustrates the stand of the true zaddikim; the dubious think otherwise.

A second problem rose from the fact that there was a large number of zaddikim but no superior authority, a multiplicity which must be understood as one of the chief bases of the hasidic movement. Historically, hasidism is the reply to the crisis in messianism. The way to hasidism, to the concentrated attempt to preserve the reality of God for the Jew, was paved by the extreme antinomian development of the Sabbatian movement, whose followers thought they could divest the God of Israel of his character of teacher of the right way and still have a Jewish God. Jacob Frank's enterprise, which ran grotesquely amuck and took the final leap into a kind of nihilism draped in mythology, had shown wakeful souls that not only sections of the Jewish people but the whole community was on the edge of the abyss, and this realization had led the most valuable forces to hasidism.

Bitter experience pointed to the necessity of preventing the people from again putting their faith in any single human. Hasidism succeeded in this, on the one hand by setting up the classical picture of biblical eschatology in contrast to the aftermath of the Sabbatian theology, by renewing the concept of the altogether human executor of the divine will to redemption. On the other hand, hasidism repudiated every possible tendency in the direction of endowing a human being with divine attributes, as had happened in those last messianic movements. Not a speck of the idea of incarnation ever attached itself to the Baal Shem, either in regard to his teachings or to the legend which grew around him.

But even more; out of a conscious or unconscious sense of danger (it does not matter which), the structure of the hasidic community was fundamentally characterized by a multiplicity which could not merge into a unity. Every congregation was autonomous and subject to no superior authority. The zaddikim were under no superior leadership. Even the Great Maggid, who headed a hasidic community composed of a number of congregations, did not desire to be anything but a teacher. While in the succeeding generations we find zaddikim competing for higher rank, the rivalry between them being reflected by their congregations, no one laid serious claim to exclusive validity.

Not until the second period did this rivalry degenerate into mutual exclusion. The most striking instance is the quarrel between "Zans" (Rabbi Hayyim of Zans) and "Sadagora" (Rabbi Abraham Yaakov of Sadagora and his brothers) which revived the methods once prevalent in altercation between hasidim and their adversaries (mitnagdim), even to the point of ban and counterban.

What lay behind all this becomes evident in the unmistakable utterances of the rabbi of Zans, who cited the legend of the rivalry between the sun and the moon and the sun's statement that it is not possible for two kings to wear the same crown. Those zaddikim who realized the danger took a firm stand against such deviations from the hasidic way. It is from this point of view that we must interpret the words of Rabbi Hirsh of Zhydatchov, a distinguished disciple of the Seer of Lublin, who said that for hasidim to regard theirs as the only true rabbi is idol worship. But we also find utterances in which plurality is raised to an absolute which verges on the ridiculous, as for example, when the grandson of a distinguished hasidic thinker said that every zaddik should be the Messiah to his hasidim.

The third relationship, that of the zaddik to his school: In the beginnings of hasidism the idea of rivalry between master and disciple never entered the mind of either. On the one hand, the disciple's devotion to his master exerted so powerful a force over his entire life that the thought of acting against the will of his teacher could never occur to him. On the other hand, the teacher, far from seeing his pupils as potential rivals, made those he considered fit for such an office heads of congregations where they served the movement as his representatives, as it were. As an example of this, read how the Great Maggid in truly biblical fashion invests Rabbi Menahem Mendel with belt and staff and appoints him rabbi.

There was a change in the very next generation, toward the end of the first period. Rabbi Elimelekh of Lizhensk, who succeeded to the Great Maggid's teachings, would not suffer his disciples to lead congregations of their own during his lifetime. When one of them, who later became the Seer of Lublin, nevertheless assumed such leadership, a deep and permanent tension resulted. Legend even has it that Rabbi Elimelekh's curse had a fatal effect on those who became the followers of his disciple.

But the same relationship, only in a more acute and complicated form, obtained between the Seer of Lublin and certain of his disciples; it brought gloomy tragedy when the Seer falsely accused the Yehudi, his noblest disciple, of competing with him, and finally—if we may trust the tradition—drove him to his death. There is an oral tradition that the Seer said repeatedly that the Yehudi was above him ("he walks on a higher plane than we"), but that he, the Seer, had been appointed to his place by Rabbi Elimelekh—an utterance which is very strange when viewed in the light of all these occurrences, but undoubtedly reflects the speaker's consciousness.

11

At this point, though a disciple's leading a congregation was disapproved, still it was endured. In the succeeding generation however, it was generally accepted almost as law that a disciple should not found his own congregation during his teacher's lifetime. Thus a fundamental principle of the hasidic movement, one we might term the inner apostolate, is abandoned. The master no longer sends forth his tried and proven disciples to supplement his work of teaching and construction with their own, each in his autonomous domain; he keeps them chained to himself and his house, and thus prejudices the activities of the movement.

These and similar phenomena are the reason for the sharp criticism which distinguished zaddikim of the second period pronounced upon the zaddikism of their time. After the Yehudi had spoken of the types of leaders who led former generations, and were followed by the zaddikim, he added: "That is why I sigh: I see that the present too will be corrupted. What will Israel do then?"

Another zaddik refuses to expound the hasidic teachings ("say Torah"), because he notes that the instruction of certain zaddikim no longer guards the original complete purity of the hasidic teachings, and that lurking demons might fall upon the teaching and drag them into their realm. It is particularly significant that some descendants of great zaddikim do not want to become rabbis—a son and a grandson of Rabbi Elimelekh's, for instance.

A zaddik of the sixth generation, the grandson of a grandson of the Great Maggid, gives vehement expression to his resentment at a decline which was already apparent. This was Rabbi Dov Baer of Leva, a son of the famous Rabbi Israel of Rizhyn, who went so far as to leave the hasidic camp for a time and fled to the camp of the "enlightened." (This was the incident which set off the quarrel between the followers of Zans and those of Sadagora.)

Rabbi Dov Baer often told a story which ostensibly was about his ancestor, the Great Maggid, but actually referred only to his and not the Maggid's situation. "A tenant farmer," so he told, "once came to the Maggid of Mezritch to ask his help in a matter having to do with his affairs. 'Is it me you are asking?' the Maggid inquired. 'Do you really mean me?' The man replied: 'I ask the rabbi to pray for me in this matter.'— 'Wouldn't it be better,' said the Maggid, 'if you were to ask me to teach you how to pray to God? Then you wouldn't have to come to me any more.' "

In these words which could not by any stretch of the imagination have come from the lips of the Great Maggid, but resemble similar utterances by zaddikim of the second period, despair over the decline of zaddikism has turned into doubt of its very basis. In the early days of hasidism the zaddik also guided his hasidim to a direct relationship with God, but he did not believe that merely teaching people how to pray meant that the man who is an intermediary between heaven and earth could be dispensed with. For, according to the hasidic concept, external help as such is not what matters; it is only the outer husk which makes an inner form of help possible.

This idea emerges most clearly in a story told by Rabbi Shalom Shakhna, the grandson of the Great Maggid and the grandfather of the rabbi of Leva. He tells how a tenant farmer came to him before the beginning of the Sabbath and confided his trouble: that one of his calves was ailing. "And from his words," says the rabbi, "I heard him imploring me: 'You are a lofty soul and I am a lowly soul. Lift me up to yourself!' " Thus the expedient of external help is not to be abandoned in the least; for teaching how to pray cannot in itself be the true "elevation," and the experience of being uplifted is not a unique event. It is by its very nature a process which is interrupted only by death and, according to a concept we occasionally encounter, not necessarily even then.

Hasidism enters upon its decline when the zaddikim no longer give their hasidim inner help along with and through external help. For here, everything is based on the relationship between zaddikim and hasidim, a living relationship which is all-inclusive and penetrates to the innermost core. When that is lacking, then indeed "the present too will be corrupted."

The series of zaddikim treated in this volume must needs begin with the descendants of the Maggid of Mezritch, with the "Sadagora dynasty." This sequence is essentially different from the succession of the Maggid's disciples, and the disciples of the disciples. Even his son Abraham—as we know from Tales of the Hasidim: The Early Masters—showed his definite opposition to him and his teachings by choosing the way of radical asceticism.

Abraham's son Shalom Shakhna (d. 1802) swerved sharply from his father's path without, however, returning to that of his grandfather. He was educated by Rabbi Nahum of Tchernobil, one of the most faithful disciples of the Baal Shem and the Maggid, and later married his granddaughter.

Shalom expressed his striving toward innovation in his every act. His rich clothing and splendid manner set him apart from his environment, but these outward manifestations apparently symbolized a definite trend and probably because of this people liked to say that his soul was a "spark" of King David's. When his father-in-law reproached him, he replied with the parable of the hen who hatched duck's eggs and then surveyed the swimming ducklings in great dismay. He emphatically rejected Nahum's miracle cures, for while he too wanted to help sufferers, it was to be with the strength of his soul and according to the needs of the moment rather than through the usual magical procedures. To him, all help that came from the outside was only the point of departure and the husk of an inner help.

He surrounded himself with a group of young men who were passionately devoted to him. The conflict between them and their fathers' generation flared up time and again, and that— according to their ideas—was as it should be, for Rabbi Shalom, so we are told, had said: "That which is a result of good cannot take place without opposition." There is even a peculiar story (which I heard in a version still stranger than the one preserved in writing) that Rabbi Shalom made himself appear sinful in public for the purpose of outwitting Satan. For Satan was considered sovereign over Israel in exile, but the secret of redemption was also supposed to have been confided to him, and so Shalom pretended to be sinful in order to gain Satan's confidence and worm the secret out of him. One is tempted to interpret this as an after effect of the Sabbatian tenet of holy sin.

There are several indications that Rabbi Shalom strove to be more than a zaddik. One is the answer he gave Rabbi Barukh, a grandson of the Baal Shem. When Barukh, a proud and imperious man, visited him and suggested: "Let us both lead the world" (world, in this connection, referred to the hasidic community as the center of Israel), he replied: "I can lead the world by myself." But in saying this he was not thinking of reviving the office of exilarch, as has been supposed. His words sprang from the belief in the potential messianic mission of a family in which the potential could become actual in every generation.

Like his father, Rabbi Shalom died young, and before his death had a vision which he told to his son Israel, which allows a deep understanding of this belief. He saw a zaddik sitting in one of the halls of heaven. On the table in front of him lay a magnificent crown shaped out of his teachings and his holiness. But the zaddik was not permitted to place the crown on his head. "I have told you about it," Rabbi Shalom added, "because some day you may need to know it."

His son, Rabbi Israel of Rizhyn (d. 1850), not only adopted his father's manner but carried it further, so that the ceremonial and ritual of his household made it appear like the court of a priest-king. He himself put into words the dynastic character implicit in his mode of life, for he compared Rabbi Abraham Yehoshua Heshel, the old rav of Apt who was generally accepted as "the leader of his generation," to Moses the teacher, but himself to Solomon the king; and the rabbi of Apt himself dubbed him a king in Israel. The throngs which swarmed to his house honored him as such.

It was in this light that his activities were reported to the Czarist regime which arrested him as a leader of the Jews, regarded by them as their king. After two years in prison (for the most part in Kiev) he was liberated and soon afterward fled to Galicia. After much wandering and travail, he settled in Sadagora (Bukovina), which became the goal of mass pilgrimages. But many zaddikim came as well, especially the younger zaddikim, paid homage to him, and delighted in his conversation. Scarcely one among them however became his disciple. He did not wish to bind anyone to himself. He wanted visitors who hung on his words, not disciples who entailed a sustained mutual relationship.

Like the Great Maggid, Rabbi Israel was a distinguished expounder of the Torah, in the hasidic manner, but his homilies are not parts of a unified thinking life. They are sudden lightning conceits—not the work of a fragmentist, like those of the Great Maggid, but of an aphorist, for they flash with the luxuriance of multi-faceted jewels, while the works of the fragmentist show the deep sparkle of plain-cut stones. Modern Western civilization would have called the rabbi of Rizhyn a brilliant improviser, and weighed in the scale of values of that civilization, he was certainly a genius; but he was no longer the vessel and the voice of the religious spirit.

His six sons were gifted epigoni. They too still had something of the spiritual world of the Great Maggid, but it no longer developed into mature personal form. Almost all of them had followers, drew crowds, held court, had congregations and influence; not one of them had disciples. The noblest of his sons, Rabbi David Moshe of Tchortkov (d. 1903), was tender and humane to all creatures. In my youth I spent several summers not far from his home, but I did not make his acquaintance.

Another of his sons, whom I have already mentioned, Rabbi Dov Baer, named for his great-grandfather, was first considered the most notable of the six and attracted the greatest number of people. Later he joined the so-called "enlightened" group and wrote letters in the nature of manifestoes against superstition. This phase, however, lasted only a short while. He returned to Sadagora and remained there from that time on in a sort of half-voluntary confinement. His life merely expressed the situation: the king's highway had come to a dead end.

Since Rabbi Mendel of Vitebsk did not found a school in Palestine, the first place among the disciples of the Maggid must be assigned to Rabbi Shmelke of Nikolsburg, a great preacher, singer of songs, and friend to all humanity. None of his disciples ever equaled him in preaching, but Rabbi Yitzhak Eisik of Kalev fell heir to his gift of song, while Rabbi Moshe Leib of Sasov inherited his love for mankind.

Rabbi Yitzhak Eisik of Kalev (Nagy-Kallo in the north of Hungary; d. 1828) came from a Hungarian village and absorbed its peasant vitality in his childhood. Tradition has it that he tended geese. He not only used the tunes he had learned from the herdsmen for sacral hymns or psalms, such as "By the waters of Babylon," but—without having to make too many changes—converted some of the texts into Jewish mystical verses. The sadness of the pastoral songs is turned into the suffering in exile, their yearning for love into the longing for the Divine Presence. The "unknown melodies" of Rabbi Shmelke played an important part in this transformation, but the rabbi of Kalev's songs were said to have been even more sensuous and enchanting, probably because of the folk elements which entered into them.

His deep attachment to the folk element is illustrated by the curious fact that he always recited the Passover Haggadah in Hungarian. It is told that on the evening of the Seder Rabbi Shmelke could hear all his disciples reciting the Haggadah in their various homes far from Nikolsburg, all except the rabbi of Kalev, because he was speaking Hungarian.

Another instance of his love for the folk element is the story that he had inherited the melody of the hymn "Mighty in dominion . . ." from the Great Maggid, who had learned it from a shepherd. But, so the tale continues, the tune had been in exile with the shepherd, for originally the Levites had sung it in the Temple. This tune, incidentally, returned to the family of the Maggid via the rabbi of Kalev, if the tradition is correct, for Rabbi David Moshe of Tchortkov was fond of singing it.

Many other songs of the rabbi of Kalev spread among his

hasidim. There was Rabbi Hayyim of Zans, for example, who on a Friday evening, when he had paced around the platform in the synagogue seven times, would sing the rabbi of Kalev's song of yearning for the reunion with the "bride," the Divine Presence, until "his bodily strength failed him, because of the vehemence of his ecstasy."

Rabbi Moshe Leib of Sasov (d. 1807) followed his teacher from one Polish village to the next, and from Poland to Nikolsburg. Legend links him with Rabbi Shmelke in miracle tales. We need hardly touch upon him in this introduction, since the stories in themselves suffice to give a clear picture of him. His soul developed the gift of the helpful love which Rabbi Shmelke had roused within him to a level of perfection unusual even in hasidism, a movement so rich in those who knew how to love. A ravishing spontaneity quickened his love and zeal toward both man and beast. In his case, the paradox of the commandment to love one's neighbor as oneself, seems resolved. (Can one love in obedience to command?) And yet even the rabbi of Sasov came up against inner obstacles. He could not love those malicious or self-assured men who disrupt the world. But that was just the sort of thing his teacher used to speak of: that one must love every soul because it is a part of God, or rather that one cannot help loving a soul the moment one grows aware that it is a part of God. And so, since he was very serious in his love for God, the rabbi of Sasov came to love His creatures more and more perfectly. The true meaning of the command to love manifests itself in the inner obstacles to its fulfilment, and in their overcoming.

In order to show the rabbi of Sasov's influence on his immediate circle, the next section of this volume deals with his disciple Rabbi Mendel of Kosov (d. 1825), whose life and work continue the line of love for humanity. He is said to have made especially radical formulations of the belief that the love for one's neighbor is only another side of the love of God. An instance of this is an interpretation he once gave to the

18

words in the Scriptures: "Love thy neighbor as thyself; I am the Lord." He explained: "If a man loves his fellow, the Divine Presence rests with them." And, on another occasion: "The union of loving neighbors effects unity in the upper world." We know that his son Hayyim never ceased in his efforts to have his hasidim live together like good neighbors, to know, help, keep one another company, and love one another.

In Tales of the Hasidim: The Early Masters, I included the Maggid of Koznitz and the Seer of Lublin, both disciples of Rabbi Elimelekh, because they were first disciples of the Great Maggid and may thus be assigned to the third generation. Two others, Rabbi Abraham Yehoshua Heshel of Apt (d. 1825) and Rabbi Menahem Mendel of Rymanov (d. 1815) belong in this volume. It is said that before he died Rabbi Elimelekh left his tongue's judging power to the rabbi of Apt and his spirit's guiding power to the rabbi of Rymanov.

The rabbi of Apt was noted for his judicious character, he discharged the office of judge and arbiter among the hasidim and even the zaddikim of his time. It was through error and effort that he arrived at his profound conception of true justice. He started out with what we usually call justice, i.e., with the wish to be just, but then he learned step by step that human justice as such fails when it attempts to exceed the province of a just social order and encroaches on that of just human relationships.
He learned that God's justice is not in the same category as his love which is the perfection of an attribute we can at least endeavor to imitate, but is something enigmatic which defies comparison with anything men call justice and law. Man should be just within the bounds of his social order, but when he ventures beyond it out on the high seas of human relationships, he is sure to be shipwrecked and then all he can do is to save himself by clinging to love.
The turning point in the life of the rabbi of Apt is, very

probably, the incident related in this book of how he publicly reproved a woman of loose morals, but then, comparing his own attitude with that of God, was overcome and became a changed man. But he did not regard his way to love as that of one individual living on earth; he saw it in connection with the migrations of his soul and realized that he had the task of perfecting that love during their course.

Rabbi Mendel of Rymanov differed from the rabbi of Apt both in his character and his life. He had fallen heir to his teacher's ability to organize, but practiced it within narrower bounds. Of the three circles which surround the zaddik, the disciples, the congregation, and the "transients," he was most concerned with the second. He issued laws to his congregation as if it were a state, and it was more real to him than the state. He did not presume to be just: he simply watched over the just order of those in his charge. When he was forced to reprove, his words penetrated like a natural force to the very heart of the incident which had evoked his censure. And so when it was necessary to preserve custom and maintain order, he who was noted for his sobriety could rise to heights of archaic majesty. This happened when, to rouse and fuse his congregation which was (as congregations always are) in danger of becoming stolid, he spoke to them as God's instituted deputy, liberated them from the compulsion exerted by the Torah and left them free to make their choice anew. To his disciples his power over "the word" made him the model of a man whose every utterance reflects his sense of responsibility.

Rabbi Zevi Hirsh of Rymanov (d. 1846), the disciple who became Rabbi Mendel's successor, was the real "self-made man" among the zaddikim of the second period. He was first apprenticed to a tailor and then became a servant in Rabbi Mendel's house. There he practiced the wisdom and art of serving on so high a plane that the zaddik soon recognized him as a rare human vessel capable of receiving teachings. He accepted young Hirsh as his disciple, but even in that capacity he went on serving the zaddik. He continued his studies for twelve years after his master's death, and then to everyone's surprise assumed the succession.

He was soon recognized by the other zaddikim and occupied a powerful position of a particular kind. Though at times he conducted himself in a haughty manner, he was very humble at heart and often said of his simple and at the same time profound sermons that he only uttered what he had been told to say; sometimes he could not even remember a sermon when he had finished preaching it.

It is also noteworthy that he often asked substantial amounts of money from persons who came to request his intercession. In such cases he named an exact sum, whose numerals were apparently chosen for their mystical significance. On the other hand, he was in the habit of distributing among the needy whatever money he had in the house. It was a sort of redistribution of goods which he practiced among his hasidim, obviously prompted by the feeling that it was his mission to direct superfluous possessions to where they were needed.

Rabbi Shelomo of Karlin, who was known for his great power in prayer, founded a school of ecstatic praying.

His most renowned disciple, who developed his teaching of giving up one's very life in prayer, was Rabbi Uri of Strelisk (d. 1826), called the "Seraph." In this connection ecstatic prayer is not a merely personal transaction; it includes both the zaddik and his hasidim. Almost all of Rabbi Uri's hasidim were poor, but not one of them turned to him in order to attain well-being. All they wanted was to pray together with him, to pray as he prayed, and like him, to give away their life in prayer.

The impression of his marvelous praying was transferred to their whole relationship to him, which became the glorification of a visionary. They really regarded him as a seraph. One hasid tells how he could see that the rabbi had more than one face, another that the rabbi grew taller and taller before his eyes, until he reached up into heaven. The hasidim relate that once when the synagogue had been polluted by the impure prayers of the Sabbatians, his mighty prayers made it burn to the ground the very next evening. But they also tell that the workday week did not begin until he had said the Benediction of Separation (Havdalah) at the close of the Sabbath. Until then the keys to hell were in his hand, and the souls released over the Sabbath could hover in the atmosphere.

Before his death Rabbi Uri ordained Rabbi Yehudah Zevi of Stretyn (d. 1844) to the succession by the laying on of hands recalling the ordination of Joshua by Moses.

Legend has it that he too had possession of the keys to hell over the Sabbath, but the motif is elaborated: all the night after the Sabbath, a hasid saw him standing at an open window, still dressed in his Sabbath clothes, and holding in his hand a great key which he could not bear to lay aside. All the while swarms of evil angels lurked around him, waiting for morning when his strength would fail.

It was his custom to take the ritual bath at night in a river outside the town, and it was said that while he stood in the water he would recite the entire Book of Psalms.

The most outstanding feature of Rabbi Yehudah Zevi's teaching was his emphatic affirmation of the unity of the attributes of God, the unity of God's Rigor and His Mercy.

Rabbi Yehudah's son, Rabbi Abraham of Stretyn (d. 1865), left the world a significant teaching of human unity: that man can bring about such unity between his faculties, that each of his senses can substitute for another and take over its function.

Besides Rabbi Uri of Strelisk, Rabbi Shelomo of Karlin had a second distinguished disciple: Rabbi Mordecai of Lekhovitz (d. 1811), who added new and concrete features to the teaching of giving one's life to prayer. He taught that he who prays should give himself up to his Lord with every word he utters, and he illustrated this by the parable of the legendary bird whose song of praise bursts its own body. Man's entire physical being must enter into every word of his prayer so that it may even "rise from his heel." It is said that Rabbi Mordecai's lung was torn by the fervor of his praying.

But his whole attitude toward life was joyful. Only in joy can the soul be truly raised to God, and "he who wishes to serve God with devotion, and divine light, and joy, and willingness, must have a spirit that is bright, and pure, and clear, and a body that is full of life."

Rabbi Mordecai's son, Rabbi Noah of Lekhovitz (d. 1834), continued along his father's lines though he was more worldly in his outlook. But even among the utterances of Rabbi Noah's grandson, Rabbi Shelomo Hayyim of Kaidanov (d. 1862), we still find sayings informed with the energy of the rabbi of Karlin's teachings on prayer.

Rabbi Shelomo's school reached a late peak in a man who was first Rabbi Mordecai's, and subsequently Rabbi Noah's disciple: Rabbi Moshe of Kobryn (d. 1858). I do not hesitate to count this little-known man among the few late-born great men which the hasidic movement produced in the very midst of its decline. While he did not enrich the teaching, his life and words and the unity between his life and his words lent it a very personal, refreshingly vital expression.

Three sayings suffice to give the gist of his philosophy: "You shall become an altar before God"; "There is nothing in the world which does not contain a commandment"; and "Just as God is limitless, so his service is limitless."

These teachings are integrated with a life which by imaging and exemplifying them, sometimes recalls the early masters of hasidism. For the rest, what is told about him in this book requires no further supplementation or explanation.

Rabbi Hayyim Meir Yehiel of Mogielnica (d. 1849), the grandson of the Maggid of Koznitz, was the most notable among the disciples of that holy man of suffering, who prophesied from the depths of his suffering. Other zaddikim besides his grandfather were his teachers, namely, the rabbi of Apt and the

Seer of Lublin, and he was also close to the Seer's disciple, the Yehudi of Pzhysha, who had so many enemies. Hayyim collected teachings without becoming an eclectic, for though he was not an independent thinker, he had a strong and independent soul which melted all matter received from the outside in the crucible of his own feeling and experience.

Two of his utterances serve to characterize him: "I have no use for spiritual rungs without the garment of the body"; and "I never wanted to win anything without working for it myself." He had insight into himself and liked to tell his hasidim what was happening within his soul. He enjoyed "telling" in any event, and talked readily and freely.

The relationship between him and his hasidim was one of great intimacy; every gesture of his made a lasting impression on them and they served him with love. The disciple for whom his influence was most fruitful was Rabbi Yisakhar of Wolborz (d. 1876).

The rest of this volume gives the story of the school of Lublin and the schools it influenced, including the significant schools of Pzhysha and Kotzk. These developed under the influence of Lublin, especially of the great personality of the Seer, and yet in opposition to both.

Tales of the Hasidim: The Early Masters included ten disciples of Mezritch. Similarly, this volume treats nine of the many disciples of the Seer of Lublin. They are: Rabbi David of Lelov (d. 1813), Rabbi Moshe Teitelbaum of Ohel (Ujhely in Hungary; d. 1841), Rabbi Yisakhar Baer of Radoshitz (d. 1843), Rabbi Shelomo Leib of Lentshno (d. 1843), Rabbi Naftali of Roptchitz (d. 1827), Rabbi Shalom of Belz (d. 1855), Rabbi Zevi Hirsh of Zhydatchov (d. 1831), Rabbi Yaakov Yitzhak of Pzhysha, known as the "Yehudi" (d. 1813), and Rabbi Simha Bunam of Pzhysha (d. 1827). (For the sake of inner relatedness, I have taken them in this non-chronological sequence; and I have not included Rabbi Menahem Mendel of Kotzk, although he was for a time a disciple of the Seer; but have dealt with him in connection with the school of Pzhysha, because he himself never failed to stress that he belonged to Pzhysha rather than to the school of Lublin.)

David of Lelov was one of the most lovable figures in hasidism. He was wise and at the same time childlike, open to all creatures, yet retaining his secret heart, alien to sin and yet protecting the sinner from his persecutors.

He is a notable example of a zaddik who could not become what he was until the truth of hasidism had freed him from his ascetic outlook on the world. He owed this liberation to Rabbi Elimelekh.

The Seer of Lublin was his next teacher, with whom he kept faith throughout his life even though he was, and could not but be, opposed to him in basic issues, while siding whole-heartedly with his friend the Yehudi in the quarrels between Lublin and Pzhysha.

For a long time he refused to be regarded as a zaddik, in spite of the fact that he had numerous reverent followers who compared this unpretentious man to King David, probably with more reason than other zaddikim. For a considerable period of his life he worked in his little shop and frequently sent customers to other shopkeepers who were poorer than he.

He liked to travel through the country, visit unknown village Jews, and warm their hearts with his brotherly words. In the small towns he gathered children about him, took them for drives, and played and made music with them. In the market place he fed and watered animals which had been left untended, as the rabbi of Sasov had done before him. He was particularly fond of horses and went into vehement explanations of how senseless it is to beat them. Because he was more devoted to his own family than to mankind at large, he declared that he was not worthy to be called a zaddik.

He believed that his most important mission was to keep peace among men; that was why—so tradition has it—he had been granted the power of making peace wherever there was enmity by his mere prayer. He taught that one should not reprimand and exhort persons whom one wishes to turn to God, but associate with them like a good friend, quiet the tumult in their hearts and through love lead them to recognize God. This was the method by which he himself led to the right way many who had strayed. (Outstanding among these was a famous physician, Dr. Bernhard, whom the rabbi of Lelov took to the Seer of Lublin, where the doctor developed into a hasid living on a very high rung.)

Rabbi David's own life provided the conclusive example for his teachings. "Everything he did, every day and every hour," said Rabbi Yitzhak of Vorki who studied with him for a time, "was the statute and the word of the Torah."

As Rabbi Elimelekh freed the rabbi of Lelov from the bonds of asceticism, so Rabbi Elimelekh's disciple, the Seer of Lublin, freed Rabbi Moshe Teitelbaum from his preoccupation with scholarliness which isolated him from the world. The Seer recognized in his soul the true flame which only lacked the proper fuel; whoever has that flame is already a hasid at heart, no matter how much he may be opposed to the hasidic way.

Many things had prepared Rabbi Moshe for this way, among others his curious dreams of which we have records, some from the time of his youth. In these dream experiences—including encounters with the masters of the Kabbalah from bygone ages, whom he watched at their secret work—he learned to realize how little good deeds avail if the man who does them is not devoted to God with all his soul, and that both paradise and hell are within the human spirit.

At that point, the Seer became his teacher and taught him the true hasidic joy, but it was not easy for him to reach that state. It was said that Rabbi Moshe was a "spark" from the soul of the prophet Jeremiah. All his life he had sorrowed very deeply for the destruction of the Temple and of Israel. When he learned joy, his hope in the Messiah triumphed over his sorrow, for this hope had an extraordinary sensuous force. No other zaddik is reported to have had such vigorous and concrete faith in the Messiah at every instant of his life.

Rabbi Yisakhar Baer of Radoshitz was known far and wide as a miracle worker and especially famed for his miraculous cures. Chief among these were his cures of "dibbukim," of those who were possessed by demons, and they even gained him the name of "the little Baal Shem." He seems to have had this tendency toward the miraculous from youth on, although for a long time he did not venture to try out his inner powers and was known only as a shy and quiet man. We are told a characteristic incident of his youth: that he accompanied Rabbi Moshe Leib of Sasov on a journey and suggested to Rabbi Moshe Leib his own magical methods of which he himself was not yet aware.

But still stranger than this is the fact that he, who went from one zaddik to another, and after leaving the Seer finally attached himself to the Yehudi, kept his reverence for miracles intact even with this new teacher, the very air around whom was hostile to the miraculous. The tradition affords some explanation for this, for we are told that when the Yehudi's son fell ill, the father himself turned to Rabbi Yisakhar Baer, whose slumbering healing powers he had apparently divined and now decided to actualize. Without any faith in his own gift, in the urgent need of the moment, Rabbi Yisakhar took the child in his arms, laid it in the cradle, rocked it, prayed, and succeeded in healing it.

Many years later, when the school of Pzhysha had produced the last great hasidic school, that of Kotzk, with its atmosphere of tragedy, and the hasidim in both camps, Kotzk and Radoshitz, were opposing one another, Rabbi Yisakhar is said to have uttered a paradox which defined the principle of Kotzk as being the surrender of one's own will, before the will of God, and that of Radoshitz as holding to one's own will, which also springs from the will of God. The saying was: "If you cannot get across it, you must get across it, nevertheless." The followers of the rabbi of Kotzk, however, claimed that in Kotzk they were taught to bring their hearts closer to their Father in Heaven, while in Radoshitz the attempt was made to bring our Father in Heaven closer to the heart of the Jews. By this they meant that instead of striving up to God in all his greatness and austerity, the school of Radoshitz was trying to make him familiar to man— by way of miracles.

This reminds us of what Rabbi Yisakhar himself once said. When one of his most promising disciples asked him why he worked miracles and if it would not be better to purify the soul, he replied that he had been sent "to make the Godhead known to the world."

Rabbi Shelomo of Lentshno was just as unique, though in a different way. He was much praised for his extreme cleanliness because it symbolized his entire mode of life. It is told that he never looked at a coin and never touched one with his fingers; that he never put out his hand to receive anything, not even when any of the zaddikim who were his teachers (viz., Rabbi Mendel of Rymanov, the Seer of Lublin, and the Yehudi) offered him something to eat from his own plate, as the zaddikim often did to their dearest followers; and that he never spoke any idle words or listened to any idle speech.

Even in his youth he made a characteristic comment on the verse in Psalms that God will not despise a broken heart: "But it must, at the same time, be whole." And it is also characteristic that whenever he spoke of the coming of the Messiah, he described the great feeling of shame that would prevail everywhere. Because of his holiness, which though secluded was sympathetic to all creatures, he was regarded as one of the epiphanies of the suffering Messiah. Once he himself said of Messiah the son of Joseph, who according to the tradition was to be killed: "That is no longer the case; he will die of the sufferings of Israel."

He too had enemies among the other zaddikim. The leader of the fight which was waged against him when he remained faithful to the school of Pzhysha was a man who differed from him in all fundamental respects. He was Rabbi Naftali of Roptchitz, who had been taught by Rabbi Elimelekh of Lizhensk and later by his four great disciples: the Rabbi of Apt, the Maggid of Koznitz, Rabbi Mendel of Rymanov, and above all the Seer of Lublin.

We hardly know of another zaddik whose soul harbored such a mass of contradictions as did that of Rabbi Naftali of Roptchitz. But if we consider them all together, they are by no means formless and chaotic, but give the picture of a real human figure. He introduces into the hasidic world a type not uncommon among the distinguished intellectuals of the modern era: a mixture of irony and yearning, skepticism and belief, ambition and humility.

From his youth on, he was given to jests, many of them bitter, and to all manner of pranks including some that were really malicious. In his youth, he reflected on his own endowments with extreme pride, in his age with doubts verging on despair. He once observed that his teacher Rabbi Mendel of Rymanov was holy and knew nothing of cleverness, and added: "So how can he understand what I am like?" On another occasion, when the Seer of Lublin grew impatient with his eternal jesting and reminded him that the verse in the Scripture reads: "Thou shalt be whole-hearted with the Lord thy God," and not "Thou shalt be clever with the Lord thy God," Naftali gave the following bold reply which is utterly out of keeping with the original fundamental point of view of hasidism: "It requires great cleverness to be whole-hearted with the Lord."

But after he himself had become a rabbi, there are more and more quite different reports of him. A number of stories told in this volume, such as "The Watchman," "The Morning Prayer," "Leader and Generation," and above all, "A Wish," the tale of his desire to be reincarnated as a cow, testifies to what had taken place and was still taking place in his soul.

A conversation of his with Rabbi Meir of Stabnitz suggests a conclusion, though rather general, which Rabbi Naftali drew from his life experience. When he met Rabbi Meir, who had been his fellow pupil in Lublin and had in the meantime become to a certain extent the Seer's successor, he told him that from now on the hasidim should stay at home and study rather than go to zaddikim. Rabbi Meir answered: "Do not worry: God will provide! If we are not able to lead the community, other and abler men will appear and be the leaders"—a reply not, however, confirmed by later events.

Together with Rabbi Naftali of Roptchitz we must consider his disciple Rabbi Hayyim of Zans (d. 1876), who, of all the distinguished talmudic scholars among the hasidim, was probably the one that continued the old line of study with the most energy or—to use a curious simile attributed to him—undertook to turn the garment, which had already been turned, back to its original side. But we must not suppose that he attempted the synthesis which the earlier periods of the movement had tried to effect again and again. This synthesis seems to have been renounced, for though Rabbi Hayyim emphasizes that in the final analysis teaching and "service" are the same thing, he admits that as far as he is concerned in learning there is nothing in the world but the Torah, and in praying nothing but service.

He was a master in talmudic debate as well as in ecstasy, and no less distinguished for his generous charities and his deep knowledge of human nature, but he did not approach the great zaddikim in certain all-important qualities, for he lacked the unity of soul, and the unity of a figure shaped by the unity of the soul.

Many great men of the later generations are characterized by the fact that they have everything except the basic unity of everything. Yehezkel of Shenyava, a son of the rabbi of Zans, was a living protest against this trend. It is told of him that he did not want to preach sermons about the Scriptures, but would only read aloud from the Torah. One of his comments on his father was that Rabbi Hayyim had the soul of Abel, but of himself he said that the good element in Cain's soul had entered into his. Another of his sayings which has been handed down to us is that every zaddik comes across men more devout than he among those who follow him, only those men are not aware of it themselves.

The profuse legendary material at my disposal did not yield what I should call a comprehensive picture of Rabbi Shalom of Belz, the famous zaddik and founder of a "dynasty." But certain of his traits are so remarkable that I cannot omit him. Two motifs emerge with peculiar clarity. One is that of confession. Rabbi Shalom had his hasidim tell him all the "alien thoughts" which passed through their minds, that is, all the temptations of fantasy which prevented them from concentrating on prayer. He listened to their confessions with intense activity and this reciprocal relation accomplished the complete liberation of the hasidim.

The other motif has to do with marriage. It is well known that in circles of devout men not merely the presence of women in general, but even that of their own wives, was regarded as a "diverting" factor. This effect was not, however, attributed to the nature of woman as such, but to original sin and that part of it in particular which was due to the female element. In the case of the rabbi of Belz original sin seems to have been conquered. We see him sitting with his wife like Adam and Eve in paradise before the fall, when woman was still man's "help meet" with all her being; the original state of creation is restored.

Rabbi Hirsh of Zhydatchov, who studied not only with the Seer but also with the rabbis of Sasov and Koznitz, presents a new and unique situation. Together with his brothers and nephews he formed a family which was at the same time a school whose leader he was. A story told about one of the five brothers demonstrates the inner connection existing in this circle. It is about one of the brothers who, when the eldest, Rabbi Hirsh, was very sick, offered himself to heaven in his place because "the world needs him more." And his sacrifice was accepted.

Not only in his work, but in his everyday life, Rabbi Hirsh was the true Kabbalist among the disciples of the Seer of Lublin. He never raised a glass of water to his lips without going through a special mystical concentration (kavvanah). Since he had no self-confidence, he feared even after the age of forty that he might be dominated by the planet Venus, in whose sphere good and evil mingle. The fact that so many hasidim came to study with him also filled him with misgivings; could Satan have a hand in it? This doubt assailed him because he took everything very seriously, including the rela-

31

tionship between outer and inner help which he felt he must give to each of his hasidim. But how could he give really personal attention to every individual in such a crowd?

His rejection of any kind of supremacy, of any exclusive claim for himself or any other zaddik, is closely tied to this general attitude. He believed that a hasid who thought that his was the only true rabbi was an idolater, and that all that mattered was for everyone to find the rabbi fitted to his character and to his particular needs, the proper rabbi to give him individual help.

Rabbi Yehudah Zevi of Rozdol (d. 1847), a nephew of Rabbi Hirsh, developed the problem of the zaddik which his uncle had newly posed, in connection with his own self-doubting. He felt that he lacked the power the great zaddikim of earlier times possessed, the power to change the world. The determining principle of his own soul was, he discovered, a kind of yielding of his own, so to speak, space, a space making. He called this element nothingness and believed that it too was necessary for the existence of the world.

Rabbi Yitzhak Eisik of Zhydatchov (d. 1873), another nephew of Rabbi Hirsh, did not make any greater claims for the zaddik, but stressed the positive factor in his relationship to the hasidim, in two ways: first, by his view that all human relationships, hence those of zaddik and hasidim as well, are based on a mutual give and take, and secondly by interpreting the frequently misunderstood moral influence of the zaddik on the hasid as an action which is not independent but conditioned by and included in the religious operation. On the whole, we may say that the school of Zhydatchov substantially contributed the critical evaluation of the entire sphere of relationship existing between zaddik and hasidim, and to their new and more precise delimitation.

The school of Pzhysha, which originated in that of Lublin, and the school of Kotzk, the offspring of that of Pzhysha, present a large, independent, communal structure. But we cannot properly understand the salient feature of these two schools without knowing that of their founder, the Yehudi.*

Like his master, the Yehudi was called Yaakov Yitzhak, but since it was not fitting to use his teacher's name in his teacher's entourage, he is said to have been known as "the Yehudi," i. e., the Jew. This became so popular that later on other zaddikim addressed the rabbi of Pzhysha simply as "holy Jew." But the name is symbolic as well and points to the special character of the man. Even as a boy Yehudi refused to pray at stated intervals and in the company of others. Neither rebukes nor blows were of any avail. But then his father noticed that after the House of Prayer had been closed the boy climbed over the roof and in through a window to say his prayer, and did this day after day. As a youth he liked to pray in a granary where no one could see him.

In those days he already had the reputation of being a great talmudic scholar but one who knew nothing of the service of the heart. It was generally supposed that he did not take the bath of immersion for he was never seen in any of the groups of ten or more who descended the ninety steps to the ice-cold pool. They went together in order to relieve the weirdness of the long slippery stair, and also to light a fire and warm the water a little. But the Yehudi went alone at midnight, immersed himself without making a fire, returned as secretly as he had come, and studied the Kabbalah. At dawn his young wife sometimes found him lying unconscious over his book.

His wife's parents lived in the city of Apt. At that time, Rabbi Moshe Leib of Sasov resided in the same city. He took an interest in the youth, became fond of him, and had a profound influence on his sensitive and reticent soul. Presently Rabbi Abraham Yehoshua Heshel of Apt also discovered the greatness of Yehudi's soul. For many years he taught children in various villages. Then he was filled with

---

*See my book *For the Sake of Heaven* (Philadelphia, 1945) which tells of the ambivalent relationship between the Seer and the Yehudi.

33

a yearning for death which he regarded as the perfection of being. He did not know whether this yearning was divine truth or self-delusion. He sought support and leadership and it is said that Rabbi David of Lelov took him to the Seer of Lublin.

There, so we are told, he was received like one who has been expected, and a feeling of deep calm came over him. When we remember the restlessness of his youth, we can understand what he meant by saying that in Lublin he learned to fall asleep. But the Seer was not like his teacher the Maggid of Mezritch. He did not have the same great clarity which evoked the confidence of those he educated. The Maggid of Mezritch helped the disciples under his care to build up the substance of their life, each out of his own particular elements. The Seer lived in the world of his own spiritual urges, the greatest of which was his "seeing." His humility—though passionate like all his other qualities—impelled him time and again to strike a compromise between his personal world and the world at large, yet he could not really understand a human being like the Yehudi or the premises of his nature, for he lacked the one essential to such a man: the confidence of one soul in another. The Yehudi, in turn, could never realize this failing in the Seer's personality. That was why the relationship between the two was one of both intimacy and remoteness.

Finally the Yehudi founded a congregation of his own, a step which though taken at his teacher's suggestion provided fuel for the Seer's suspicions. With the help of Rabbi Bunam, who had been a fellow student of the Yehudi's and had then become his disciple, this congregation grew into the school of Pzhysha. But the focal point in the Yehudi's life continued to be his disturbed and bitter relations with the rabbi of Lublin, and time and again he felt a compulsion to bridge the unbridgeable gap.

He started out on his own way in the shadow of this conflict, and after years of struggle, the people flocked to him. "Turn!" he cried to them. "Turn quickly, for the day is near, there is not time for new migrations of souls; redemption is close at hand!" What he meant by this was that redemption was so imminent that people had no more time to strive toward perfection in new incarnations, that they had to take the decisive step now, with one stupendous effort, in the great turning. The Yehudi kept on the other side of the realm of magic which the Seer and his friends entered at that time in an attempt to reach the messianic sphere by affecting current events; he did not wish to hasten the end, but to prepare man for the end.

Rabbi Uri of Strelisk, the "Seraph," said of him that "he wanted to bring a new way down to men: to fuse teaching and prayer into one service." He went on to say that that had never happened before, but I think that it had happened in the beginnings of the hasidic innovation, but had by that time disappeared. And Rabbi Uri continued: "But he died in the midst of his work and did not complete it."

The gravest accusation the Yehudi's enemies proffered against him was that he did not pray at the prescribed hours, but waited until he was filled with the desire to pray. This was however nothing but the first necessary consequence of his will to concentrate. He did not have the opportunity to draw the further consequences, for he died in the fulness of his strength, before he was fifty, some two years before his teacher. According to one legend, the Seer had bidden him die, so that through the Yehudi the Seer might learn from the upper world what next step to take in the great messianic enterprise.

According to another legend, the upper world gave him the choice of either dying himself or having his teacher die— and he chose. There is still another version which suggests that the secret of his youth which had expressed itself in a yearning for death was at that time renewed on a higher plane, and that the highest "unification" is bound up with bodily death when it is performed by those who are uprooted— and this late bloom of hasidism no longer had any true roots. The story of his death is enveloped in more mystery than that of any other zaddik.

He himself once formulated the teaching which took shape in his life in a few terse words which are a commentary on the verse in the Scriptures: "Justice, justice shalt thou follow." They were: "We ought to follow justice with justice and not with unrighteousness." In this volume the passages about the Yehudi are supplemented by stories selected from a mass of kindred material about his sons and grandsons intended to show that here a peculiarity of character is preserved through several generations.

Rabbi Simha Bunam of Pzhysha was the greatest of the Yehudi's disciples and assumed the succession. He had traveled about as a copyist, lumber merchant, and pharmacist, went to Hungary to study the Talmud, and also made repeated business trips to Danzig. Wherever he went he kept his eyes open and experienced life sympathetically and freely. "I know all about sinners," he once said. "And so I also know how to straighten a young tree that is growing warped."

When Bunam first grew aware of the hasidic truth, he studied with the Maggid of Koznitz whom he frequently visited. Later he journeyed to Lublin where the Seer immediately became fond of this "worldly" man. Finally he made the acquaintance of the Yehudi and was soon his most trusted disciple.

After the Yehudi's death, the great majority of the hasidim of Pzhysha chose Bunam for their rabbi, but he was very reluctant to follow the call and let many who came to see him wait for days because he found it so difficult to practice his new vocation. He had no contact with the masses, not even that which the Yehudi had with his followers during the last period of his life: that of accepting their enthusiasm. But once he began seriously to teach, his teaching became his most vital function and one he discharged with a strong sense of responsibility. He shook and revolutionized the entire lives of the young men who came from everywhere and begged permission to remain near him. Since these youths were leaving their homes and business for his sake, families from far and wide expressed more enmity to him than to any other zaddik.

Many zaddikim of his time were hostile to him for objective reasons. Rabbi Naftali of Roptchitz, who had fought most vehemently against the Yehudi, once told a young man who had come to ask his blessing on his marriage to a girl from the neighborhood of Pzhysha: "I am not saying anything against the rabbi, for he is a zaddik: but his way is dangerous to the disciples who follow him. We serve so many years to arrive at the power and fervor they acquire in so short a time. With those methods 'the other side' may slip in—God forbid!—with the help of the demoniacal planet Venus." Finally, at the great zaddikim wedding at Ostila there was something very like a court session, in which the rabbi of Apt presided and dismissed the case, which was however more legitimate than the accusation guessed.

Bunam tried to continue to lead his hasidim along the way the Yehudi had taken, but he could not maintain it, for he did not share his teacher's belief that man must be prepared for redemption here and now and that redemption was really so close at hand. The Yehudi had tried to strike roots in the *goal*. But Bunam could no longer conceive this goal as the direct aim of his own personal actions, and so the heritage of his master was left hanging in air. The prospect of a new fusion of teaching and prayer, which had brightened the horizon for a brief moment, now vanished. It passed because the old rootedness was no more and it had proved impossible to strike new roots. Wisdom could still prosper in the atmosphere of "individualism," of abandonment which now became the abandonment of the goal, but holiness could not ripen in it. Wise Bunam was known as "the man versed in the mystery" but he was no longer close to the mystery itself, as the Yehudi like the early zaddikim had been. His profound table talk and crystalline parables bear powerful witness to the religious truth, but he cannot be regarded as the body and voice of the religious spirit. Prayer, which the Yehudi had "delayed," i.e., subjectivized, was made subsidiary to teaching—a natural result of the supremacy of the school over the congregation. And under the influence of rootlessness, teaching

itself ceased to be the transmission of the unutterable and again
became mere preoccupation with the study of contents.

The sinister quality of this later period of disintegration,
which was only glossed over by Rabbi Bunam's clear wisdom,
plainly comes out in the legend about his son, Rabbi Abraham
Moshe, who died before his thirtieth year, soon after his
father. He was all awareness of death and longing for death.
His father said of his son that he had the soul of King
Jeroboam I who separated Israel from Judah; that now his
way could lead either to utter evil or to perfect goodness
and an early death—and it led to the second.
What the young rabbi says concerning the sacrifice of Isaac
has a dark personal ring: Abraham's love for his son was
expressed in his very readiness to sacrifice him, for Isaac
dwelt in Abraham's house "only as a son," while in reality
he was the sacrificial lamb of God.
There is a strange story that before his wedding—he married
one of the Yehudi's granddaughters—Rabbi Bunam sent him
to the graveyard to invite one of the dead, and Moshe made
a mistake and invited the wrong one. He did not remain at
home after he was married, but took to the woods with a
group of youths "attached to him" and with them "learned
the hasidic way." (We know of a youth group of this kind
around Rabbi Shalom Shakhna, and shall find the same
situation in the case of Rabbi Mendel of Vorki.) It was the
same wood through which the Seer of Lublin had once driven,
where he had said that "the entire manifest and hidden
teachings together with the Divine Presence" would once
be present there. His father came to fetch him home to his
young wife. As if waking from sleep, he said: "I forgot."

The story entitled "The Secrets of Dying" tells how he was
involved in the death of his father, who "all his life had
learned to die." He hesitated to become his father's successor,
for he knew that by so doing he would cut short his own
life. Yet in the end he decided for it. Only two years later,
however, he "craved" death, and died. He was as beautiful in

death as he had been in life. A zaddik who approached as he was being carried to the grave cried: "Alas for the beauty which must rot in the earth," and then lapsed into a silence which he did not break the whole of that day.

It is said that Rabbi Abraham Moshe was a great musician. As far as we know, he was Rabbi Bunam's only son.

If we follow Rabbi Hanokh in regarding Rabbi Bunam's disciples as commentaries on his teachings, then we must consider Rabbi Menahem Mendel of Kotzk (d. 1859) as that commentary which was itself in need of a commentary; but he never found one, for his disciples were not such a commentary.

From childhood on Rabbi Mendel was a rebel who zealously guarded his own independent way. It is told that when the Seer of Lublin sent for the youth and according to his custom asked him questions which revealed his own gift of "seeing," Mendel answered only under protest, and later when the Seer rebuked him for his way because it led to melancholy, Mendel left Lublin and went to Pzhysha. There he did indeed submit to the Yehudi's guidance, but soon after his master's death his irrepressible soul again revolted, not only in anger at the swarms of idle visitors: it was mutiny of the spirit.

When he himself became a rabbi, it grew quite clear that he was fanatically intent on a fundamental renovation of the movement. Hasidism was to remember the purpose of man's creation: "To lift up the heavens." He declared: "Holy revelation has deteriorated into habit," and every ounce of strength had to be concentrated to press on to revelation, to that point from which the heavens can be "lifted up."

This could no longer be the task of the congregation; it was the task of the disciples. The bond between congregation and school seems to be definitely severed. The congregation still had prayer, and prayer had as superior a significance at Kotzk as anywhere else. The rabbi himself was praised for having prayed without effort or ostentation "like one conversing with his friend." But in order to deceive the world—and at Kotzk they were always intent on dissembling in the sight of the world—prayers were "quickly gotten over with." Indeed, there was no longer any real feeling for congregational prayer as such. Prayer and teaching had finally become two worlds which were related only through knowledge of the goal, but not through the warmth of the heart and enthusiasm of practice. The "temple of love," where the great love between the hasidim once lived, was closed because of the abuse of the holy fire, and could not be opened again. Everything depended on the discipleship as an elite which was to press forward to revelation.

Toward the end of his life Rabbi Mendel hinted at what he had originally had in mind, saying that he had intended going "into the woods" with four hundred hasidim and giving them "manna" so that they might know the kingly power of God. This is the vision of a new wandering through the desert to receive the new revelation. Rabbi Mendel interpreted the words in the Talmud that "the Torah was given only to those who eat manna" as referring only to those who had no care for the morrow (Exod. 16:19 ff.) In this connection it is significant that even as a child he insisted that he remembered standing at Sinai, and as a rabbi, he enjoined everyone to imagine the stand at Sinai in his heart.

Certain of his utterances which have been transmitted indicate his hope that every member of his selected group would be able to "see straight into heaven" and become like the Baal Shem. This was quite consistent, for he regarded himself as the Sabbath on which the work of the great week, begun with the Baal Shem, reached its culmination. But these visions soon faded. The overwhelming disappointments he had suffered in his early years led him to concentrate on learning with fanatic intensity. His disciples (most of whom, incidentally, had to gain their livelihood by manual labor) thought themselves far above the rest of the world, and this led to undesirable developments.

After his first bold hopes had been wrecked, his only concern was to maintain, internally and externally, what he considered the truth, which was not a content, but a personal quality, something "which cannot be imitated." He expounded the words in the psalm that God is close to all who call on him in truth, by interpreting it to mean: Who call on him by the quality of truth dwelling in their soul, and he refused to make peace even with the school of a friend, if it had to be on terms that violated this quality.

He was even more uncompromising in his defense of inner truth. God's commandment, he taught, must not be made an idol to hide the truth, and when we say "God" we must mean the true God and not a "molten image" of our fantasy. It is quite understandable that only a few of his disciples— disciples and former companions, such as the rabbi of Ger, who saw in Mendel a "spark of the true fire" and "lay down under it"—incorporated the stern teaching of personal truth in their lives and made it live. (One disciple later defined this teaching to mean: "There is no truth until one's entire person is internally one and unified in His service, until one's entire person is one truth from the first to the last of the letters of the Scriptures.")

Most of them probably enjoyed listening to Rabbi Mendel's utterances, such as his praise of Pharaoh because he "was a man" and had remained steadfast in the face of the plagues, but they did not realize the implications of his utterances. His disappointment in his hasidim certainly did much to make him somber and aloof for the last twenty years of his life.

But it would be taking this tragic figure of hasidic agony too lightly if we were to explain the events of his life in terms of his personal experiences, without analyzing the change in faith itself. It seems to me that the decline of a great movement, above all of a great religious movement, is the most severe test to which the faith of a really believing man can be put, a far more difficult test than any personal fate. And Rabbi Mendel was a really believing man. He once said to himself: "I have faith; faith is clearer than vision."

To me the most important of all questionings of fate is how such closeness to God could change into such remoteness from God. In the history of hasidism, this question appears in the school of Pzhysha. The Yehudi's words: "This too will be corrupted," are evidence that he had already sensed it; he tried to combat it by powerfully calling for a turning. This question also threw its shadow over Rabbi Bunam—as we know, among other things, from his radical elaboration of the theme of "Satan's hasidim"—and he answered it by teaching that the shepherd is there even when the sheep do not see him. In Rabbi Mendel's time the decline had advanced so far and he was so sensitive to it, that the question felled him with cruel force, and he succumbed to its blows.

The crisis came on a Friday evening on which the rabbi did not pronounce the Benediction of Sanctification (Kiddush) until midnight and did not leave his room to come to the Sabbath table until that time. The oral reports, almost all of which have been preserved, differ considerably on what happened then, but all agree on a certain more or less outspoken antinomian note, on the transference of Rabbi Mendel's inner rebelliousness to his relation to the Torah. This holds even though we do not know whether he really said the words attributed to him by the so-called "enlightened" group; that man with all his urges and lusts is part of God; and whether he finally cried out: "There is no judgment and there is no judge!" —or whether he only touched the candlestick and thus ostentatiously sinned against the law of the Sabbath.

At all events something profoundly shocking must have occurred, for otherwise we could not explain one incident on which all the reports are fairly agreed. It is that Rabbi Mordecai Joseph, once Rabbi Mendel's fellow student at Rabbi Bunam's, later his disciple, and always his secret rival, called to the hasidim: "The tablets and the broken tablets were both preserved in the Ark of the Covenant, but when God's name is desecrated, there is no place for consideration of a rabbi's honor—tie him up!" Rabbi Mendel's brother-in-law, the faithful rabbi of Ger, opposed Rabbi Joseph and succeeded in quieting a large number of hasidim.

The rest left Kotzk after the Sabbath, Rabbi Mordecai Joseph at their head. He settled in the town of Izbica and later declared that "Heaven had commanded" him to leave his former teacher.

From that time on, throughout the remaining twenty years of his life, Rabbi Mendel kept to his room behind two doors which were almost always closed. Two holes were bored through one door, through which he heard the service in the adjoining House of Prayer, sometimes probably watching. The other door he occasionally opened himself, when hasidim were gathered outside. On such occasions he stood on the threshold without his kaftan. His face was awful to behold. He cursed them in choppy words that burst from his lips with such force that they were seized with terror and fled from the house through doors and windows. But sometimes, on a Friday evening, he issued from his room dressed in his white pekeshe and greeted his visitors, whom he otherwise gave only the tips of his fingers through the hole in the door. But he never sat down at the Sabbath table and almost never ate more than a plate of soup in the evening. When called to read the Torah on a Sabbath, he would go to the pulpit, his prayer shawl drawn over his face, and would go back again as soon as he had read the scriptural portion. Mice came and went in his room as they pleased, and when the hasidim heard them scuttling about, they whispered to the newcomers that these were souls who had come to the rabbi for redemption. And if you were to ask a hasid of Kotzk what the rabbi did about the bath of immersion, you would be told to this day that the legendary well of Miriam, which, locked in stone, once accompanied the Jews on their journey through the desert, had opened up in the rabbi's room.

I have told the story of the rabbi of Kotzk in such detail because it is so striking an illustration of the end of a process; it gives the impression of being the final act in a drama. But to regard it as an end from the purely chronological point of view would be a mistake. On the contrary: Kotzk became a focus for hasidic life and work which went on as though this were not the close of a phase, but the middle.

Three zaddikim who were close friends of Rabbi Mendel are a good example of this. They were: Yitzhak of Vorki, who died a decade before Mendel (1848), and must be considered together with his son whose name was also Mendel (d. 1868); and Yitzhak Meir of Ger (d. 1866), and Hanokh of Alexander

(d. 1870), who both survived Rabbi Mendel of Kotzk by almost ten years. But if we listen intently, we can hear midnight striking in the lives of these disciples too—though much more slowly.

I shall take Rabbi Hanokh—the last of the three—first, because of them all he was a disciple of the rabbi of Kotzk in the truest sense of the word. Rabbi Mendel and these three had all studied together at Rabbi Bunam's. When their teacher died, the rabbi of Ger, who was then twenty-eight and had already attained to his own spiritual position and his own sphere of work, deliberately subordinated himself to the rabbi of Kotzk after talking with him in the woods all through one night— so tradition has it—because he saw "the light shining from Tomashow" (Rabbi Mendel's first home).

The rabbi of Vorki, who was twenty years older than the other two, visited the Seer of Lublin when he was a mere boy and later studied with David of Lelov and Bunam. When Rabbi Bunam died, he attached himself to Abraham Moshe for the brief period of his rabbinate and then headed a congregation of his own, for a time even in Pzhysha. All through his life, however, he was a true friend to Rabbi Mendel. But Rabbi Hanokh was the disciple par excellence of the rabbi of Kotzk who had once been his fellow student in Rabbi Bunam's House of Study. Rabbi Hanokh always said that prior to the rabbi of Kotzk no one had taught him that a hasid was a human being who asked for the meaning. Even in Kotzk he continued to hide his deep and burning nature under all sorts of foolery.

He actually developed in the teachings of Rabbi Mendel only the old, the original hasidic element. His main contribution was that he gave a more concrete and perfect form to the concept of "lifting up the heavens." He taught that the so-called two worlds, heaven and earth, are in reality one single world which has split apart but will grow whole again if man makes the earth entrusted to him like heaven. (Here he seems to demand the opposite of "lifting up the heavens," and yet it is the same thing, for a heaven which is no longer separate from earth, no longer deprived of earth, a heaven which has no gaps, must certainly have been "lifted.") All men, moreover, have the possibility of making the earth like heaven, for at the bottom of every heart there is a residue of the substance and the power of heaven, which can operate from its human habitation. Israel is in exile; man is in exile, but it is the exile of his own baseness, to which he lends the control of his heavenly heart. This must be taken as the point of departure for man's sharing in the redemption. Here we have the classical hasidic teachings in a new form approaching the views even of the era in which we are living. The parable of the Maggid's disciple, Rabbi Aaron of Karlin, about the negation of the ego reappears in a new practical form when we hear that Rabbi Hanokh never referred to himself as "I" because that pronoun belongs to God alone. But melancholy, though not despairing utterances, such as his words concerning the aging of melodies, testify to his deep insight into the decline of hasidism and its need for regeneration.

In contrast, the brilliant sayings of Rabbi Yitzhak Meir of Ger cannot be worked into a unified and relatively independent doctrine like those of Rabbi Hanokh. The rabbi of Ger was an aphorist somewhat like Rabbi Israel of Rizhyn, whom he resembled in other respects as well. He too was a representative zaddik of far-reaching influence, but he concerned himself with and represented the social and cultural affairs of Polish Jewry to a far greater extent than the rabbi of Rizhyn, and he spoke of himself with a humble self-criticism quite foreign to Rabbi Israel.

His critical and yet not hopeless attitude toward the movement, whose decline he recognized, is expressed very clearly in a certain description—surely not without reference to his own experience—which he drew in his old age of a congregation which had everything: a leader and members and a House of Study and all the appurtenances. Suddenly Satan bore out the innermost point. "But everything else remained just as it was, and the wheel kept on turning, only that the innermost point was lacking." He was speaking intimately to his grandson, but suddenly the description wrested a cry from him: "God help us! We must not let it happen!"

Rabbi Yitzhak of Vorki, the third of the three disciples of Kotzk, was also given to self-criticism, but he did not have such clear-cut resolution in the face of the declining movement. This noble man, who among all the disciples came closest to the mature wisdom of Rabbi Bunam, seems not to have realized the problems of that late hour. But I think that what he said about the seemingly hopeless and yet not hopeless turning of the great sinner goes beyond the sphere of personal experience.

His son Mendel of Vorki, on the other hand, gave direct and forceful expression to the crisis, not so much in one or the other of his sayings, as through his silence. The variations handed down to us on the theme of his "silence" form a curious picture. With him silence is not a rite, as with the Quakers, nor is it ascetic practice, as with some Hindu sects. The rabbi of Kotzk called it an "art." Silence was his way. It was not based on a negative principle; nor was it merely the absence of speech. It was positive and had a positive effect. Mendel's silence was a shell filled with invisible essence, and those who were with him breathed it. There is a story of how he met another zaddik for the first time, how they sat opposite each other for an hour in complete silence, somewhat like Aegidius, St. Francis' disciple, and St. Louis of France, and both derived benefit from this experience. He spent a night of silence with his hasidim, and they felt themselves uplifted toward the One.

There is no doubt that silence was his special kind of fervor, of hasidism. But it was not only that. When he himself spoke of silence—though not of his own, which he never touched on directly—he did not interpret it as soundless prayer but as soundless weeping or as "a soundless scream." The soundless scream is the reaction to a great sorrow. It is in general the Jew's reaction to his own great sorrow; it "befits us." By reading between the lines we discover that it is particularly his, Mendel of Vorki's reaction to the hour in which "the present too is corrupted." The time for words is past. It has become late.

THE DESCENDANTS OF

THE GREAT MAGGID

SHALOM SHAKHNA OF PROBISHTCH

The Hen and the Ducklings

Rabbi Shalom Shakhna, the son of Abraham the Angel, lost both his parents when he was very young, and grew up in the house of Rabbi Nahum of Tchernobil, who gave him his granddaughter to wife. However, some of his ways were different from Rabbi Nahum's and unpleasing to him. He seemed to be very fond of show, nor was he constant in his devotion to the teachings. The hasidim kept urging Rabbi Nahum to force Rabbi Shalom to live more austerely.

One year during the month of Elul, a time when everyone contemplates the turning to God and prepares for the Day of Judgment, Rabbi Shalom, instead of going to the House of Study with the others, would betake himself to the woods every morning and not come home until evening. Finally Rabbi Nahum sent for him and admonished him to learn a chapter of the Kabbalah every day, and to recite the psalms, as did the other young people at this season. Instead, he was idling and loafing in a way particularly ill becoming to one of his descent.

Rabbi Shalom listened silently and attentively. Then he said: "It once happened that a duck's eggs were put into a hen's nest and she hatched them. The first time she went to the brook with the ducklings they plunged into the water and swam merrily out. The hen ran along the bank in great distress, clucking to the audacious youngsters to come back immediately lest they drown. 'Don't worry about us, mother,' called the ducklings. 'We needn't be afraid of the water. We know how to swim.'"

The Powerful Prayer

Once on the eve of the New Year in the House of Prayer, while Rabbi Nahum of Tchernobil was reciting the Afternoon Prayer with great fervor, his grandson-in-law Rabbi Shalom, who used to recite this prayer at the reader's desk, suddenly felt a sinking of the spirit. All around him were praying with great concentration, but it needed all the strength he had just to utter one word after the other, and to grasp the simple meaning of each word. Afterward Rabbi Nahum said to him: "My son, how your prayer took Heaven by storm today! It lifted up thousands of banished souls."

In Peace

Once when Rabbi Shalom Shakhna happened to be staying in a small town of the district of Kiev, the old zaddik Rabbi Zev of Zhytomir arrived to spend the sabbath there. On Thursday evening Rabbi Shalom prepared to leave and went to bid Rabbi Zev farewell. The zaddik inquired when Rabbi Shalom expected to reach his destination. "Tomorrow, around three in the afternoon," was the reply.

"Why do you plan to be on the road after the noon hour on the day before the sabbath?" Rabbi Zev asked in surprise.

"At twelve o'clock I usually put on my sabbath clothes and start singing the Song of Songs, which is Solomon's, king of peace. By that time the sabbath peace has already begun for me."

"And what am I to do," replied Rabbi Shalom, "if a tenant farmer comes to me toward evening and tells me his troubles, tells me that his calf has fallen sick, and from his words I gather that he is saying to me: 'You are a lofty soul, and I am a lowly soul; lift me up to you!' What am I to do then?" From off the table the old man took the two candlesticks with the lighted candles, and grasping them in his two hands, he accompanied his young guest through the long corridor to the outer door. "Go in peace," he said. "Go in peace."

The Streets of Nehardea

Rabbi Shalom said:

"The Talmud tells of a wise man versed in the lore of the stars and relates that the paths of the firmament were as bright and clear to him as the streets in the town of Nehardea where he lived. Now if only we could say about ourselves that the streets of our city are as clear and bright to us as the paths of the firmament! For to let the hidden life of God shine out in this lowest world, the world of bodiliness, that is the greater feat of the two!"

With the Same Passion

It is written: "A Psalm of David," and following: ". . . after he had gone in to Bathsheba." This is how Rabbi Shalom expounded the verse: "David returned to God and said his psalm to him with the same passion with which he had gone to Bathsheba. That was why God forgave him on the instant."

On the Highest Rung

A hasid of Rabbi Shalom living in a certain town happened to be present when the "Rav," Rabbi Shneur Zalman, on a visit to the town in the course of a journey on the Sabbath, said Torah with great fervor. But suddenly it seemed to the hasid that the "Rav" grew less fervent, that what he said now appeared to lack the admirable passion of what had gone before. The next time the hasid was with his teacher Rabbi Shalom, he told of the incident, and openly stated his surprise. "How can you venture to judge such matters!" said the zaddik. "You don't know enough to do that. But I shall tell you: There is a very high and holy rung, and he who reaches it is freed of all the stuff of earth and can no longer kindle to flame."

ISRAEL OF RIZHYN

The New Heaven

When the rabbi of Rizhyn was a child, he was once walking up and down in the yard on a Friday toward evening time, when the hasidim had already gone off to pray. A hasid went up to him and said: "Why don't you go in? The sabbath has already begun."

"The sabbath hasn't begun yet," he replied.

"How do you know that?" asked the hasid.

"On the sabbath," he answered, "there always appears a new Heaven, and I can't see any sign of it yet."

On Earth

Rabbi Israel of Rizhyn, the son of Rabbi Shalom Shakhna, and Rabbi Moshe of Savran had quarreled. The rabbi of Savran, prompted by the wish to make peace, paid his adversary a visit. Rabbi Israel asked him: "Do you believe there is a zaddik who clings to God unceasingly?" The other answered as one who wants to hide a doubt: "There might well be." To which the rabbi of Rizhyn replied: "My grandfather was like that; my grandfather Rabbi Abraham, whom they called the Angel." Then the other said: "He did not, come to think of it, spend many days on this earth." And the rabbi of Rizhyn: "And my father Rabbi Shalom was like that." And again the rabbi of Savran remarked: "He too, come to think of it, did not spend many days on this earth."

Then the rabbi of Rizhyn replied: "Why speak of years and days! Do you think they were on earth in order to dry up here? They came, accomplished their service, and returned."

The Tale about Smoke

Once Rabbi Moshe of Kobryn came to visit the rabbi of Rizhyn on the eve of the sabbath. He found his host standing

in the middle of the room, his pipe in his hand and clouds
of smoke wreathing round him. The rabbi of Rizhyn immediately began to tell a story:
"There was once a man who lost his way in the woods at
twilight on the eve of the sabbath. Suddenly he saw a house
in the distance. He walked toward it. When he entered he
found himself face to face with a robber, a fierce-looking
robber, and on the table in front of him lay a gun. The
robber jumped up, but before he could get hold of the
gun the man had seized it, and quick as lightning he thought:
"If I hit him, it will be well, if I miss, the room will at least be
full of smoke and I can escape.' "
When the rabbi of Rizhyn reached this point in his story he
put down his pipe and said: "Sabbath!"

Two Kinds of Zaddikim

The rabbi of Rizhyn told how the people of Jassy sneered
at the rabbi of Apt after his sermons. He added: "In every
generation there are people who grumble about the zaddik
and look askance at Moses. For the rabbi of Apt is the Moses
of his generation." He paused, and after a while he continued:
"There are two kinds of service and two kinds of zaddikim.
One sort serves God with learning and prayer, the other
with eating and drinking and earthly delights, raising all
this to holiness. This is the kind the grumbling is about. But
God has made them as they are because he does not want
man to be caged in his lusts, but to be free in them. That is
the calling of these zaddikim: to make men free. Those others
are the lords of the manifest, these are the lords of the hidden
world. It is to them that secrets are revealed and the meaning
of dreams unfolded, as it was to Joseph, who curled his beautiful hair and served God with the delights of this world."
On another occasion he spoke about the verse: "The heavens
are the heavens of the Lord; but the earth hath He given to
the children of men," saying: "There are two kinds of zaddikim.
Those of the one sort learn and pray the livelong day and
hold themselves far from lowly matters in order to attain to
holiness. While the others do not think of themselves, but only

of delivering the holy sparks which are buried in all things back to God, and they make all lowly things their concern. The former, who are always busy preparing for Heaven, the verse calls 'the heavens,' and they have set themselves apart for the Lord. But the others are the earth given to the children of men."

Zaddikim and Hasidim

The rabbi of Rizhyn said:

"Just as the holy letters of the alphabet are voiceless without the vowel signs, and the vowel signs cannot stand without the letters, so zaddikim and hasidim are bound up with one another. The zaddikim are the letters and the hasidim who journey to them are the vowel signs. The hasidim need the zaddik, but he has just as much need of them. Through them he can be uplifted. Because of them he can sink—God forbid! They carry his voice, they sow his work in the world. Suppose that one of the hasidim who come to me is on the road and meets a carriage full of so-called enlightened passengers. He persuades the coachman to let him ride beside him, and when the time comes to say the Afternoon Prayer he gets down from his seat, and makes ready, and prays while the carriage waits. And the passengers are annoyed and revile the coachman and shout at him. In the midst of all this, perhaps through all this, they experience a change of soul."

The Roof

Jacob Ornstein, the rav of Lwow, opposed the hasidic way. And so once when the rabbi of Rizhyn was calling on him, he thought his visitor would launch into subtle interpretations of the Scriptures in order to impress him with the scholarship of the hasidim. But the zaddik only asked: "What are the roofs of the houses in Lwow made of?"

"Out of sheet iron," said the rav.

"And why out of sheet iron?"

"To be protected against fire."

"Then they might just as well be made of brick," said Rabbi Israel and took his leave. When he was gone, the rav laughed and exclaimed: "And that is the man people flock to!"

54

A few days later Rabbi Meir of Primishlan came to Lwow to see the rabbi of Rizhyn, who was his friend, but found he had already left. They told him what he had said. His face lit up and he said: "Truly, the roof, the heart of the man who watches over the congregation, should be of brick: so shaken with all their sorrows that it threatens to break every moment, and yet endures; but instead it is of sheet iron!"

The Other Way

Once when the Jews were passing through a period of great stress, the rabbi of Apt who was then the eldest of his generation issued a command for a universal fast, in order to call down God's mercy. But Rabbi Israel summoned his musicians, whom he carefully selected from a number of different towns, and night after night he had them play their most beautiful melodies on the balcony of his house. Whenever the sound of the clarinet and the delicate tinkle of the little bells floated down from above, the hasidim began to gather in the garden, until there was a whole crowd of them. The music would soon triumph over their dejection and they would dance, stamping their feet and clapping their hands. People who were indignant at these doings reported to the rabbi of Apt that the day of fasting he had ordered had been turned into a day of rejoicing. He answered:

"It is not up to me to call him to account who has kept the memory of the command in the Scriptures green in his heart: 'And when ye go to war in your land against the adversary that oppresseth you, then ye shall sound an alarm with the trumpets; and ye shall be remembered before the Lord your God.'"

The Counterruse

Several mitnagdim of Sanok came to the rabbi of Rizhyn when he was passing through their city, and complained to him: "In our congregation we pray at dawn, and after that we sit wrapped in our prayer shawls, with our phylacteries on head and arm, and learn a chapter of the Mishnah. Not so the hasidim! They pray after the hour set for prayer has passed, and when they have finished praying they sit down together and drink schnapps. And yet they are called the 'devout' and we the 'adversaries.' ''

Leib, the rabbi of Rizhyn's servant, was seized with an irresistible desire to laugh as he listened to this complaint, and not troubling to conceal the reason for his laughter, he said: "The service and prayer of the mitnagdim are ice-cold and have no warmth at all, just like a corpse, and when you watch by the side of a body you study the chapter from the Mishnah prescribed for this occasion. But when the hasidim have done their bit of service, their heart glows and is warm like one who is alive, and whoever is alive must drink schnapps."

The rabbi said: "We'll let the jest pass. But the truth of the matter is this: You know that ever since the day our Temple was destroyed, we pray instead of making sacrifice. And just as the sacrifice was disqualified if the thought was impure, so it is with prayer. That is why the Evil Urge devises ruse upon ruse to confuse him who prays with thoughts alien to prayer. Now for this the hasidim have invented a counter-ruse. After praying they sit down together and drink to one another. 'To life!' Each tells what is burdening his heart and then they say to one another: 'May God grant your desire!' And since—so our sages say—prayers can be said in any language whatsoever, this speaking and answering of theirs while drinking is also regarded as prayer. But all the Evil Urge sees is that they are eating and drinking and using everyday speech, and so he stops bothering his head about them."

"Thee"

The hasidim were once sitting together and drinking, when the rabbi entered the room. It seemed to them that he did not eye them with favor. "Are you displeased to find us drinking, rabbi?" they asked. "Yet it is said that when hasidim sit together over their cups, it is just as though they were studying the Torah!"

"There is many a word in the Torah," said the rabbi of Rizhyn, "which is holy in one passage and unholy in another. So for instance, it is written: 'And the Lord said to Moses: Hew thee two tables of stone,' but also: 'Thou shalt not make unto thee a hewn image.' Why is it that the same word is holy in the first passage and unholy in the second? It is because there the word 'thee' comes after, and here it precedes. So it is with all we do. Whenever the 'thee' comes after, all is holy, when it precedes, all is unholy."

The Judgment of the Messiah

Many heads of families of Berditchev complained to the rabbi of Rizhyn that their sons-in-law had left wives and children in order to become his disciples, and when they asked him to persuade the youths to return home, he told them about a young man who had lived in the days of the Great Maggid. He had quitted his father-in-law's house to go to the maggid. They had fetched him back and he had pledged on a hand-clasp that he would stay at home. Yet shortly thereafter he was gone. Now his father-in-law got the rav of the town to declare that this broken promise was cause for divorce. The young man was thus deprived of all means of subsistence. Soon he fell ill and died.

When the zaddik had finished his story, he added: "And now, my good men, when the Messiah comes, the young man will hale his father-in-law before his court of justice. The father-in-law will quote the rav of the town, and the rav will quote a passage from the commentary on the Shulhan Arukh. Then the Messiah will ask the young man why after giving his hand on it that he would remain at home he broke his promise just the same, and the young man will say, 'I just had to go to the rabbi!' In the end the Messiah will pronounce judgment. To the father-in-law he will say: 'You took the rav's word as your authority and so you are justified.' And to the rav he will say: 'You took the law as your authority and so you are justified.'

"And then he will add: 'But I have come for those who are not justified.'"

The Zaddik and the People

The rabbi of Rizhyn said:
"As when someone prepares to split a tree with an ax, and

takes a great swing at it but misses, and the ax goes into the earth, so it is when the zaddik talks to people in order to rouse their hearts to the service of God, but they do not heed him, and admire only the cleverness and artfulness of his sermon."

The Hidden Teachings

Concerning the verse: "For instruction shall go forth from Me," the rabbi of Rizhyn said:

"The teachings will never be altered. The first book of Moses will forever be the book of beginnings, which tells what happened to our fathers from the day God created the world. But there is something which is hidden from us: what God wrought before he created the world. And that is what is meant by the words: 'Now will it be said to Jacob and of Israel, what God hath wrought.' And the same is meant by the words: 'For instruction shall go forth from Me'—telling what I wrought before I created the world."

Ezekiel and Aristotle

Once when many wise men were gathered about his board, the rabbi of Rizhyn asked: "Why are the people so set against our master Moses ben Maimon?" A rabbi answered: "Because in a certain passage he asserts that Aristotle knew more about the spheres of Heaven than Ezekiel. So why should we not be set against him?"

The rabbi of Rizhyn said: "It is just as our master Moses ben Maimon says. Two people entered the palace of a king. One took a long time over each room, examined the gorgeous stuffs and treasures with the eyes of an expert and could not see enough. The other walked through the halls and knew nothing but this: 'This is the king's house, this is the king's robe. A few steps more and I shall behold my Lord, the King."

The Road Makers

When the rabbi of Ger visited the rabbi of Rizhyn in Sadagora, his host asked: "Are there good roads in Poland?"
"Yes," he replied.

"And who," the rabbi of Rizhyn continued, "is responsible for the work and directs it, Jews or non-Jews?"

"Jews," answered the rabbi of Ger.

"Who else," exclaimed the rabbi of Rizhyn, "could be versed in the work of making roads!"

Who May Be Called Man?

Concerning the words in the Scriptures: "When any man of you bringeth an offering to the Lord . . ." the rabbi of Rizhyn said: "Only he who brings himself to the Lord as an offering may be called man."

The Right Kind of Altar

It is written: "An altar of earth thou shalt make unto Me . . . and if thou make Me an altar of stone, thou shalt not build it of hewn stones, for if thou lift up thy tool upon it, thou hast profaned it."

The rabbi of Rizhyn expounded this as follows: "The altar of earth is the altar of silence which is most pleasing to God. But if you do make an altar of words, do not hew and chisel them, for such artifice would profane it."

The Nature of Service

The rabbi of Rizhyn said:

"This is the service man must perform all of his days: to shape matter into form, to refine the flesh, and to let the light penetrate the darkness until the darkness itself shines and there is no longer any division between the two. As it is written: 'And there was evening and there was morning—one day.' "

And another time he said:

"One should not make a great to-do about serving God. Does the hand boast when it carries out the will of the heart?"

Walking the Tight Rope

Once the hasidim were seated together in all brotherliness, when Rabbi Israel joined them, his pipe in his hand. Because he was so friendly, they asked him: "Tell us, dear rabbi, how should we serve God?" He was surprised at the question and replied: "How should I know!" But then he went right on talking and told them this story:

There were two friends, and both were accused before the king of a crime. Since he loved them he wanted to show them mercy. He could not acquit them because even the king's word cannot prevail over a law. So he gave this verdict: A rope was to be stretched across a deep chasm and the two accused were to walk it, one after the other; whoever reached the other side was to be granted his life. It was done as the king ordered, and the first of the friends got safely across. The other, still standing in the same spot, cried to him: "Tell me, my friend, how did you manage to cross that terrible chasm?" The first called back: "I don't know anything but this: whenever I felt myself toppling over to one side, I leaned to the other."

Breaking Impulses

A young man gave a note of request to the rabbi of Rizhyn. He had written to ask God's help in breaking his evil impulse. The rabbi's eyes laughed as he looked at him: "You want to break impulses? You will break your back and your hip, yet you will not break an impulse. But if you pray and learn and work in all seriousness, the evil in your impulses will vanish of itself."

Suffering

A man who was afflicted with a terrible disease complained to Rabbi Israel that his suffering interfered with his learning and praying. The rabbi put his hand on his shoulder and said: "How do you know, friend, what is more pleasing to God, your studying or your suffering?"

God the Forgiver

The time the rabbi of Rizhyn followed the advice of his physicians and went to Odessa to bathe in the sea, a grandson of the famous Rabbi Jacob Emden was living there. His name was Meir and he had strayed from the path of his fathers. When Rabbi Israel heard about him, he sent for him and invited him to come to Rizhyn. He promised that all his expenses would be taken care of. Meir agreed.

He had sat at the rabbi's table in Rizhyn only a short time when he made complete penance. One day, however, the zaddik noticed that he was looking depressed, and asked: "Meir, my son, what is troubling you? If it is your sins, remember that the turning makes up for everything."

Meir answered: "Why should I not be troubled? After doing penance I keep returning to sin over and over again as a dog returns to his vomit—and how can I know whether my penance is still accepted?"

The rabbi of Rizhyn touched his arm and said: "Have you never wondered why we read in the prayer: '. . . For thou art a forgiver of Israel and a pardoner of the tribes of Jeshurun.' Would it not be enough to write: 'You forgive and pardon'? But just as it is man's way and compulsion to sin and sin again and again, so it is God's way and his divine compulsion to forgive and pardon again and again."

Penance

A confirmed sinner who allowed no evil desire to pass him by came to Rabbi Motel of Tchernobil, handed him a slip on which he had listed the sins he had committed in his life, and asked to have a penance imposed on him. When Rabbi Motel had read the slip of paper, he said: "I am too old to assume the burden of someone who requires such heavy penance. Go to the rabbi of Rizhyn. He is young, he will take it upon himself." So the man went to the rabbi of Rizhyn and gave him the list. And now the rabbi of Rizhyn read the whole long column, the big items and the small, and the sinner waited.

Finally the zaddik said: "This shall be your penance. No matter what word of prayer you utter, from now until you die, you shall not utter a single word of prayer with empty lips; but you shall preserve the fulness of every word."

God and Gladness

Concerning the words in the Scriptures: "And it shall be, if thou shalt forget the Lord thy God . . ." the rabbi of Rizhyn said: "It is well known that by every 'and it shall be' in the Scriptures, gladness is meant. Here too this is what is meant. Here we are told: 'If you forget gladness and fall into a depression, you are forgetting the Lord your God.' For it is written: 'Strength and gladness are in His place.'"

The Child Thinks of His Father

The rabbi of Rizhyn said:

"In certain prayer books we do not read: 'Cause us, O Lord our God, to lie down,' but 'Cause us, our Father, to lie down.' For when man thinks of God as God, whose glory fills the world and there is no thing in which God is not, then he is ashamed to lie down on a bed in his sight. But if he thinks of God as his father, then he feels like a fond child whose father sees after him when he goes to bed, and tucks him in, and watches over his sleep. As we pray: 'Spread over us the covering of thy peace.'"

Afar Off

This question was put to the rabbi of Rizhyn: "Of the children of Israel standing at the foot of Mount Sinai, it is written: 'And the people saw it and stirred and stood afar off . . .' How shall we interpret this? Is not the entire earth filled with the glory of God? How can one stand 'afar off' from him?"

He expounded: "Miracles are for those who have little faith. When Israel saw that God was performing miracles, they knew that they had still to stand afar off; their hearts stirred, and—in spirit—they stood afar off at a place which was still befitting to them, but at the same time they yearned for perfect faith with all the strength of their stirring hearts."

To Walk with One's Own Light

A young rabbi complained to the rabbi of Rizhyn: "During the hours when I devote myself to my studies I feel life and light, but the moment I stop studying it is all gone. What shall I do?"

The rabbi of Rizhyn replied: "That is just as when a man walks through the woods on a dark night, and for a time another joins him, lantern in hand, but at the crossroads they part and the first must grope his way on alone. But if a man carries his own light with him he need not be afraid of any darkness."

Holy Spirit

The rabbi of Rizhyn was asked: "What does it mean when they say of some person or other that he has a holy spirit?"
He answered: "If a man really has spirit and he does not allow it to grow impure, that is called holy spirit."

Controversy for the Sake of Heaven

The rabbi of Rizhyn said:
"When the hasidim see one rabbi carrying on a controversy with another, they too begin to argue with one another. But in reality only the zaddikim are permitted to carry on a controversy, for it is a controversy for the sake of Heaven. That is why it says in the Talmud: 'Which controversy was for the sake of Heaven? That of Hillel and Shammai.' It does not say 'of the school of Shammai and the school of Hillel,' for a controversy for the sake of Heaven can be waged only by the teachers, not by their disciples."

The Time for Prayer

Once when Rabbi Israel was visiting the rabbi of Apt, he waited a long time before saying the Morning Prayer—something he did quite frequently. When they asked him when he was going to pray, he said he did not know just yet, and told this story:
A king had set an hour at which every one of his subjects was to have a free hearing. One day a beggar came to the palace at another hour and asked to be taken to the king. The guards snapped at him, and demanded whether he was not acquainted with the ruling. The beggar said: "I know all about it, but it only holds for those who want to talk to the king about the things they have need of; but I want

to talk to the king about what the realm has need of." The beggar was instantly admitted.

"And so," the rabbi of Rizhyn ended his story, "how am I to know when I shall pray?"

A Dish of Beans

A number of young men came to Rizhyn from a distant town in order to spend the Days of Awe near Rabbi Israel. When they noticed that he did not keep the prescribed hours for prayer but waited until he was seized with fervor, they wanted to imitate him and also waited, though they did not quite know what for. After the Feast of the Rejoicing in the Law, they went to the rabbi to take leave of him. He gave them his blessing and said: "See to it that you do not delay your prayers, but say each at its proper time. I shall tell you the story of the man whose wife served him a dish of beans for dinner year in, year out, day after day. Once she was delayed and the meal was put on the table an hour late. When her husband saw the beans, he grew angry and cried: 'I thought that today you were going to serve me an especially fine dish, and that the cooking of it had taken up so much time because it required many ingredients and particular care. But I am not in the mood to wait for the beans I eat every day!' " With that the zaddik ended his tale.

The young men bowed, and started on their homeward journey. In an inn, where they stopped on the way, they met an old man whose face was unfamiliar to them, but with whom they immediately entered into conversation. When they told him what the rabbi had said to them in parting, he smiled and said: "The cause of the man's anger was that there was as yet no perfect love between him and his wife. If there is such love, the man is well pleased if his wife lets him wait a long time, and then serves him a dish he eats every day, and there is nothing his heart does not regard as new and good."

These words struck the young men deeply. When they went to Rizhyn again on the Days of Awe, they told the rabbi of the incident. He was silent for a time, and then said: "What the old man said to you he also said to me, and he also said it to God."

In the Attic

This story is told:
Every night the rabbi of Rizhyn was in the habit of climbing to the attic and staying there for two hours. During that time his servant Shmulik who accompanied him waited sitting on the stairs. Once the zaddik's daughter wanted to fetch something from a cupboard which was in the attic, and found Shmulik sitting there and weeping. She asked him what was the matter. "Someone," he said, "slipped me a lot of money so that I should let him go in to the rabbi, and now he is inside." He opened his hand and showed her the money. Just then the rabbi came out at the door. There was no one in the room. In Shmulik's palm lay a few shards of clay.

Of a Hidden Zaddik

This story is told:
A hasid of the rabbi of Rizhyn had a daughter who was afflicted with serious eye trouble which no doctor knew how to cure. Time and again he begged the rabbi to help him, but no help was granted him. Finally, when the girl was stricken blind, the zaddik said to him unasked: "Take your daughter to Lwow, and when you get there, wait for the vendors who go about the streets and call out their wares, each with his own singsong cry, for instance: 'Fine pretzels, fresh pretzels!' He whose cry you like best is the one who can heal your daughter."
The hasid did as he was told and soon discovered the man who sang out his wares most to his liking. He bought a pretzel from him and asked him to bring some to the inn the next day. When the vendor entered his room, the hasid locked the door, and repeated the words of the rabbi of Rizhyn. The vendor's eyes snapped and he shouted: "You let me out of here, or I'll make a heap of bones of you along with your rabbi." The hasid opened the door in terror. The man disappeared, but the girl was cured.

This is what Rabbi Israel of Rizhyn said on the "Sabbath of the Turning":

"Hosea says: 'Return, O Israel, unto the Lord thy God.' That was said to the whole world and to all the creatures of Heaven and earth. For everything that has been created, below and above, all the servants of the Most High, the angels, the seraphim, the heavenly creatures, the holy wheels, all up to the throne of God himself, must accomplish the turning. And that is what the words 'unto the Lord thy God' mean: all creatures of all rungs to the very highest, up to the throne of God, must accomplish the turning."

But when he had said this, Rabbi Israel addressed himself: "O Israel, return Israel, unto the Lord thy God."

Turning and Redemption

The rabbi of Rizhyn said:

"They say that the zaddik of Spola, the Grandfather, once called out: 'Messiah, why don't you come? What are you waiting for? I swear to you by my beard that the Jews will not atone.' And I shall not contradict the Grandfather of Spola. But this I promise you, Lord of the world, I promise you that they will atone just as soon as Messiah, the king, appears. And they have some justification. For before ever we sinned, You in your covenant with Abraham between the section of the sacrifice sentenced us to four exiles; therefore you must redeem us before we do penance."

On another occasion the rabbi of Rizhyn laid the fingers of his right hand on the table after the morning meal, and said: "God says to Israel: 'Return unto me . . . and I will return unto you.'" Then he turned his right hand palm up and said: "But we children of Israel reply: 'Turn Thou us unto Thee, O Lord, and we shall be turned; renew our days as of old.' For our exile is heavy on us and we have not the strength to return to you of ourselves." And then he turned his hand palm down again and said: "But the Holy One, blessed be he, says: 'First you must return unto me.'" Four times the rabbi of Rizhyn turned his hand, palm up and palm down. But in the end he said: "The children of Israel are right, though, because it is true that the waves of anguish close over them, and they cannot govern their hearts and turn to God."

The Time to Come

It was on a sabbath and the rabbi of Rizhyn sat at his table surrounded by his hasidim. Then he said to them: "The days are near when all will be well with the common man both in body and in soul, but all will not be well with the extraordinary man, not in body and not in soul, and he will not even be able to recite one psalm."

And he concluded: "Why do I tell you this? So that your hearts shall not grieve: it ought to be so, it must be so."

Another time he said: "In the last three hours before redemption it will be as difficult to cling to Jewishness as to climb a smooth wall of ice. That is why in the Hoshanot prayer we say: 'Three hours—pray help!' Those are the last hours."

Labor Pains

The rabbi of Rizhyn said:

"If a pregnant woman goes into labor in the eighth month when her time is not yet come, they try to stop her labor. But not so in the ninth month. If the woman goes into labor then, they try to hasten it, so that she may soon give birth. That is why formerly when people called to Heaven begging God to free the earth of some misery, their prayer was granted, for the time was not yet come. But now that redemption is near, no prayer which ascends in behalf of the sorrowful world is of avail, but sorrow is heaped upon sorrow so that the birth may soon be accomplished."

Blowing the Ram's Horn on the Sabbath

On a New Year's Day which fell on a sabbath the rabbi of Rizhyn said:

"On a New Year's Day which falls on the sabbath, the ram's horn which summons the world to the new year must not be blown. On that day God himself blows the ram's horn. And he certainly knows how to blow! That is why on this day our hope is so wide-awake; the source of mercy itself has wakened it."

The Two Caps

Rabbi David Moshe, the son of the rabbi of Rizhyn, once said to a hasid:

"You knew my father when he lived in Sadagora and was already wearing the black cap and going his way in dejection; but you did not see him when he lived in Rizhyn and was still wearing his golden cap." The hasid was astonished. "How is it possible that the holy man from Rizhyn ever went his way in dejection! Did not I myself hear him say that dejection is the lowest condition!"

"And after he had reached the summit," Rabbi David replied, "he had to descend to that condition time and again in order to redeem the souls which had sunk down to it."

The Sound of the Ram's Horn

Rabbi David Moshe told this story:

The year he died my father could no longer go to the House of Prayer on New Year's Day. I prayed with him in his room. His service was more wonderful than ever before. When he had ended, he said to me: "Today I heard the Messiah blow the ram's horn."

The Meal at the Close of the Sabbath

In his old age the rabbi of Rizhyn spent his summers in the little town of Potok. Once Rabbi Moshe of Kobryn visited him over the sabbath. That day, the rabbi of Rizhyn did not eat the meal at the close of the sabbath, but sat in his garden in the evening, and the rabbi of Kobryn kept him company. For a long time the rabbi of Rizhyn was silent. Then he said: "We could eat the fruits of this tree in place of the meal, couldn't we?" Then he touched the rabbi of Kobryn's belt and said: "Let's take a little walk." And as they walked, he repeated what he had said before: "Dear Rabbi Moshe, you are a learned man. Is it not true that we are permitted to replace the meal at the close of the sabbath with fruits?" Then the rabbi of Kobryn understood that the rabbi of Rizhyn was speaking of his own end and of his sons, and cried out: "Our holy rabbi, the world still has need of you!" But a month and a half after this sabbath, Rabbi Israel died.

ABRAHAM YAAKOV OF SADAGORA

Creatures

On the fifteenth day of the month Shevat, the "New Year of the Trees," when they were placing fruit on the table, as is the custom on this day, Rabbi Abraham Yaakov, the eldest son of the rabbi of Rizhyn, said:

"It is written: 'When any man of you bringeth an offering unto the Lord, ye shall bring your offering of the cattle, even of the herd or of the flock.' All creatures and plants and animals bring and offer themselves to man, but through man they are all brought and offered to God. When man purifies and sanctifies himself in all his members as an offering to God, he purifies and sanctifies all the creatures."

Of Modern Inventions

"You can learn something from everything," the rabbi of Sadagora once said to his hasidim. "Everything can teach us something, and not only everything God has created. What man has made has also something to teach us."

"What can we learn from a train?" one hasid asked dubiously.

"That because of one second one can miss everything."

"And from the telegraph?"

"That every word is counted and charged."

"And the telephone?"

"That what we say here is heard there."

Bird Song

On the Sabbath of Song when the song from the Torah is read, which Moses and Israel sang at the Red Sea, the rabbi of Sadagora was asked: "Why is it customary to scatter buckwheat grits for the birds on this day?"

"A king," he replied, "had a little pavilion where he could be quite alone. It was built well away from all his palaces. Nobody was allowed to enter it but himself, nor could any of his servants set foot in it. Only a songbird shared the room with him, and the king listened to his song which was dearer to him than all the music of his singers.

"In the hour when the waters of the Red Sea were divided, all the angels and seraphim sang praise to the Lord. But he was listening to the song of his little bird Israel.

"That is why we feed the birds on this day."

On the Sabbath of Song

On the Sabbath of Song when the song sung beside the Red Sea was read, the rabbi of Sadagora said:

"It is not written that they sang the song immediately after they crossed the sea. First they had to reach the rung of perfect faith, as it is written: . . . 'and they believed in the Lord, and in his servant Moses.' Only after that come the words: 'Then sang Moses and the children of Israel . . .' Only he who believes can sing the song."

All the Melodies

Rabbi Abraham Yaakov said:

"Every people has its own melody, and none sings that of another. But Israel sings all of them, in order to bring them to God. Thus in the Section of Songs all the creatures that live on the earth and all the birds utter each his own song, but Israel makes a song out of all of their songs in order to bring them to God."

Testimony

One Friday evening a group of so-called enlightened men entered the house of the rabbi of Sadagora uninvited, to hear him say the Kiddush and then to make fun of it. When the zaddik noticed this, he said: "The words from Genesis which we say to inaugurate the sabbath: 'And the heaven and the earth were finished,' are spoken here, as we all know, in testimony of the work of creation of the one and only God, and where could testimony be more in place than where there is denial? So let us testify in the face of these who deny that God created the world and that he guides it." He rose and said the Kiddush.

Everyone Has His Place

Rabbi Abraham was asked:
"Our sages say: 'And there is not a thing that has not its place.'
And so man too has his own place. Then why do people sometimes feel so crowded?" He replied: "Because each wants to
occupy the place of the other."

Sufferings and Pangs

Once the rabbi of Sadagora sat at his midday meal, and sighed,
and did not eat. His sister asked him what was troubling him
and repeated her question several times. At last he answered
her with a question of his own: "Have you heard the reports
about the sad condition of our brothers in Russia?"
"It seems to me," she answered, "that these sufferings might
be the birth pangs that herald the coming of the Messiah."
The zaddik considered this. "Perhaps, perhaps," he finally
said, "but when suffering is about to reach its peak, Israel
cries out to God, saying it can bear it no longer, and God is
merciful and hears them: he relieves the suffering and post-
pones redemption."

The Wandering Light

A friend once asked the rabbi of Sadagora: "How can this
be? A number of holy men who lived before our time alluded
to a date on which redemption was to come. The era they
indicated has come and gone, but redemption has not come
to pass."
The zaddik replied: "My father, may his memory be a blessing
unto us, said this: 'In the Talmud we read that all the calculated dates of redemption have passed. But just as the
Divine Presence left the sanctuary and went into exile in the
course of ten journeys, so she cannot return all at once, and
the light of redemption loiters between Heaven and earth. At
every date it descended one rung. The light of redemption
is now dwelling in the lowest Heaven, which is called the
"curtain." ' That is what my father said. But I say: the light
of redemption is spread about us at the level of our heads. We
do not notice it because our heads are bowed beneath the
burden of exile. Oh, that God might lift up our heads!"

NAHUM OF STEPINESHT

Playing Checkers

On one of the days of Hanukkah, Rabbi Nahum, the son of the rabbi of Rizhyn, entered the House of Study at a time when he was not expected, and found his disciples playing checkers, as was the custom on those days. When they saw the zaddik they were embarrassed and stopped playing. But he gave them a kindly nod and asked: "Do you know the rules of the game of checkers?" And when they did not reply for shyness he himself gave the answer: "I shall tell you the rules of the game of checkers. The first is that one must not make two moves at once. The second is that one may only move forward and not backward. And the third is that when one has reached the last row, one may move to where he likes."

The Choice

Rabbi Nahum once said to the hasidim gathered about him: "If we could hang all our sorrows on pegs and were allowed to choose those we liked best, every one of us would take back his own, for all the rest would seem even more difficult to bear."

The Pious Man

In a certain city lived a man whose piety was so much talked of that the people had given him the byname of "the Pious One." He fell ill, and when his family heard that several people in the town were going to Rabbi Nahum to beg his blessing, they asked them to mention "the Pious One" when they got to the zaddik. The people agreed. Along with the slips of paper on which they had written their names they also gave Rabbi Nahum a slip bearing the name of the sick man, and told him this was a man who was famed far and wide for the austere life he led, and went by the name of "the Pious One." The rabbi commented: "I do not know what a pious man is, and I never learned anything about it from my father either. But I fancy it must have to do with a kind of cloak: the material is made of arrogance, the lining of grudges, and it is sewed with the threads of dejection."

DAVID MOSHE OF TCHORTKOV

Who Makes the Bands of Sleep to Fall

The hasidim tell this story:
When Rabbi David Moshe, a son of the rabbi of Rizhyn, was
seven years old, a fire broke out in his father's house one night.
The children were assembled, and David Moshe was found to
be missing. His father sent a servant to fetch him. The servant
found the boy lying in bed fully awake and asked whether
he had not noticed that there was a fire. David Moshe said
nothing but gave the servant to understand through signs that
he had of course noticed it, but that since he had already said
the nightly prayer beginning: ". . . who makes the bands of
sleep to fall upon mine eyes," he did not want to interrupt his
falling asleep and was certain he would be saved. While the
servant was reporting this to the father, the fire died down.

The Faithful Servant

Rabbi Nahum of Stepinesht once said this of his brother, Rabbi
David Moshe of Tchortkov:
"When my brother David Moshe opens the Book of Psalms
and begins to recite the praises, God calls down to him: 'David
Moshe my son, I am putting the whole world into your hands.
Now do with it just as you like.' Oh, if he only gave me the
world, I should know very well what to do with it! But David
Moshe is so faithful a servant that when he gives the world
back it is exactly as it was when he received it."

The Birth of a Melody

The rabbi of Tchortkov once said:
"Sometimes it happens that war breaks out between two
kingdoms, and the war drags on for thirty years. Then out of
the groans of those who fell in battle and the cries of the
victors a melody is born so that it may be sung before the
zaddik."

In a Thick Cloud

Rabbi David Moshe said:

"God says to Moses: 'Lo, I come unto thee in a thick cloud that the people may hear when I speak with thee.' There is always danger that the spirit of the zaddik may mount too high and lose touch with his generation. That is why God masses the dark cloud of sorrow over the zaddik and sets limits to his soul, and then the word which he received can get to the people again. But when sorrow descends upon the zaddik, he finds God even in the sorrow, as it is written: '. . . but Moses drew near unto the thick darkness where God was.' "

The Meekness of Moses

Once Rabbi David Moshe said with tears in his eyes:

"It is written that Moses was meek above all men. How are we to interpret this? He with whom God spoke face to face and whose work was so mighty—how could he think himself less than all others? The reason is this: In those forty days which Moses spent on the heights his body had become pure and luminous like that of the ministering angels. After that time he said to himself: 'Of what importance is it, if I, whose body was purified, give service to God? But if one of Israel who is still clad in his turbid flesh serves God—how much greater is he than I!' "

The Scroll of the Torah

Once a new Torah Scroll was being dedicated in the House of Prayer. Rabbi David Moshe held it in his hands and rejoiced in it. But since it was large and obviously very heavy, one of his hasidim went up to him and wanted to relieve him of it. "Once you hold it," said the rabbi, "it isn't heavy any more."

The Natural Way

Rabbi David Moshe once asked after one of his hasidim who was in great straits and in need of the help of God. The rabbi wanted to know whether that help had been accorded him. He was told that that was not the case, and that the nature of his trouble was such it was hardly possible to imagine that help could come in a natural way.

"Most likely the man has not perfect faith," said the zaddik. When he saw that the hasidim did not understand him, he continued: "At first glance it seems as though there were no reason to separate the natural way from the supernatural. This event was sent by God and that other too was sent by God—so why make a distinction? But the distinction is real nevertheless. You know, when the world was created, the flood of light was so unbounded that the world could not bear it, and the vessels broke. And so the light was limited in order that it might be received and contained. And that is the meaning of the natural way: the limiting of the abundance into the bounded measure of the vessels. Now such a vessel is the readiness of man, and the readiness of man is faith. But just as all men have not the same faith, and no man has the same faith at all times, so the bounds of the natural way differ. He whose faith is stronger, whose vessel is more spacious, is accorded a greater measure of the natural way, for that way reaches to the bounds of faith. Yesterday when your faith was small, you had to seek the help you had need of beyond nature, but today your faith has grown great and so all the help you are accorded is possible by the natural way. This is the meaning of what is told of Nahshon, the son of Amminadab: When Israel stood by the Red Sea he leaped into the waters before they were divided, and when they reached his throat, he said: 'Save me, O God, for the waters are come in even unto the soul.' He did not cry aloud, he spoke in a gentle voice, for his faith was great, and so everything that took place was natural."

Praise of This Generation

Once on the eighth day of the Feast of Booths there was great rejoicing at the table of the rabbi of Tchortkov. He laughed and asked: "Why are you people so exceedingly happy? Have you had a drop to drink?"

"There hasn't been time to drink," they replied. "We stayed in the House of Prayer for a long time, and then we came straight to the rabbi's table. We are just happy because of the festival and because we are with our rabbi."

"It is true," said he, "that the moment the people of Israel feel the least bit of revelation, they are filled with an overwhelming joy." And after a while he went on: "I say that this generation of ours from whom God hides in great secrecy is better than the wilderness generation. They were vouchsafed that great revelation, of which a serving-maid, so it is told, saw more than the prophet Ezekiel saw later on, and they had tremendous spiritual powers, and their master was Moses. But now God is hidden, and our strength is slight, and yet the moment we sense the least bit of revelation we are uplifted and full of joy. That is why I say: This generation is better than the wilderness generation."

FROM THE SCHOOL OF

RABBI SHMELKE OF NIKOLSBURG

MOSHE LEIB OF SASOV

By Night

In his youth Moshe Leib sometimes secretly changed his dress
of an evening, left the house unobserved, and shared in the
amusements of some young men of his own age, singing and
dancing with them. They all loved him, and his most casual
word was their law; yet he never commanded them. When he
went to Nikolsburg to study with Rabbi Shmelke, they gave up
their revelry because without him they took no pleasure in it.
After many years, one of them who had been traveling in
foreign lands stopped in Sasov on his way home. In the inn
and on the street everyone he talked to told him about a
wonderful man, the great zaddik Moshe Leib. When he heard
the name, which was quite a common one, it did not occur
to him that this could be his companion in the delights of
days gone by, but his curiosity got the better of him. He went
to the rabbi and instantly recognized him. And the thought
crossed his mind: "My, my, he is certainly an adept at deceiv-
ing the world!" But as he looked into Rabbi Moshe Leib's
face, a face he knew so well and that yet commanded his
reverence, he realized the implication of his memories and
suddenly understood that in those nights he and his friends
had been guided without knowing it, and that time and again
their celebrations had been uplifted under the influence of
a law they could not grasp.
He bowed before the zaddik, who was regarding him with
kindness, and said: "Master, I thank you."

The Rod

Moshe Leib's father was bitterly opposed to the hasidic way.
When he learned that Moshe Leib had left the house without
his knowledge and gone to Rabbi Shmelke's House of Study
in Nikolsburg, he flew into a rage. He cut a vicious rod and
kept it in his room against his son's return. Whenever he

81

saw a more suitable twig on a tree, he cut a new rod which he thought would be more effective, and threw the old one away. Time passed and many rods were exchanged. In the course of a thorough house-cleaning a servant once took the rod up to the attic.

Soon afterward Moshe Leib asked his teacher's leave to absent himself for a short while and went home. When he saw his father jump at sight of him and start on a furious search, he went straight up to the attic, fetched the rod, and laid it down in front of the old man. The latter gazed into the grave and loving face of his son and was won over.

The Khalat

Moshe Leib spent seven years in the House of Study of the holy Rabbi Shmelke of Nikolsburg. When the seven years were up, the rabbi summoned him and said nothing but: "Now you may go home." Then he gave him three things to take with him: a ducat, a loaf of bread, and the kind of long white robe that is called khalat, and he added: "May the love of Israel enter your heart."

Moshe Leib walked all day and grew very tired. In the evening, as he approached a village where he intended to eat his bread and pass the night, he heard the sound of groaning and found that it came from behind a barred cellar window. He went up to it, spoke to the person inside, and soon learned that it was a Jewish innkeeper who had been imprisoned because he had not been able to pay his three hundred gulden rent to the lord of the estate. The first thing Moshe Leib did was to throw his loaf of bread through the bars.

Then without asking the way, just as though he were at home in that region, he made straight for the manor house, asked to be taken to the lord, and requested him to release the Jew. He offered his ducat as ransom. The manor lord merely looked over this impudent fellow who was attempting to settle a debt of three hundred gulden with a ducat, and sent him packing. But the instant Moshe Leib was outside, he was so overcome with the suffering of the imprisoned Jew that he burst in at the door again and cried: "But you must let him go! Take my ducat and let the man go free!"

Now in those days every lord in the state of Poland was a king on his own estate and had the power of life and death. So the lord ordered his servants to seize Moshe Leib and throw him into the kennel. And because Moshe Leib saw death in the eyes of the dogs who rushed at him, he quickly put on his white khalat, so as to die in a festive robe. But at sight of the khalat the dogs backed toward the wall and howled. When the lord entered the kennel, Moshe Leib was still leaning close to the door, and the dogs stood around in a wide circle, howling and shivering. He was told to get out and be off, but Moshe Leib insisted: "Not until you take my ducat and let the man go free!" Then the lord took the ducat and himself went to the house where the Jew was imprisoned, opened the cellar door, and bade the man go home in peace. And Moshe Leib continued his journey.

The rabbi of Tchortkov loved to tell this story, and when he had finished he always added: "Oh, where can that kind of khalat be found!"

A Jew Lives Here!

When Moshe Leib visited Rabbi Elimelekh for the first time, his host honored him at the sabbath meal by asking him to say Torah. Now on this particular sabbath the passage of the Scriptures to be read dealt with God's smiting the Egyptians and passing over the houses of the Israelites. Moshe Leib said: "This cannot possibly mean that God passed over a certain place, because there is no place where he is not. But when he passed through the Egyptians' houses, and saw the corruption of their souls, and then came to a house full of piety and goodness, he was overjoyed and cried: 'A Jew lives here!' "

When Rabbi Elimelekh heard this explanation, he jumped on the table, danced upon it, and sang over and over: "A Jew lives here! A Jew lives here!"

When Moshe Leib was young, he and his wife and children lived in great poverty. One of his neighbors who wished him well offered him a sum of money so that he might ride to market, buy goods, and sell them in his home town. Rabbi Moshe Leib rode to market with the other dealers. When they arrived at their destination they all attended to their business, but he went to the House of Study. When he left it and went to the market place, without realizing how many hours had passed, they were just getting ready to start for home, and when he said he wanted to buy some goods, they laughed at him. So he went home with the rest.

His children were waiting for him in front of his house and called: "What did you bring us?" At these words he fainted.

Just as Moshe Leib regained consciousness, the well-to-do neighbor arrived to inquire how he had made out. He saw how wretched Moshe Leib looked and asked: "What's the matter, Rabbi? Have you lost the money? But don't let that worry you: I'll give you more." Rabbi Moshe Leib only said: "Oh, what shall I do if in the future I come home, and they ask, 'What have you brought us?'"

"Well, if that's the way it is," said the neighbor, "you had better carry on your business at home."

After this, he made known to the world that Rabbi Moshe Leib was a zaddik.

How Long?

Long after Rabbi Moshe Leib's death, his son, Rabbi Shmelke of Sasov, was asked to tell about his father. He said: "He died when I was still a boy and at that time I did not have the understanding to grasp his actions. But there is something I can tell you anyway. I must have been about five years old. It was New Year's and my father was praying at the reader's desk. I had crept under his prayer shawl and heard how in the middle of his low-voiced Prayer of Benedictions he complained to God in the half-coaxing, half-affectionate tone of a child and the language used by the common people. He said something like this: 'Dear God, please send us the Messiah sometime! How long are you going to let us suffer in the dark exile? We can't stand it any more!' "

How a Thief Instructed the Rabbi of Sasov

The rabbi of Sasov once traveled about trying to collect money to ransom persons in the debtors' prison, but he did not succeed in getting together the sum he needed. Then he regretted having wasted time he might have spent studying and praying, and resolved that henceforth he would stay home. On the same day he heard that a Jew who had stolen an article of clothing had been soundly beaten and put in jail. Rabbi Moshe Leib interceded with the judge and gained the thief's release.

When the zaddik went to fetch the thief from jail, he warned him: "Remember the beating they gave you and don't ever do anything like that again!"

"Why not?" said the thief. "If you don't succeed the first time, you may succeed the next."

"If that's the case," said the rabbi to himself, "then I must keep trying at my job, too."

Interruption

One midnight when Rabbi Moshe Leib was absorbed in the mystic teachings, he heard a knock at his window. A drunken peasant stood outside and asked to be let in and given a bed for the night. For a moment the zaddik's heart was full of anger and he said to himself: "How can a drunk have the insolence to ask to be let in, and what business has he in this house!" But then he said silently in his heart: "And what business has he in God's world? But if God gets along with him, can I reject him?" He opened the door at once, and prepared a bed.

Imitatio Dei

The rabbi of Sasov once gave the last money he had in his pocket to a man of ill repute. His disciples threw it up to him. He answered them: "Shall I be more finicky than God, who gave it to me?"

How the Rabbi of Sasov Learned How to Love

Rabbi Moshe Leib told this story:

"How to love men is something I learned from a peasant. He was sitting in an inn along with other peasants, drinking. For a long time he was as silent as all the rest, but when he was moved by the wine, he asked one of the men seated beside him: 'Tell me, do you love me or don't you love me?' The other replied: 'I love you very much.' But the first peasant replied: 'You say that you love me, but you do not know what I need. If you really loved me, you would know.' The other had not a word to say to this, and the peasant who had put the question fell silent again.

"But I understood. To know the needs of men and to bear the burden of their sorrow—that is the true love of men."

His Own Suffering

Whenever the rabbi of Sasov saw anyone's suffering either of spirit or of body, he shared it so earnestly that the other's suffering became his own. Once someone expressed his astonishment at this capacity to share in another's troubles.

"What do you mean 'share'?" said the rabbi. "It is my own sorrow; how can I help but suffer it?"

At the Fair

Rabbi Moshe Leib used to go to the fair and keep a sharp lookout for anyone who might need his help. On one such occasion the traders had left the stalls to watch the performance of a troop of jugglers or some other spectacle, and their cattle remained in the market place, untended. The calves were thirsty and hung their heads. When the rabbi noticed this he took a bucket and watered the animals as if that had been his job all his life. Just then one of the traders returned, and when he saw a man tending the cattle of the others he asked him to see to his cattle, too. They were standing in one of the side streets, he said, and he wouldn't argue over the cattle tender's fee. The rabbi obeyed and stayed on his job until he had finished.

The Love of Man

The rabbi of Sasov used to visit all the sick boys in the town, sit at their bedside, and nurse and take care of them. Once he said: "He who is not willing to suck the pus from the sore of a child sick with the plague has not climbed even halfway up the mountain to the love of his fellow men."

The Delay

On the eve of the Day of Atonement, when the time had come to say Kol Nidre, all the hasidim were gathered together in the House of Prayer waiting for the rabbi. But time passed and he did not come. Then one of the women of the congregation said to herself: "I guess it will be quite a while before they begin, and I was in such a hurry and my child is alone in the house. I'll just run home and look after it to make sure it hasn't awakened. I can be back in a few minutes."
She ran home and listened at the door. Everything was quiet. Softly she turned the knob and put her head into the room— and there stood the rabbi holding her child in his arms. He had heard the child crying on his way to the House of Prayer, and had played with it and sung to it until it fell asleep.

Lamentations at Midnight

Rabbi Moshe Leib was unusually tall and broad but a protracted disease was sapping his strength. However, even when he had retired exhausted with pain, he rose from his bed every midnight, left his room wide-awake and with a firm step, and recited the lamentation over Jerusalem. That was why his hasidim said that the words in the Song of Songs: "Hark! my beloved knocketh," applied to him. For it was clear that the voice of the mournful Divine Presence was knocking at his heart and waking him.
Rabbi Hirsh of Zhydatchov had heard of the rabbi of Sasov's strange doings at midnight. Once when he was a guest in his house he hid so that he might watch him. At midnight he saw the rabbi of Sasov put on peasant's dress, go into the snow-covered yard, fetch a load of wood out of the cellar, lash the logs together, and hoist them on his back. Then he

walked away and Rabbi Hirsh followed him in the crackling cold of the winter night to the end of the town. There Rabbi Moshe stopped in front of a miserable hut and unloaded the wood. His disciple crept up to a back window and looked into a bare room. The stove was out. On the bed lay a woman pressing a newborn child to her breast with a gesture of utter despair.

But at that moment the rabbi of Sasov entered the room. Rabbi Hirsh saw him go up to the woman and heard him address her in Ruthenian: "I have a load of wood for sale and don't want to carry it any further. Will you buy it at a bargain price?" The woman answered: "I haven't a penny in the house." But the rabbi refused to be put off. "I'll come back for the money some other time," he said. "If you'll just take the wood!" The woman objected: "What shall I do with the wood! I can't chop it up myself and there isn't an ax anyway." The rabbi of Sasov replied, "You just let me take care of that," left the room, took his ax, and chopped the wood into small pieces.

And while he was chopping, Rabbi Hirsh heard him reciting that part of the Lamentations at Midnight associated with the name of our Mother Rachel. He caught the words: "Shake thyself from the dust; arise, and sit down, O Jerusalem!" Then the rabbi took the wood, stooped in order to enter through the low door, and made a fire in the stove. While he put in the wood, he softly recited the other part of the lamentations associated with the name of our Mother Leah, and ended with: "Thou wilt arise, and have compassion upon Zion; build Thou Jerusalem." Then he left the room and went home, walking very quickly.

Below and Above

The rabbi of Sasov was entertaining two singers at his house. Their singing was excellent, but—as is so often the case with singers—they were mischievous fellows. Once his wife put some coffee on the table for him, but while he was getting ready the two of them drank it up and filled the pot with water. His wife did not have another warm drink to serve him, for things were none too plentiful in that house. She grew very angry at the ne'er-do-wells and cried: "What do you need singers for! All they give you is trouble!" He said: "Their beautiful songs waken my heart so that I can hear the angels sing."

God and Man

A woman who lived next door to Rabbi Moshe Leib lost one child after another before they were a year old. Once when she was in the zaddik's house, she cried aloud: "A God who gives you children just to take them away again is not good: he is a cruel God!" Rabbi Leib's wife scolded her: "That's no way to talk! What you should say is: 'We cannot fathom God's mercy, and what he does is well done.'"

"Oh, no!" said the rabbi, who heard them talking from where he sat in his room and came out to join them. "You must not be resigned. Take courage, woman, and take strength. A year from now you will have a son, and in time to come I shall lead him under the bridal canopy." And so it was.

When It Is Good to Deny the Existence of God

Rabbi Moshe Leib said:

"There is no quality and there is no power of man that was created to no purpose. And even base and corrupt qualities can be uplifted to serve God. When, for example, haughty self-assurance is uplifted it changes into a high assurance in the ways of God. But to what end can the denial of God have been created? This too can be uplifted through deeds of charity. For if someone comes to you and asks your help, you shall not turn him off with pious words, saying: 'Have faith and take your troubles to God!' You shall act as if there were no God, as if there were only one person in all the world who could help this man—only yourself."

Pouring the Mead

Rabbi Hayyim of Zans told this story:

"When I was a little under three, a great fire broke out in Brody, the town where I was born, and my nurse took me and fled to Sasov. She stayed there with me over the last days of the Feast of Booths. Now on the Day of Rejoicing in the Law, Rabbi Moshe Leib of Sasov was in the habit of going to the market place together with his entire congregation. This time, too, tables and benches had been set up, and they all sat around the tables while the rabbi—blessed be his memory!— took a pitcher of mead, walked from one to the other, and poured. The women came to the market place to watch, and on this occasion my nurse joined them, carrying me in her arms. The rabbi said, 'The women shall stand to one side,' and they did so, my nurse along with them. At that I craned my head across my nurse's shoulder and watched. I watched carefully and I still know everything I saw."

A zaddik who was among his listeners asked: "Does the rabbi really remember how he craned his head across his nurse's shoulder?" Rabbi Hayyim replied: "It was imposed on me to remember, for I had got a beautiful little soul and if I had not spoiled it later on, it would have amounted to something. So I was given this memory to keep on my way."

The Dance of Healing

News was brought to Rabbi Moshe Leib that his friend the rabbi of Berditchev had fallen ill. On the sabbath he said his name over and over and prayed for his recovery. Then he put on new shoes made of morocco leather, laced them up tight and danced.

A zaddik who was present said: "Power flowed forth from his dancing. Every step was a powerful mystery. An unfamiliar light suffused the house, and everyone watching saw the heavenly hosts join in his dance."

The Bridal Dance

A hasid related:

"I was at the wedding of Rabbi Moshe Leib's grandson and there were many guests. When they formed the ring for the bridal dance, a man in a short peasant's smock with a short peasant's pipe in his mouth suddenly leaped into the ring and danced alone in the very middle. I was just about to take him by the sleeve, for I thought he must be out of his mind to break into a circle of zaddikim; but when I saw them all watching him in silence, I let him be. After the dance, I found out that it was the rabbi."

This Is the Time to Dance

A zaddik who was near death got up and danced. And when those around him tried to get him to stop, he said: "This is the time to dance." Then he related: "When Rabbi Uri of Strelisk was traveling around to collect money for some charitable purpose, he called on the rabbi of Sasov. 'I have no money,' said the rabbi, 'but I'll dance a bit for you.' He danced the whole night through and Rabbi Uri did not take his eyes off him, for in every step was a holy meaning. When morning dawned Rabbi Moshe Leib said: 'Now I'll go and collect some money in the market places and streets.'

"He left and did not return until after two days. When they asked him where he had been, he said: 'When I was young, I once needed money to ransom prisoners and started out to collect it with a boy who was to show me where the rich people lived. The boy did his job so cleverly and well that I soon had the required sum. Because of this I promised him that I should once dance at his wedding. Now when I arrived in Zlotchov I heard the sound of gay music, followed it, and learned that the boy I had traveled with was celebrating his wedding. And so I danced and made merry with the merry until now.'

"And that is why I say," the zaddik who was telling the story added, "when they come to you with a demand, it is time to dance."

How the Rabbi of Sasov Helped a Woman Bear Her Child

The story is told:

In a certain village a woman had been lying in labor for days, and the hour of her delivery would not come. They sent a messenger to the rabbi of Sasov to ask him to beg God to have mercy on her. At dead of night the man arrived in the city where he knew no one, not even the zaddik, and could not find his way in the dark. Only one house was still lit. The messenger knocked. An old man opened the door, poured him a glass of brandy to refresh him, and asked why he had come. When he heard the cause of the journey, he said: "It is too late to go there now. You just sleep here and in the morning I'll take you to the rabbi." He gave him something to eat and prepared a bed for him.

The man woke up early in the morning and was sorry that he had given in to his own weariness and the words of the old man, and postponed his pressing errand. Just then his host came up to him and said: "Be of good cheer! I have just learned that the woman has given birth to a healthy boy. Go to the nearby villages and tell her relatives." When the man was outside the house, he discovered from the questions people asked him that he had been a guest of the rabbi; but he did not venture to go back in.

The Way of Life

Rabbi Moshe Leib said:
"The way in this world is like the edge of a blade. On this side is the netherworld, and on that side is the netherworld, and the way of life lies in between."

An Hour

Rabbi Moshe Leib said:
"A human being who has not a single hour for his own every day is no human being."

Depending on God

Rabbi Moshe Leib said:
"How easy it is for a poor man to depend on God! What else has he to depend on? And how hard it is for a rich man to depend on God! All his possessions call out to him: 'Depend on us!' "

Generations

The rabbi of Rizhyn related:
"Once when the holy Baal Shem Tov wanted to save the life of a sick boy he was very much attached to, he ordered a candle made of pure wax, carried it to the woods, fastened

it to a tree, and lit it. Then he pronounced a long prayer. The candle burned all night. When morning came, the boy was well.

"When my grandfather, the Great Maggid, who was the holy Baal Shem's disciple, wanted to work a like cure, he no longer knew the secret meaning of the words on which he had to concentrate. He did as his master had done and called on his name. And his efforts met with success.

"When Rabbi Moshe Leib, the disciple of the disciple of the Great Maggid, wanted to work a cure of this kind, he said: 'We have no longer the power even to do what was done. But I shall relate the story of how it was done, and God will help.' And his efforts met with success."

The Love of Israel

Rabbi Moshe Leib wanted most earnestly to acquire only one of all the virtues of his teacher Rabbi Shmelke of Nikolsburg: his love of Israel. And he did acquire it and in abundance. For when he fell very ill and lay on his bed for two and a half years, racked with pain, he grew more and more certain that he was suffering for the sake of Israel, and his pain did not grow less, but it was transfigured.

The Wedding Tune

Once Rabbi Moshe Leib married off two orphans and saw to it that they did not feel deserted on their wedding day. When the two young people stood under the bridal canopy, the rabbi's face was transfigured with radiance, for at that moment he felt himself a father twice over. He listened to the tune the musicians were playing. Then he said to the people standing around him: "I wish it were vouchsafed me to go to my eternal home on the day destined to the sound of this tune."

After many years, when this hour and these words were long forgotten, a number of musicians were traveling to play at a wedding in Brody, on a snowy winter's day. Suddenly the horses began to pull harder and broke into a rapid trot. The driver could not slow them up. They went faster and faster, jolted the sleigh worse and worse, and ran unerringly toward some goal. They finally stopped at a cemetery. The musicians saw many people gathered there, and asked where they were, and who was being buried. When they heard the name of Rabbi Moshe Leib, they remembered how years ago when they were young they had played before him at the wedding of the two orphans. And now the people too recalled the incident and they all cried: "Play the wedding tune!"

After Death

It is told:

When Rabbi Moshe Leib had died he said to himself: "Now I am free from fulfilling the commandments. What can I do now that will be in obedience to the will of God?" He thought for a while. "It must surely be God's will that I be punished for my countless sins!" And immediately he began to run with all his might and jumped straight into hell. Heaven was very much perturbed at this, and soon the prince of hell was told not to stoke his fires while the rabbi of Sasov was down there. Thereupon the prince begged the zaddik to take himself off to paradise, for this was clearly not the place for him. It just would not do to call a holiday in hell for his sake.

"If that is the case," said Moshe Leib, "I won't stir from here until all the souls are allowed to go with me. On earth I made it my business to ransom prisoners, and so I certainly will not let this big crowd suffer in this prison." And they say that he had his way.

The Dancing Bear

Some guests who had attended the wedding of the daughter of Rabbi Shmelke of Sasov, who was Rabbi Moshe Leib's son, paid a visit to Rabbi Meir of Primishlan on their way home. He questioned them eagerly as to what special thing they had seen at the celebration, refused to be satisfied with what they told him, and kept on asking: "And what else happened?" Finally they said: "While the traditional dances with the bride and groom were going on, an enormous man completely disguised as a bear leaped into the circle and did a most magnificent bear's dance. Everybody marveled at his really wonderful bounds, and there was a great clapping of hands. And then just as suddenly as he had come, he was gone. No one knew him."

"I'll tell you," said Rabbi Meir. "That was none other than our holy teacher Rabbi Moshe Leib of Sasov—may his memory help us—who came down from the uppermost paradise to rejoice with his family."

His Heart

Once Rabbi Bunam was asked: "Have you ever known a zaddik whose heart was broken and crushed and yet sound and whole?" Rabbi Bunam replied: "Yes, I did know such a zaddik. It was Rabbi Moshe Leib of Sasov."

He Who Lives Forever

The hour before he died Rabbi Shmelke of Sasov saw his father Rabbi Moshe Leib and his great teacher Rabbi Mikhal, the maggid of Zlotchov, standing beside him. Then he began to sing the hymn: "Glory and faithfulness are His who lives forever." When he came to the verse, "Cognition and expression are His who lives forever," he stopped singing and said: "When a man approaches his end, when the power of expression and the power of cognition are being taken from him, he shall give these two, cognition and expression, to Him who lives forever."

MENAHEM MENDEL OF KOSOV AND HAYYIM
OF KOSOV

"Wherefore?"

Once when they asked Rabbi Mendel of Kosov with great insistence, "Why doesn't the Messiah come?" he replied: "It is written: 'Wherefore did the son of Jesse not come neither yesterday nor today?' Why does he not come? Because today we are no different from what we were yesterday."

Destroying a Man

A deputation came to Rabbi Mendel of Kosov to complain of a certain slaughterer in their town. After they had enumerated a long list of misdeeds the people asked the zaddik to relieve this objectionable person of his office. But one who had come along with the rest disputed their testimony, saying that it was slander and sprang from hatred. Rabbi Mendel decided in favor of the slaughterer. The others reproached him bitterly because he had believed the words of one single man and ignored the majority.

"The Scriptures relate," he said, "that God bade Abraham offer his son as a burnt-offering, and Abraham prepared to obey. But an angel stopped him and instantly he heeded the angel's voice even though God had not himself revoked his command. What the Torah teaches us thereby is this: None but God can command us to destroy a man, and if the very smallest angel comes after the command has been given and cautions us: 'Lay not thy hand upon . . . ' we must obey him."

The Right Kind of Help

Among Rabbi Mendel's hasidim was a man by the name of Rabbi Moshe, who was both well-to-do and fond of doing good deeds. And then the wheel of fortune turned—to use a popular phrase—and he lost all his money and fell into debt. He went to the zaddik and told him about his predicament. "Go to my brother-in-law, the Seraph of Strelisk," said Rabbi Mendel, "and pour your heart out to him." The man did so. When Rabbi Uri of Strelisk had heard his story he said: "I shall take the bath of immersion for you and the merit of this bath will accrue to your benefit." The man returned to his master and reported what had happened. "Go back to my brother-in-law," said the rabbi of Kosov, "and say to him: 'The bath of immersion will not serve to pay my creditors.' "

The man rode to Strelisk a second time and said what he had been told to. "Very well, my son," the Seraph replied. "In that case I shall also dedicate to your welfare the merit of the phylacteries which I shall put on today." When the man repeated this in Kosov, Rabbi Mendel said: "Give my brother-in-law this message from me: 'The phylacteries can't get rid of tormentors, either.' "

The man did as he was bidden. The Seraph reflected. "Well," said he, "if that is the case, I shall do my utmost for you. I shall dedicate to you the merit of all the prayers I say today, and thus from this hour on the three merits will unite in giving you help." Rabbi Moshe returned to Kosov and gave his report.

"Go," said the zaddik, and he spoke as softly as always, only more slowly, and when he spoke slowly the effect on those who were listening was greater than if he had raised his voice, "go, speak to my brother-in-law in my name and say: 'All this will not settle a single debt.' "

When the Seraph received this message, he immediately put on his fur coat and set out for Kosov. The moment he arrived at his brother-in-law's he asked: "What do you want of me?" "What I want," said Rabbi Mendel, "is for both of us to travel around for a number of weeks, and collect money from our people. For it is written: 'Thou shalt uphold him.' " And that is what they did.

The Snuffbox

Once when Rabbi David of Zablotov, the son of Rabbi Mendel of Kosov, was visiting Rabbi Zevi Hirsh in Zhydatchov, he happened to pull his snuffbox out of his pocket to take a pinch. Hardly had Rabbi Hirsh laid eyes on the box when he asked: "Where did you get that?"

"From my father," said Rabbi David.

"This box," said the rabbi of Zhydatchov, "conjures up for me the Tent of Meeting, and it conjures up all the secret holy meanings which Bezalel the builder had in mind when he put up the Tent of Meeting."

Rabbi David replied: "They told me this about my father: When he had this box made he gave the silversmith a piece of solid silver and told him exactly what to do. He even told him how many times he was to strike with his hammer— just so many and no more. And he stood by the entire time and saw to it that everything was done just as he said."

"Now everything is perfectly clear," said the rabbi of Zhydatchov.

The Gift to His Adversary

A Jew from Kosov who was known to be opposed to the hasidic way once came to Rabbi Mendel and complained that he was about to marry off his daughter and did not have the money for her dowry. He begged the rabbi for advice on how to earn the sum he needed. "How much do you need?" asked the rabbi. It came to a few hundred gulden. Rabbi Mendel opened a drawer in his desk, emptied it, and gave the money to the man.

Soon after, the zaddik's brother learned what had occurred. He came and took the zaddik to task, saying that whenever something was needed in his own house he said he had no money to spare, yet now he had given such a large sum to an adversary. "Someone was here before you," said Rabbi Mendel, "and said exactly the same thing, except that he expressed himself much better than you."

"Who was it?" asked his brother.

Rabbi Mendel replied: "It was Satan."

Dancing and Pain

On every sabbath eve Rabbi Hayyim of Kosov, the son of Rabbi Mendel, danced before his assembled disciples. His face was aflame and they all knew that every step was informed with sublime meanings and effected sublime things.

Once while he was in the midst of dancing, a heavy bench fell on his foot and he had to pause because of the pain. Later they asked him about it. "It seems to me," he said, "that the pain made itself felt because I interrupted the dance."

In Every Generation

One evening several of Rabbi Hayyim of Kosov's hasidim sat together in his House of Study and told one another stories about zaddikim, above all about the Baal Shem Tov. And because both the telling and the listening were very sweet to them, they were at it even after midnight. Then one of them told still another story about the Baal Shem Tov. When he had ended, another sighed from the bottom of his heart. "Alas!" said he, half to himself. "Where could we find such a man today?"

At that instant, they heard steps coming down the wooden stair which led from the zaddik's room. The door opened and Rabbi Hayyim appeared on the threshold, in the short jacket he usually wore in the evening. "Fools," he said softly, "he is present in every generation, he, the Baal Shem Tov, only that in those days he was manifest while now he is hidden." He closed the door and went back up the stair. The hasidim sat together in silence.

YITZHAK EISIK OF KALEV

The Song of the Gooseboy

Rabbi Leib, the son of Sarah, the roving zaddik who never stayed in one place for any length of time, was always on the search for souls, the souls of the dead which longed for redemption, and living souls which needed to be discovered and uplifted.

The story goes that once when he was in the north of Russia, he heard of a holy soul in the south of Hungary which was hiding rather than becoming manifest in the body of a boy. He immediately set out on one of his wonderfully swift journeys. When he arrived in the little town he had been told of, he prayed in the House of Prayer and then went into the adjoining wood and walked until he came to a clearing which was threaded by a stream. There he found a boy of about eight walking slowly along the bank with eyes and ears only for his flock, which obeyed his every whistle and gesture. Rabbi Leib followed unobserved, and soon the boy began to hum a little song, repeating the few words over and over:

> "Shekhinah, Shekhinah, how far, how far!
> Galut, Galut, how endless you are!
> But if the Galut were taken away,
> We could be together, together to stay."

After listening for a while, Rabbi Leib approached the boy and asked him where he had learned his song. "Why, all the herdsmen here sing it," answered the boy. "Do they really sing those words?" the zaddik insisted. "Well," said the boy, "they say 'beloved' instead of 'Shekhinah,' and 'wood' instead of 'Galut,' but that's just stupid. For who could our beloved be if not the Shekhinah and every child knows that the wood which separates us from her is the Galut, so why not say so in the first place?"

Then Rabbi Leib went with the boy and his flock of geese to the poor widow who was his mother and offered to take her son with him and see to it that he grew up to be a rabbi. He brought him to Rabbi Shmelke of Nikolsburg and the boy grew up in his House of Study. Rabbi Shmelke's melodies formed his soul, but to the end of his days he sang to himself the songs of the Hungarian herdsmen, changing only a word here and there.

Miriam's Well

This story was told by a grandson of Jacob Fisch, a man both rich and devout, whom the Baal Shem had blessed with both hands and wished a very long life, and who actually lived to the age of one hundred and thirteen years, his face remaining youthful to the day of his death.

"My grandfather's estate was close to the town of Kalev. Once in the late afternoon before the Day of Atonement, when everybody was already assembled in the House of Prayer, wearing shrouds and reciting the Prayer of Purity with much weeping, the rabbi of Kalev called my grandfather and said to him: 'Rabbi Jacob, have your horses harnessed; let us go for a drive.' My grandfather was very much surprised, but since he was well acquainted with the zaddik's ways he said nothing, but sent word home to have the carriage brought around. They got in and drove across my grandfather's fields. In one place there was a narrow body of water. Quickly the rabbi took off his clothes and immersed himself again and again. My grandfather stood beside him and did not know what to do. But the zaddik was already putting on his clothes. They drove straight to the House of Prayer, and the zaddik went up to the reader's desk.

"My grandfather could not get over his amazement, for never before had he seen any water in that place in his fields. When the Day of Atonement was over, he went back there and looked around, but nowhere could he find a trace of the stream. Then he went to the zaddik and said: 'Rabbi, you know that I never ask you about your own concerns, but now I beg you to explain to me what happened.'

" 'Rabbi Jacob,' answered the zaddik, 'if Miriam's Well, which accompanied Israel in the wilderness, comes through our part of the country unexpectedly, why in the world do you just stand there instead of immersing yourself in it along with me?' "

Immersion without Water

Once on the afternoon before the Day of Atonement, when the time for the ritual bath had come, the rabbi of Kalev went to the stream near which the town is situated. But instead of immersing himself in it he lay down on the grassy bank and said: "Oh, what a good place to sleep!" When it was almost evening, and the hasidim who had accompanied him had all dipped down in the stream, he awoke and stretched. Then without immersing himself, but looking and moving as though he were quickened with new life, as he always appeared after the bath, he returned to the town with the rest.

Enduring Pain

From youth until old age Rabbi Yitzhak Eisik suffered from an ailment which was known to involve very great pain. His physician once asked him how he managed to endure such pain without complaining or groaning. He replied: "You would understand that readily enough if you thought of the pain as scrubbing and soaking the soul in a strong solution. Since this is so, one cannot do otherwise than accept such pain with love and not grumble. After a time, one gains the strength to endure the present pain. It is always only the question of a moment, for the pain which has passed is no longer present, and who would be so foolish as to concern himself with future pain!"

Like Lye

One sabbath, after Rabbi Yitzhak Eisik had sung the song, "When I the sabbath keep," which contains the words: "That is why I wash my heart like lye," he paused and said: "One does not wash lye; one washes with lye!" Then he replied to his own objection: "But the holiness of the holy sabbath can make a heart so pure that it becomes strong enough to purify other hearts, as lye purifies objects."

The disciple who related this incident, later—when he had become a zaddik—told his own hasidim: "Do you know how I became a Jew? My teacher, the holy rabbi of Kalev, took the soul out of my body and soaped and beat it and rinsed it and dried it and rolled it, like women washing clothes at a brook, and then he put this cleansed soul back into me."

"And the Fire Abated"

The tale is told:

The rabbi of Kalev once spent the sabbath in a nearby village as the guest of one of the hasidim. When the hour to receive the sabbath had come, someone suddenly screamed, and a servant rushed in and cried that the barn in which the grain was stored was on fire. The owner wanted to run out, but the rabbi took him by the hand. "Stay!" he said. "I am going to tell you a story." The hasid stayed.

"When our master Rabbi Zusya was young," said the zaddik, "he stoked the stoves in the house of the Great Maggid, for this duty was always assigned to the youngest disciples. Once when he was saying the psalms with great fervor just before the coming of the sabbath, he was startled by screams from within the house. Sparks had fallen from the stove which he had filled with wood, and since no one was in the living room, a fire had started.

" 'Zusya!' he was reproached. 'There's a fire!'

" 'No matter,' he replied. 'Is it not written: And the fire abated!' At that very same moment the fire abated."

The rabbi of Kalev fell silent. The hasid, whom he still held by the hand, did not dare move. A moment passed and someone called in at the window that the fire in the barn had gone out.

The Visit on the Seder Evening

They tell this story:

Reizel, the daughter of Rabbi Zevi Hirsh of Zhydatchov, who had married a son of the rabbi of Kalev, lived with him in her father's house. Once they received an invitation to spend the Passover in Kalev. She was against it since she did not want to be absent from her father's Seder, but her husband kept urging her to accept, until finally she consented.

The customs in her father-in-law's house were different from those she was familiar with. But what vexed her more than anything else was that the rabbi did not sit down at the table early on the Seder evening as her father did, but walked back and forth in the room for a long time without saying a word. Suddenly he threw open the window. A carriage drawn by two great white horses stopped in front of the house. In it were three men and four women of princely appearance. The rabbi went out to them. They embraced and kissed him, exchanged a few words: then the coachman cracked his whip and the carriage was gone. The rabbi re-entered the room, closed the window and sat down at the table. Reizel did not dare to question him.

When the festival was over and she was back home, she told her father all that had happened. "You must know," he instructed her, "that those were the patriarchs and the matri-archs. The holy rabbi did not want to sit down to the Seder before the advent of salvation, and he besieged the upper worlds with his prayers. And so the fathers and the mothers had to appear and tell him that the time was not yet come."

FROM THE SCHOOL OF

RABBI ELIMELEKH OF LIZHENSK

ABRAHAM YEHOSHUA HESHEL OF APT

Knowing the Future

When young Heshel walked across the field, he heard the future in the rustle of growing things; and when he walked through the street, he heard the future in men's footsteps. But when he fled from the world and withdrew to the silence of his room, his own limbs told him the future. Then he began to fear, being uncertain whether he could keep to the true way now that he knew where his feet were taking him. So he gathered courage and prayed that this knowledge be taken from him. And God in his mercy granted his prayer.

The Bribe

In his youth Rabbi Abraham Yehoshua was head of the law court in Kolbishov, and there were five cities in his district. Once he was to decide a lawsuit together with two judges who had been bribed. Since he obstinately opposed all their suggestions, they finally advised the person who had bribed them, who knew as well as they that the rabbi was incorruptible, to slip a considerable sum of money into the pocket of the special coat which Rabbi Abraham Yehoshua wore only on the day of the New Moon. The man took their advice and managed it unobserved. At the next court session the rabbi felt himself inclining to the opinion of his fellow judges. For a while he was silent. Then he postponed decision for a day, went to his room and cried his heart out to God. On the day of the New Moon he put on his special coat and found the money. He summoned the man and forced him to confess what he had done.

Whenever the rabbi of Apt related this incident, he would cite a verse from the fifth book of Moses: "For a gift doth blind the eyes of the wise, and pervert the words of the righteous."

Rabbi Shmelke of Sasov, the son of Rabbi Moshe Leib of Sasov, was still a child at the time of his father's death. Once when he was a young man, he visited the rabbi of Apt. In honor of his guest the rabbi had the candles lit in the House of Study and received him with such kindness that the youth was embarrassed. The moment he had rather reluctantly seated himself in the armchair drawn up for him, the rabbi of Apt turned to him and told him the following:

"I owe it to your father that I began to serve God in the right way. At that time I was rav in the little town of Kolbishov and thought the finest thing in the world was to learn for the sake of learning. One afternoon when I was sitting over my books I heard a carriage drive past. I left the room and found two men just getting off, the older short and frail, the younger a veritable giant. They walked up to me, but since I resented being disturbed in my studies I did not ask who they were. I only offered them some pastries and a sweet liqueur and went back to my books. They sat and talked to each other without paying any attention to me.

"I took myself firmly in hand and tried to go on studying without being distracted, yet I could not help hearing some of their words, especially as there was something majestic and solemn in their voices and the expression of their faces. They were indeed speaking of solemn matters, apparently continuing a discussion they had begun on their journey. But in my soul I rejected the idea of having anything to do with it, for I said to myself: 'That is not my way—so why should I concern myself with it?' Later I accompanied them to the House of Prayer. After the prayer, they asked me whether I could put them up for the night. At that time there was not much room in my house, but it was impossible to turn away men such as these—that was perfectly clear to me. So I said yes, served them coffee, and went on studying. And the same thing happened as before: they continued their discussion and my mind was torn between trying to concentrate on my reading and fighting against listening. Then I prepared a place for them to sleep and I too lay down. Around midnight

I rose as always and began to study. In the next room I heard them talking about sublime matters.

"Early in the morning they came to bid me farewell and asked me in a way that seemed quite casual what passage in the Talmud I was studying at the moment. When I told them, they began to discuss that passage. The older man made a remark about it, the younger raised an objection, and when half an hour was up, between them they had completely illuminated the passage and I realized that I had not understood it properly until then. Then to cite an example for something he had said the older man told a story about the Baal Shem Tov and in the same way the younger told one too.

"When they had finished their stories they took leave of me, and even then I did not ask them anything, for I was glad to continue my studies undisturbed. But as, in my usual custom, I was walking up and down the balcony a little before going to the House of Prayer, I suddenly thought: 'Why didn't I ask those men who they were and why they came?' And then, bit by bit, the words I had caught while I was studying came back to me and formed a connected whole. Only then did I know with certainty that what they had said had been sublime. From that time on I could do nothing but think of them. I repeated their words to myself and saw that they were intended to be properly learned. But then I noticed that from day to day my prayer was becoming purer and stronger. The words I had heard surrounded the prayer and purified and strengthened it. I grew sadder and sadder at the thought that I had let the men go without becoming acquainted with them, and my longing to see them again increased.

"Another early morning, two weeks afterward, I was walking up and down the balcony with just a skullcap on (for I was in the habit of putting on my fur cap only before going to the House of Prayer), when I saw a carriage passing the house. Evidently it was not going to stop. The two men were in it. I rushed out with only my cap on my head and called a word of greeting. The carriage stopped, they returned my greeting indifferently, and the older man added: 'We are in a hurry. We want to pray in the next village.'

" 'Can't I get you something to eat?' I asked.

" 'Well, all right,' said the younger, a little more cordially.

" 'Get us a few pretzels, but quickly.'

"It took a few moments to fetch them, and when I came out of the house the carriage was making off at full speed. I swiftly snatched up prayer shawl and phylacteries and holding them in one hand and the pretzels in the other, I ran after the carriage in my skullcap and shouted to them to stop. But they did not seem to hear me, and not until I had mustered all my strength to catch up with them did the carriage stop. I got in and we began to talk. I found out that the older man was the rav of Berditchev and the younger Rabbi Moshe Leib of Sasov, your father. After we had prayed in the next village, I offered them the pretzels and they said the blessing and ate, and I with them. Then they wanted to send me home but I begged to be allowed to accompany them a short way. So we drove off together and they spoke to me, and then I asked questions and they answered. The talk continued and the carriage rolled along and I was not aware that the hours were passing. When the carriage stopped, I discovered that we were in Lizhensk, in front of Rabbi Elimelekh's house. 'Here you are,' said your father. 'This is where your light lives.'

"And so I stayed on in Lizhensk."

Temptations

Joseph Landau, the rabbi of Jassy in Rumania, had rejected a bribe offered him by a prominent member of his congregation whom he had opposed because the man had violated a religious law. Shortly after this he visited the rabbi of Apt, and with a self-satisfied air told him how he had resisted temptation. When the zaddik bade him farewell he blessed him and expressed the hope that he would become an honest and God-fearing man. "I am delighted with the blessing of my teacher and master," said Rabbi Joseph Landau, "and what more could I ask! But why did you wish me this just at this time?"

The rabbi of Apt replied: "It is written: 'Also unto Thee, O Lord, belongeth mercy; for Thou renderest to every man

110

according to his work.' Those who expounded these verses asked themselves time and again why paying a hired man his proper wages should be called 'mercy.' But the truth of the matter is that God has mercy when he leads every man into the temptation befitting his inner level: the common man into petty, the superior man into grave, temptation. The fact that you were exposed to so slight a temptation is a sign that you have not yet reached one of the upper rungs to perfection. That is why I blessed you asking God to let you ascend to them and be found worthy of a greater test."

In Hell

The rabbi of Apt said to God:
"Lord of the world, I know that I have no virtue and no merit for which, after my death, you could set me in paradise among the righteous. But if you are thinking of putting me in hell among the evil-doers, please remember that I cannot get along with them. So I beg of you to take all the wicked out of hell, so you can put me in."

The Turning Point

A respected woman once came to ask the advice of the rabbi of Apt. The instant he set eyes on her he shouted: "Adulteress! You sinned only a short while ago, and yet now you have the insolence to step into this pure house!" Then from the depths of her heart the woman replied: "The Lord of the world has patience with the wicked. He is in no hurry to make them pay their debts and he does not disclose their secret to any creature, lest they be ashamed to turn to him. Nor does he hide his face from them. But the rabbi of Apt sits there in his chair and cannot resist revealing at once what the Creator has covered." From that time on the rabbi of Apt used to say: "No one ever got the better of me except once—and then it was a woman."

The Proud and the Humble

Once the rabbi of Apt came to a city in which two men competed for the privilege of giving him lodgings. Both houses

111

were equally roomy and comfortable and in both households all the rules were observed with pious exactness. But one of the men was in ill repute for his many love affairs and other sinful doings and he knew quite well that he was weak and thought little of himself. The other man, however, no one in the whole community could accuse of the slightest breach of conduct. With proud and stately steps he walked abroad, thoroughly aware of his spotless purity.

The rabbi selected the house of the man with the bad reputation. When he was asked the reason for his choice, he answered: "Concerning the proud, God says: 'I and he cannot live together in this world.' And if God himself, blessed be he, cannot share a room with the proud, then how could I! We read in the Torah, on the other hand: ' . . . who dwelleth with them in the midst of their uncleannesses.' And if God takes lodgings there, why shouldn't I?"

The Golden Scale

Rabbi Naftali, a disciple of the rabbi of Apt, who later became the rabbi of Roptchitz, asked a fellow pupil to find out what their teacher thought of him. For half a year his friend made every effort to get the rabbi to say something, but he said nothing about Naftali, nothing good and nothing bad. So his fellow disciple told Naftali, saying: "You see, the master has a golden scale in his mouth. He never passes judgment on anyone, for fear he might wrong him. Has he not forbidden us to judge even those who are supposed wicked through and through? For if anyone were to wrong them, he would be wronging God himself."

Tall Stories

The rabbi of Apt liked to tell tall stories. You might have taken them for meaningless exaggerations, and yet not only his disciples but others too saw meaning in them and found enlightenment.

Once when he was visiting Rabbi Barukh of Mezbizh, a grandson of the Baal Shem, and was just about to begin a story, Rabbi Barukh asked him to accompany him to the well which was called "the spring of the Baal Shem." The moment they reached the well the rabbi of Apt started talking and Rabbi Barukh stood by, leaning on his cane and listening. Among other things, the rabbi of Apt told about his son's wedding: "The batter for the noodle dish was spread on leaves over the fences and even hung down from the roof-tops!"

The Mezbizh hasidim who surrounded the two watched the wise lips of their rabbi and prepared to burst out laughing as soon as he did, but they saw that he was listening attentively and his lips were not twitching. Later, when the rabbi of Apt had left, Rabbi Barukh said: "Never have I heard such a golden tongue!"

On another occasion, when the rabbi of Apt went to Berditchev to call on Rabbi Levi Yitzhak, the people came in droves to see and greet him. Scarcely had he tasted the sweet liqueur and the cakes that had been set before him, when he began to walk up and down the room telling a story. He told how when he was a rav in the town of Jassy they had wanted to build a big bridge in front of his house, and what huge quantities of wood they had carted to the spot. A merchant who often went to Jassy to trade was among the listeners, and nodded eagerly: "Yes, Rabbi, that's just the way it was!" The rabbi of Apt turned to him in surprise. "And how do you know about it?" he asked.

Denunciation

Two young men who had been friends from childhood on lived in the same city. After they married they decided to be partners in a business, and their business throve. But the wife of the one, who was clever and smooth in her dealings with customers, was displeased that her husband's friend who had a good but somewhat stupid wife should have half the profits. Her husband did indeed tell her that it is not our shrewdness or strength that matters, but only that which pleases God. She however would not accept his instruction and pressed him more and more until finally he said to his friend: "We must separate, dear friend, for I cannot stand this any longer."

They divided up the business, but from that time on the man with the dull wife had all the luck, while the clever wife made nothing but blunders in her buying and selling. She grew more and more malicious and finally hit on the idea of having two bribed witnesses take a false oath that the other woman had committed adultery.

The matter came before the religious court. When Rabbi Abraham Yehoshua had examined the witnesses, he sent for his son and said to him: "Have this posted all over the district: 'Whoever from this time on gives the rabbi of Apt a ruble is a sinner in Israel.' For it says in the Torah: 'At the mouth of two witnesses . . . shall he that is to die be put to death.' But I can see that this woman is without guilt. Thus what I see is contrary to the holy Torah, and whoever pays me taxes sins."

When the rabbi of Apt had uttered these words with all solemnity, the witnesses were seized with terror. They nudged each other with their elbows and then confessed the truth.

The World of Illusion

Once the rabbi of Apt spoke of the world of illusion in which the souls of all those who die deluded by their own vanity stray. And he told this story:

"A few years ago during a very cold winter a poor man went to buy wood in the market place of our town. He wanted to warm the room for his wife who had just borne a child. There were only a few fagots left and he was just about to purchase them when the head of the community appeared and outbid him. The poor man who could not pay a higher price begged him in vain to have pity on his wife and child. That night the woman and baby fell sick, and they died a few days later. The man survived them for only a short while; but on the very day he died the head of the community died too.

"Then the souls of both men appeared to me in a dream. For the poor man had summoned his opponent to my court. I pronounced the judgment. Many times in the course of his life the head of the community had been brought before worldly judges on the complaints of those he had oppressed and tormented, but since he was well versed in all the intricacies of the law, he had always had the suits referred to one higher

court after another until he managed to get himself acquitted.
Even now, in the world of illusion, he seemed just as sure
of himself as he had been on earth and appealed to a higher
judge. He came without delay, but contrary to expectations
he not only agreed with my judgment but pronounced an even
harsher sentence.

" 'I'll teach the judge!' shouted the accused and again appealed
to a still higher court. But when the court convened, his
sentence was again raised.

" 'If I have to go to the emperor himself, I'll see this thing
through!' shouted the head of the community.

"By now he has gotten as far as the governor."

Those Who Are to Hear, Hear

Once a great throng of people collected about the rabbi of
Apt to hear his teachings.

"That won't help you," he cried to them. "Those who are to
hear, will hear even at a distance; those who are not to hear,
will not hear no matter how near they come."

Ways

A disciple asked the rabbi of Apt: "It is written: 'For the
Lord regardeth the way of the righteous; but the way of the
wicked shall perish.' The two parts of this sentence do not
seem to belong together."

The rabbi explained: "The righteous have many and devious
ways, and the wicked have also many and devious ways. But
the Lord knows the ways of the righteous by the fact that
they are all one way and that is the Way. But the ways of the
wicked are numerous and manifold, for they are nothing but
many ways of losing the one way. In the end they themselves
realize that each is losing his own way and all the ways.

"It is as though someone were walking through a wood and
keeping to a certain path not knowing why he has taken this
particular path rather than another. He keeps walking day
and night until he comes to a tall beech standing at the end
of the path and at that point the way is lost. The man cannot

go forward and he does not dare to go back, for he has lost the way."

Freedom of Choice

Rabbi Heshel said:

It is God's will that there be freedom of choice. That is why he has waited until this day. For in the days of the Temple they had the death penalty and whipping, and so there was no freedom. After that Israel had penal codes, so there was still no freedom. But now everyone can sin openly and without shame, and prosper. And so whoever leads a good life today is worthy in the eyes of God, and redemption depends on him.

A Great Nation

The rabbi of Apt was asked: "The Midrash points out that God said 'Go' twice to Abraham, once when he bade him leave his father's house, and once when he commanded him to sacrifice his son. The explanation in the Midrash is that the first bidding as well as the second was a test. How are we to understand that?"

He replied: "When God bade Abraham leave his father's house, he promised to make of him 'a great nation.' The Evil Urge observed with what eagerness he prepared himself for the journey and whispered to him: 'You are doing the right thing. A great nation—that means power, that means possessions!'

"But Abraham only laughed at him. 'I understand better than you,' he said. 'A great nation—means a people that sanctifies the name of God.' "

Every Day

The rabbi of Apt said:

"Every one of Israel is told to consider himself to be standing at Mount Sinai to receive the Torah. For man there are past and future events, but not for God; day in, day out, he gives the Torah."

Two Kinds of Love

This question was put to the rabbi of Apt: "It is written: 'And Jacob served seven years for Rachel; and they seemed unto him but a few days, for the love he had to her.' How shall we interpret this? One would think that the time seemed overlong for the lover and that a day seemed as long as a year!"

The rabbi of Apt explained: "There are two kinds of love. The first attaches itself to the loved object and returns to the lover, and so every hour is long and hangs heavy on his hands because the lover longs to go to his beloved. But the second, the love for one's true mate, does not return to the lover. So it does not matter whether he lives one or a thousand miles away from his beloved. That is why we read: 'And Jacob served seven years for Rachel; and they seemed unto him but a few days, for the love he had to her.' It was her he loved; his love clung to her and did not return to him. He was not concerned with himself and his desire. His was the true love."

Like a Vessel

Rabbi Heshel said:

"A man should be like a vessel that willingly receives what its owner pours into it, whether it be wine or vinegar."

We Shape a Human Likeness for God

Our sages said: "Know what is above you." This is how the rabbi of Apt expounded those words:

" 'Know what is above, is from you.' And what is it that is above you? This is what Ezekiel says: 'And upon the likeness of the throne was a likeness as the appearance of a man upon it above.' How can this be said with reference to God? For is it not written: 'To whom then will ye liken Me, that I should resemble him?' But the truth of the matter is that it is we who make 'a likeness as the appearance of a man.' It is the likeness we shape when we serve with devout hearts. With such a heart we shape a human likeness for our Creator, for him, blessed be he and blessed be his name, who can be likened to none. When a man is merciful and renders loving help he assists in shaping God's right hand. And when a man fights the battle of God and crushes Evil, he assists in shaping

God's left hand. He who is above the throne—it is you who have made him."

The Widow

A disciple of the rabbi of Apt related this story:

"Once I was present at a conversation my teacher carried on with a widow. He spoke to her of her widowhood in good, comforting words, and she allowed her soul to be comforted and found new strength. But I saw that he wept and I too began to weep; for suddenly I knew that he was speaking to the Divine Presence, that is forsaken."

The Soul

On the Day of Atonement, when Rabbi Abraham Yehoshua would recite the Avodah, the prayer that repeats the service of the high priest in the Temple of Jerusalem, and would come to the passage: "And thus he spoke," he would never say those words, but would say: "And thus I spoke." For he had not forgotten the time his soul was in the body of a high priest of Jerusalem, and he had no need to learn from the outside how they had served in the Temple.

Once he himself related: "Ten times have I been in this world. I was a high priest, I was a prince, I was a king, I was an exilarch. I was ten different kinds of dignitary. But I never learned to love mankind perfectly. And so I was sent forth again and again in order to perfect my love. If I succeed this time, I shall never return again."

Tears and Laughter

A man once confessed a sin to the rabbi of Apt and told him with tears how he had atoned for it. The zaddik laughed. The man went on to tell what more he intended doing to atone for his sin; the rabbi went on laughing. The man wanted to speak on, but the laughter robbed him of his speech. He stared at the zaddik in horror. And then his very soul held its breath and he heard that which is spoken deep within. He realized how trivial all his fuss about atoning had been and turned to God.

Later the rabbi of Apt told his hasidim: "Two thousand years ago, before I became a high priest in the Temple of Jerusalem, I had to learn the service step by step. First I was accepted into the company of young priests. At that time this man who has just gone was one of those who lived remote from the rest. He was stern with himself, pure and proven in the practice of all the virtues. But unexpectedly he was snared in a serious sin. In accordance with the law he prepared to bring a sin-offering.

"This was the custom in those days: When a man came to the keeper in charge to choose an animal for the sacrifice, the official asked him what sin he was about to atone for. When the man would begin to speak, the sorrow of his secret would spill over, and he would pour his heart out like water. Then he would take the animal and walk through the streets of Jerusalem to the hall of the Temple where the animal was to be slaughtered. There the young priests would come to meet him and they too would inquire what his sin had been, and again his heart would melt like wax in fire. By the time such a man would reach the high priest and confess his innermost secret, he would be wholly transformed.

"Now when this man entered the Temple hall with his sacrificial animal, I took pity on his ravaged and tear-stained face. I comforted him, wept with him, and eased his heart, until he began to regain his composure and his sin weighed on him less and less. When he came to the high priest he did not experience the turning to God, and his offering was not graciously accepted. So, in the course of time, he had to come down to earth once more and appear before me again. But this time I loved him more."

The Servant of the Lord

The rabbi of Apt was asked:
"In the last chapter of the fifth book of Moses we read: 'So Moses, the servant of the Lord, died there . . .' And we read again in the first chapter of Joshua: ' . . . After the death of Moses, the servant of the Lord.' Why should Moses be desig-

nated a servant of the Lord in the hour of his death and after it, just as if this were something new? For chapter after chapter before this we read how he served his Lord with all his heart and substance."

The rabbi of Apt expounded: "Before Moses died, the Lord showed him the land from the top of Mount Nebo and said to him: 'This is the land which I swore unto Abraham, unto Isaac, and unto Jacob.' Rashi comments on this: 'God sent Moses forth and said: Go and tell the patriarchs that I shall now fulfil the oath which I swore unto them.' So even in his death Moses was the messenger and faithful servant of God, and he died in order to serve in all eternity."

The Table

On the day of the New Moon in the month he was to die, the rabbi of Apt discussed at his table the death of the righteous man. When he had said grace he rose and began to walk back and forth in the room. His face glowed. Then he stopped by the table and said: "Table, pure table, you will testify in my behalf that I have properly eaten and properly taught at your board."

Later he bade that his coffin be made out of the table.

The Inscription

Before he died the rabbi of Apt ordered his sons to have no other words of praise carved on his tombstone than: "He who loved Israel." That is the inscription on the stone.

In Dying

When he lay dying the rabbi of Apt cried out: "Why does the son of Jesse delay?"

He wept and said: "Before his death the rabbi of Berditchev promised that he would disturb the peace of all the holy men, and that he would not stop until the Messiah came. But then they showered him with such delights in hall after hall that he forgot. But I shall not forget. I do not want to enter paradise before the coming of the Messiah."

120

After the rabbi of Apt's death, two zaddikim met, Rabbi Yitzhak of Radzivil, the son of the maggid of Zlotchov, and Rabbi Israel of Rizhyn, the rabbi of Mezritch's great-grandson. Rabbi Israel asked: "What did he mean by saying that he did not want to enter paradise before the coming of the Messiah?" Rabbi Yitzhak replied: "In the psalm we read: 'We have thought on Thy lovingkindness, Elohim, in the midst of Thy temple.' My reading of this verse is this: 'We thought of Elohim. Your lovingkindness is in the midst of your temple.' The name Elohim refers to the divine attribute of rigor. So, when we 'think,' we think of our troubles *here*, seeing in them only the divine attribute of rigor, or Elohim. But *there*, 'in the midst of Thy temple,' everyone who comes, if only to the threshold, knows that everything there is the 'lovingkindness' of God."

The Vision of the Vegetable Vendor

Rabbi Yitzhak of Neskhizh, the son of Rabbi Mordecai of Neskhizh, told this story:

"On the day before the rabbi of Apt suddenly fell ill and died, an old woman who sold vegetables in the market place said to her neighbor: 'This morning at dawn—I don't know whether I was awake or dreaming—I saw my husband, may he rest in peace, who has been dead these many years. I saw him rush past without looking at me. Then I burst into tears and cried to him: "First you go and leave me to a miserable life with my orphaned children and now you don't even look at me!" But he kept on running and didn't turn to give me a glance. As I sat there crying, I saw him coming back. He stopped and said: "I couldn't take any time off before. We had to fumigate the road and cleanse the air because the zaddikim from the Land of Israel cannot stand the air here, and they will soon be coming to receive the rabbi of Apt and escort him to the other side." '

"Isn't that a fine story?"

This tale is told:

Once the rabbi of Apt sat deep in thought. He looked bewildered and a little sad. When his hasidim asked whether anything was troubling him, he said: "Up to now, during my soul's every sojourn on earth I occupied some post of honor in Israel: but this time I have none." At that very moment a messenger from the Land of Israel arrived and handed the rabbi an official letter. In it was stated that the Palestinian community made up of emigrants from Volhynia whose seat was in Tiberias, nominated him their head. The rabbi of Apt had a feast prepared to celebrate his happiness. Then he gave the messenger a sum of money for the purpose of acquiring a plot of ground for him beside the grave of the prophet Hosea, and of the same size.

The night Rabbi Abraham Yehoshua died, a knocking was heard at the window of the Volhynia meeting house in Tiberias: "Go out and escort the rabbi of Apt to his eternal rest," it said. When the caretaker opened the door he saw a bier being borne through the air. Thousands of souls were swarming around it. He followed it to the cemetery and watched them lower the body into the grave.

MENAHEM MENDEL OF RYMANOV

The Song of Praise

The only way young Mendel could manage to travel from his home to the city where Rabbi Elimelekh lived was to hire himself out as servant to a coachman. His duties included watching the carriage and the horses during the stops on the journey. It was a bitterly cold day. The driver and his passengers were warming themselves in the inn, eating and drinking. Rabbi Mendel in his thin coat and his shoes full of holes walked back and forth beside the carriage and rubbed his hands. "Praise be to the Creator," he sang to himself, "that I am cold. Praise be to the Creator that I am hungry." He hopped from one foot to the other, and sang his song of praise as though it were a dance tune.

A guest coming toward him from the inn saw and heard him, and was amazed. "Young man," said he, "what are you mumbling to yourself?"

Mendel answered: "I am thanking God that I am in good health and can be so enormously hungry."

"But why don't you eat until you are full?" asked the man.

Mendel thought this over. "You have to have money for that," he said.

The man called a servant to watch the carriage, took Mendel into the inn, and had food and a warm drink brought to him. Then he saw to it that he got sturdy shoes and a short sheepskin coat of the sort the village Jews wear.

When Mendel reached Lizhensk he immediately went to Rabbi Elimelekh's house and, so quickly that the servants did not notice him, walked into the room of the zaddik, who was sitting over a book, absorbed in the profundities of the teachings. His son Eleazar motioned to the unmannerly stranger to go and wait outside until his presence would not disturb the zaddik in his studies. But Rabbi Elimelekh had already looked up. He took his son by the arm and said almost singing, as though he were chanting a song of praise: "Lazar, Lazar, what do you want of that little Jew? Why, sparks of fire are flying all around his head."

Barter

Rabbi Mendel's wife's parents kept urging their daughter to get a divorce from a husband who turned away from this-world things and whose inefficiency in business only equaled his dislike for it. When she refused, they put out the couple, who up to this time had been living with them, as was customary. Then the two were in bitter need. Occasionally with the cook's connivance the woman managed to steal a few provisions from her father's kitchen, or a few fagots from her father's cellar. But once when her parents were away on a trip and the tradesmen refused to give her anything more on credit, she could not bring Rabbi Mendel, who was sitting over his books in the House of Study, a thing to eat for three days. On the third day she ventured to cross the baker's threshold one more time. He turned her away. Silently she left the shop. But he followed her and offered her bread and other food, as much as she could carry, if she on her part would promise him her share in the world to come. She hesitated only an instant. Then she accepted his offer.

When she entered the House of Study she saw her husband sitting in his seat. He was almost unconscious, but the book was gripped firmly in both his hands. She spread the cloth, served him, and watched him while he ate. He looked up, for never before had she remained. They looked at each other. When their eyes met, she saw he knew what she had done. And then she saw that at that moment she had received a new share in the coming world.

The Hungry Child

Once when there was not a piece of bread in Rabbi Mendel's house, his son ran to him crying and complained his hunger was so great he could bear it no longer.

"Your hunger is not so great as all that," said his father. "For otherwise I should have something to quiet it."

The boy slunk off without a word. But before he reached the door, the rabbi saw a small coin lying on the table.

"I wronged you," he called out. "You are really very hungry indeed."

The Spoon

Rabbi Elimelekh's servant once forgot a spoon for Rabbi Mendel who was a guest at Rabbi Elimelekh's table. Everyone ate except Rabbi Mendel. The zaddik observed this and asked: "Why aren't you eating?"

"I have no spoon," said his guest.

"Look," said Rabbi Elimelekh, "one must know enough to ask for a spoon, and a plate too, if need be!"

Rabbi Mendel took the word of his teacher to heart. From that day on his fortunes were on the mend.

In Youth

Rabbi Mendel once boasted to his teacher Rabbi Elimelekh that evenings he saw the angel who rolls away the light before the darkness, and mornings the angel who rolls away the darkness before the light. "Yes," said Rabbi Elimelekh, "in my youth I saw that too. Later on you don't see those things any more."

The Call

A man came to Rabbi Mendel and begged him to confirm him in the feeling that he had the call to be a rabbi. He said he felt that he had reached that rung and was capable of pouring blessings upon Israel. For a time the zaddik looked at him in silence. Then he said:

"When I was young the voice of a man used to wake me every night at midnight. It would call to me: 'Mendel, rise for the Lamentations at Midnight!'

"I had grown accustomed to the voice. But one night I heard another voice call. 'Rabbi Mendel,' said the voice, 'rise for the Lamentations at Midnight.' I was terrified. I trembled until dawn and all day I was seized by terror. 'Perhaps I heard wrong,' I said to calm my heart. But the next night the voice again said: 'Rabbi Mendel!'

"For forty days afterward I mortified my flesh and prayed without ceasing that the voice be taken from me. But the gates of Heaven remained closed to me, and the voice kept calling. So I resigned myself."

The Testament

Before he died Rabbi Elimelekh laid his hands on the heads of his four favorite disciples and divided what he owned among them. To the Seer of Lublin he gave his eyes' power to see; to Abraham Yehoshua, his lips' power to pronounce judgment; to Israel of Koznitz, his heart's power to pray; but to Mendel he gave his spirit's power to guide.

Nothing to Offer

After Rabbi Elimelekh's death a number of his younger disciples agreed to go to Rabbi Mendel, who at that time was still living in Prystyk. They arrived at his house on a Friday afternoon. On the table were two sabbath loaves made of rye flour and two small candles in crude clay holders. They asked his wife where he was and were told that he had not yet returned from the ritual bath. Naftali, later the rabbi of Roptchitz, at once went to the city and bought all the necessary things: a white tablecloth, real white sabbath loaves both large and small, and tall candles in handsome holders. The table was set properly and they all sat down to it.

When Rabbi Mendel entered the room, they all rose to show him that they accepted him as their father. He fixed one after the other with a long, searching gaze.

Then he said: "If you bring the right things with you, you may come even to me, who have nothing to offer."

Refusal

On the eve of the New Year Rabbi Mendel entered the House of Prayer. He surveyed the many people who had come together from near and far. "A fine crowd!" he called out to them. "But I want you to know that I cannot carry you all on my shoulders. Every one of you must work for himself."

Women's Wear

The first ruling Rabbi Mendel had made in Rymanov was that the daughters of Israel should not parade up and down the streets in gay-colored, lavishly trimmed dresses. From then on the Jewish girls and women of Rymanov faithfully followed the zaddik's orders. But the daughter-in-law of the wealthiest man in town, the wife he had just fetched for his son from the capital of the district, refused to let her finery turn yellow in her chest with none to admire it.

When Rabbi Mendel saw her strutting up and down the main street, dressed in her best, he sent for the most mischievous guttersnipes and gave them permission to call after the woman whatever went through their heads. The rich man, who was one of the pillars of the community, came to the rabbi in a rage and tried to make clear to him that his ruling was con-trary to the Torah, for Ezra the Scribe had included in his ordinances permission for traders to travel from place to place so that the daughters of Israel might adorn themselves.

"Do you think," asked Rabbi Mendel, "that Ezra meant them to parade up and down the streets? Do you think he did not know that a woman can receive the honors due her nowhere save in her home?"

Weights and Measures

On the last day of every month Rabbi Mendel had the weights and measures in every Jewish shop examined. Once in the place of business of a rich man his agents discovered a liquid measure which had been declared invalid. The proprietor asserted that he no longer used it for measuring. "Even if you only use it for a spittoon, the law forbids you to have it on your premises," said one of the investigators, Rabbi Hirsh, the faithful "Servant" of Rabbi Mendel, whom the zaddik had secretly chosen for his successor. He hurled the measure to the ground and smashed it with his foot.

"Is Saul also among the prophets?" sneered the merchant. "Are you already competent to lay down the law?"

When Hirsh returned to the zaddik he reported that everything was in good order, but the others told Rabbi Mendel what had happened. He immediately sent out a crier to hammer on the doors of all the people and summon them to a sermon in the House of Prayer. But he forbade the man to knock at the rich merchant's door.

The congregation assembled. Rabbi Mendel preached on the subject of just weights and measures. Only then did the rich man, who had come along with the others, realize why he had not been summoned. The fact that the rabbi was speaking about him to everyone but him, wounded him to the heart. After the sermon he went up to Rabbi Mendel and begged to be given a penance and pardoned.

Concerning Hospitality

A man came and complained to Rabbi Mendel that he could not fulfil the commandment to be hospitable because his wife did not like to have guests, and whenever he brought people to the house it gave rise to quarrels which threatened his domestic peace.

The rabbi said, "Our sages say: 'Welcoming guests is a greater virtue than welcoming the Divine Presence.' This may sound exaggerated to us. But we must understand it properly. It is said that when there is peace between husband and wife the Divine Presence rests in their minds. That is why welcoming guests is described as being more important than welcoming the Divine Presence. Even if hospitality destroys the peace that exists between a man and his wife, the commandment to be hospitable is still the more important."

Guest Loaves

During a period when the cost of living was very high, Rabbi Mendel noticed that the many needy people whom he entertained as guests in his house received smaller loaves than usual. He gave orders to make the loaves larger than before, since loaves were intended to adjust to hunger and not to the price.

The Leaky Roof

Government officials came to Rymanov to requisition a house in which to store provisions for the army. The only house

128

suitable for their purpose proved to be the House of Prayer
of the Jewish congregation. When the heads of the community
heard of this, they did not know what to do and consulted
Rabbi Mendel in great dismay. But one of them recalled a
circumstance which might lead to a change in the decision: the
roof of the House of Prayer had been leaking for quite a
while and if a heavy rain were to fall, the provisions would
certainly have to be stored elsewhere.

"Then the decision to make a storehouse of the House of
Prayer is just," said the rabbi. "For it is a judgment upon
your idleness and neglect. Have the roof mended at once!"

The roof was mended the same day. From that time on nothing
further was heard concerning the decision of the officials. Only
after some weeks did the people of Rymanov hear that on
that very day the officials had decided in favor of another town.

At Court

When the rabbis of Apt and Rymanov were staying with the
Seer of Lublin in the city of Lantzut where he lived before
going to Lublin, his enemies denounced his guests to the
authorities, who had them jailed. They decided that since
Rabbi Mendel could speak the best German and German was
the language used in the court, he was to do the talking for all
when they were examined.

The judge asked: "What is your business?"

The rabbi of Rymanov replied: "Serving the king."

"What king?"

"The King over all kings."

"And why did you two strangers come to Lantzut?"

"To learn greater zeal in serving, from this man here."

"And why do you wear white robes?"

"It is the color of our office."

The judge said: "We have no quarrel with this sort of people."
And he dismissed them.

The Two Lights

Rabbi Mendel of Rymanov was asked: "Why cannot two
zaddikim have their seats in the same city?"

He replied: "Zaddikim are like the lights up in Heaven. When God created the two great lights of Heaven he placed both in the firmament, each to do its own special service. Ever since, they have been friends. The great light does not boast of being great and the small light is content with being small. And so it was in the days of our sages: there was a whole skyful of stars, large stars and small stars, and they lived together in all brotherliness. Not so the zaddikim of our day! Now no one wants to be a small light and bow to a greater. So it is better for each to have his own firmament all for himself."

The Acceptance of the Torah

One morning on the first day of the Feast of Weeks, before the reading from the Torah, Rabbi Mendel left the prayer room to go into his own room. After a time he returned to the prayer room and said: "When Mount Sinai was raised to hang above you like a huge hollow bell, you were compelled to accept the Law. Today I release you from this compulsion and from this responsibility. You are once more free to choose."

Then all cried aloud: "Now too we accept the Torah!"

A disciple of the rabbi of Lublin, who happened to be there because he had been unable to go as usual to his teacher over the holidays, added the following whenever he told this story: "And all their impurities melted away as they had that time, at Mount Sinai."

At a Time of Good Will

Rabbi Mendel was asked: "On the sabbath, when we say the Afternoon Prayer, why do we speak the words of the psalm: 'And as for me, may my prayer unto thee, O Lord, be at a time of good will.'"

He replied: "Because the will of the Most High to create the world for the good of his creatures already existed on the afternoon of the sabbath before the first day of creation. Every sabbath at this same time, it is as if that original will again wakes, and so we pray that this time before the sabbath draws to a close, the will to do good to His creatures may manifest itself once more."

A Day's Portion

Rabbi Kalman of Cracow asked Rabbi Hirsh the Servant, Rabbi Mendel's successor: "What is your way in the service of prayer?"
He replied: "My way was shown to me by my holy teacher, may he merit life in the world to come. Concerning manna, it is written: 'And the people shall go out and gather a day's portion every day.' Every day has its own portion of prayer, and one must concentrate on the particular meaning of each portion every day."

Belief and Trust

Rabbi Mendel of Rymanov was asked how to interpret the words God added when he told Moses that the people were to gather a day's portion of manna every day: " . . . that I may prove them whether they will walk in my law or not."
He explained: "If you ask even a very simple man whether he believes that God is the only God in the world, he will give the emphatic answer: 'How can you ask! Do not all creatures know that He is the only one in the world!' But should you ask him if he trusts that the Creator will see to it that he has all that he needs, he will be taken aback and after a while he will say: 'Well, I guess I haven't reached that rung yet.'

"But in reality belief and trust are linked, and one cannot exist without the other. He who firmly believes, trusts completely. But if anyone—God forbid—has not perfect confidence in God, his belief will be faint as well. That is why God says: 'I will cause to rain bread from heaven for you'; that means 'I *can* cause bread to rain from heaven for you.' But he who goes in the path of my teachings, and that means he who has belief in me, and that means, he who has trust in me, gathers a day's portion every day and does not worry about the morrow."

131

At the Seder, on the night of Passover, Rabbi Mendel of Rymanov liked to tell the following story after the song about "one only kid":

A peasant stood in the market place and offered a calf for sale. Along came the lord of the manor and asked: "What do you want for that dog?" Said the peasant: "That's a calf and not a dog." Each insisted that he was right and so they wrangled for a while, until the lord gave the peasant a box on the ear, saying: "Here's something to help you remember that when the lord say it's a dog, it *is* a dog." The peasant replied: "I shall remember."

Some time later, a friend of the peasant came running into the village which adjoined the manor. He was all out of breath and shouted for the firemen. It seemed that where he lived, quite a distance away, the community threshing barn and the house of the mayor, who was popular for miles around, had caught fire. The entire squad of firemen set out and took all their equipment with them. In the meantime the peasant set fire to the four corners of the manor and it burned down.

A few weeks later, when he heard that the lord was going to rebuild his house, he disguised himself, pretended to be an architect and told the lord he would draw up a plan. This he at once proceeded to do, for he was a clever peasant. They sat over the plan, calculated the amount of wood necessary for the building, and decided to go into the forest which belonged to the lord to measure the circumference of the trees which were suitable for lumber.

When they reached the forest, the peasant was contemptuous of the trees standing at the edge. There were better trees farther along, said the lord; they walked on, keeping a sharp lookout, until they were right in the middle of the forest. There the architect stopped and pointed enthusiastically to a giant of a tree, saying it was so and so many ells around and would make splendid planks.

"That's a lot more ells than you think," said the lord. The architect went up to the tree and put his arm about the trunk. "Just as I figured!" he cried.

Then the lord went up to the tree and did just as the other before him. The peasant pulled out his measuring cord, tied the lord to the trunk by his arms and legs, gave him a sound drubbing and said: "This is the first reminder, so that you'll know when the peasant says it's a calf, it *is* a calf and not a dog." Then he went his way, but the lord howled for hours until someone happened along and cut his bonds.

When the lord got home he felt ill and went to bed. He grew worse from day to day and had doctor after doctor called, but none of them could give him any relief. At that time a rumor spread through the neighboring town that a great miracle-healer would stop there for a day in the course of his travels and would heal all the sick who came to consult him.

Soon after, the peasant disguised as a doctor arrived in the town, and gave out very good advice—for he was a clever peasant. The lord, who had heard of him, had him summoned to his bedside and promised to pay him whatever he asked if he would cure him.

The doctor came, took one look at the patient, and said peremptorily to the persons around him: "You must leave me alone with him and not disturb me in my rather severe but infallible cure—not even if he should scream." As soon as they were gone, he bolted the door and gave the lord another first-rate drubbing.

Those who stood outside heard the pitiful shrieks and said: "There's a real fellow for you! He is doing a thorough job." But the peasant was saying to the lord: "This is a second reminder, so you'll be sure to know once and for all: when a peasant says it's a calf, it *is* a calf and not a dog." Then he went off with such ease and self-confidence that no one even thought of stopping him.

When the lord recovered from his illness and his bruises, he set out to find the peasant, but did not succeed, for the latter had not only dyed his skin and changed the cut of his hair but had also assumed manners and gestures that were so different that he was quite unrecognizable. Early in the morning on the next market day, he saw the lord sitting in his coach close to the market place which was still almost empty, peering in all directions. The peasant turned to an acquaintance of his who had come with his horse and had the reputation of being a good rider, and said: "Do you want to do me a favor, friend?" "Surely," said the other, "if it isn't anything too difficult."

"All you have to do," answered the peasant, "is to ride up to that gentleman in the coach, bend down and whisper to him: 'If the peasant says it's a calf, it *is* a calf.' Then ride off as fast as you can, and don't stop until you have left those who will pursue you far behind. After that, meet me at the inn—you know which—and I'll have them serve you the best old plum brandy ever."

His friend did as he had been told. When the lord heard his words, he started up, for he was sure the man he had been looking for was there in front of him. He shouted to his coachman and servant to unhitch the horses and make after the fellow. They mounted the horses and galloped off.

When the peasant saw the lord alone in his coach, he went up to him, boxed his ears soundly and said: "This is the third reminder, and now I guess you have learned that when the peasant says it's a calf, it *is* a calf and not a dog." Then he went off to the inn.

And the calf—so Rabbi Mendel ended his tale at every Seder— the calf remained a calf and never became a dog.

And when the children asked: "And what was the name of the clever peasant?" Rabbi Mendel answered, "Michael."

When they asked: "What was the name of the bad lord?" he said: "Sammael."

And when they asked: "What was the name of the calf that never became a dog?" he replied: "That is the well-known calf, Israel."

Roads

Rabbi Mendel often complained:

"As long as there were no roads, you had to interrupt a journey at nightfall. Then you had all the leisure in the world to recite psalms at the inn, to open a book, and to have a good talk with one another. But nowadays you can ride on these roads day and night and there is no peace any more."

134

Fulfilling the Law

A disciple asked Rabbi Mendel of Rymanov:

"The Talmud says that Abraham fulfilled all the commandments. How is that possible, since they had not yet been given?"

"You know," said the rabbi, "that the commandments of the Torah correspond to the bones, and the prohibitions to the sinews of man. Thus the entire Law includes the entire body of man. But Abraham had made every part of his body so pure and holy that each of itself fulfilled the command intended for it."

The Heart

Rabbi Mendel of Rymanov used to say that during the time he was silently reciting the Eighteen Benedictions, all the people who had ever asked him to pray to God in their behalf would pass through his mind.

Someone once asked how that was possible, since there was surely not enough time. Rabbi Mendel replied: "The need of every single one leaves a trace in my heart. In the hour of prayer I open my heart and say: 'Lord of the world, read what is written here!'"

The Pause

Rabbi Hirsh the Servant related:

"When my holy teacher recited the Penitential Prayers at the Reader's desk on the day before the New Year, he would always pause after saying the prayer with the phrase: "When everyone has truly turned to you with all his heart and soul," and would stand a moment in silence before he resumed. Many thought that during this time he busied himself with the permutations of the names of God, but his intimates knew he only waited until he saw that everyone in the congregation was determined to turn with all his heart and soul.

The Sounds of Work

This question was put to Rabbi Mendel: "The Scriptures say that when Moses was told that the people were bringing far too many offerings for the building of the sanctuary in the wilderness, he issued the command that no one henceforth was to work at the sanctuary. How does that follow? All Moses had to do was to command that no further offerings be brought."

Rabbi Mendel expounded: "It is well known that those who worked at the sanctuary were most holy men, and that their work had a holy effect. When one of them struck the anvil with his hammer, and another split wood with his ax, the sounds echoed in the hearts of all those who heard, and the people were driven by a holy desire to bring more than was needful. That is why Moses bade the workers stop their work."

The Disciples Band Together

Rabbi Mendel's disciples formed an association. They wrote a charter which began with these words: "We wish to found an association of comrades who seek the truth and strive to be righteous and humble; who strive to turn to God with a whole heart, with a heart rendered pure, so that we may no longer be barred by a wall from his holiness."

Whenever they made a new resolution as to how they should conduct themselves, they inscribed it on the roll which began with the above charter. One of their resolutions read: "To beware of untoward words, concerning which our holy rabbi has said that their utterance is a violation of the commandment: Thou shalt not murder."

Rabbi Mendel's utterance which is here cited was: "Every word has a perfect shape of its own, and he who casts the sound of the word to the demons is sinning against it, like one who rises against his neighbor and slays him."

The Ark of the Covenant and Its Carriers

Rabbi Mendel said:

"When a man wants to serve God in the right way and does not succeed, walls rise up before him. His prayer lacks tone, his learning light. Then his heart rises up against him, and he comes to the zaddik as one whom his own heart has cast out, and stands trembling, waiting for the zaddik to help him— then his own humility makes the zaddik humble as well. For

136

he who is to give help sees the bowed and fervent soul of him who has come for help, and thinks: 'He is better than I!' And at that instant, the zaddik is lifted to the very heights by his service and has the power to loosen that which is bound. To this we may apply the phrase: 'The Ark of the Covenant carried its carriers.'"

They Blessed Each Other

Rabbi Feivish of Zbarazh once came to Rabbi Mendel in order to spend the sabbath near him. On Sunday when he took his farewell he wept and said: "I am seventy-four years old and I still have not truly turned to God."
Weeping, Rabbi Mendel replied: "That troubles me too."
Then they decided to bless one another with the blessing that they might be able to accomplish the true turning.

The Ultimate Joy

Soon after the death of Rabbi Mendel's wife, his daughter also died. People whispered to one another not to tell him of it just yet, but when his son-in-law entered the House of Prayer weeping, while the rabbi was saying the Morning Prayer, he at once realized what had happened. He finished the Prayer of Benedictions, and said: "Lord of the world, you took my wife from me. But I still had my daughter and could rejoice in her. Now you have taken her from me too. Now I have no one left to rejoice in, except you alone. So I shall rejoice in you." And he said the Additional Prayer in a transport of joy.

ZEVI HIRSH OF RYMANOV

Genealogy

When the rabbi of Rizhyn betrothed his grandson to the
daughter of Rabbi Hirsh of Rymanov, before the writing of
the marriage contract he said: "It is the custom in my family
to recite our genealogy at the time of betrothal. And that is
what I shall now do. My grandfather's father was Rabbi Baer,
my grandfather was Rabbi Abraham the Angel, and my father
Rabbi Shalom Shahkna." He had given merely the names
of the Great Maggid, his son, and his grandson, without adding
the usual honorary titles. Then he said to Rabbi Hirsh: "Now
it is your turn to tell us from whom you are descended."
Rabbi Hirsh replied: "My father and mother left this earth
when I was ten years old, and so I did not know them well
enough to be able to speak of them, but I have been told
that they were upright and honest folk. When they died, my
relatives apprenticed me to a tailor. I stayed with him for
five years, and even though I was very young I worked well.
I was careful not to ruin what was new, and to repair what
was old."
"The marriage is agreeable to both sides," cried the rabbi
of Rizhyn.

Bed-Making

One of the duties of Rabbi Menahem Mendel of Rymanov's
servant was making his bed, and he never let anyone else do
this in his stead. Now when young Zevi Hirsh quitted the
tailor's trade and was taken into the zaddik's house as a
stoker, he begged the servant to let him make the zaddik's bed,
but the man refused, saying that the rabbi would certainly
notice that another's hand had performed this service. Once,
however, the servant was called away before evening, and
since he had to go at once, he transferred his duties to the
young stoker and gave him minute directions on how to

make the bed. Hirsh promised to do exactly as he had been told.

When Rabbi Mendel rose the following morning he called his servant and asked who had made the bed. Trembling, the man answered, and begged forgiveness.

"I never knew," said the zaddik, "that one could sleep so sweetly. From now on the stoker is to make my bed."

The Power to Cleanse

Rabbi Nathan Yehudah, the son of Rabbi Mendel of Rymanov, told this story.

"The morning after Rabbi Hirsh the Servant had celebrated his wedding, I entered the House of Study and found the bridegroom cleaning out the place with the same devotion to his task as ever. I was annoyed, went to my father, and said: 'Father, it isn't right for your Servant to ignore his marriage and do such lowly work on the Seven Days of the Feast!'

"My father replied: 'You have made me happy, my son. I was much troubled as to how I should be able to pray today if Zevi Hirsh the Servant did not clean the House of Study himself. For when he does the cleaning he drives out all the demons, and the air grows pure, and then that house is a good place to pray in.'

"On that very day my father accepted Rabbi Hirsh as his disciple."

The Loftiest Prayer

Rabbi Hirsh once complained to his teacher that whenever he prayed he saw fiery letters and words flash before his eyes. "These," said Rabbi Mendel, "are the mystical concentrations of our sacred master Rabbi Isaac Luria. So what cause have you to complain?"

"But I want to pray concentrating only on the meaning of the words," answered Rabbi Hirsh.

"What you have in mind," said Rabbi Mendel, "is a very high rung which only one man in a whole generation can reach: that of having learned all secret wisdom and then praying like a little child."

There are many reports on how Rabbi Hirsh became the successor of his teacher and master. One of them says that Rabbi Mendel dreamed that the angel Metatron, "the prince of the innermost chamber," led Hirsh the Servant to the zaddik's chair. Afterward the zaddik observed that Hirsh saw the souls of the dead who came to him for redemption as clearly as the zaddik himself. This lessened his uneasiness, yet from that time on he no longer permitted the Servant to live in his house and perform personal services for him. The only thing he allowed him to do was to help him put on his phylacteries— for Hirsh had begged this of him as a very great favor.

According to another account, Rabbi Mendel's two sons drove to Rabbi Naftali of Roptchitz after their father's death to ask him to decide which of them should become his father's successor. They took Rabbi Hirsh with them as their servant, and were already agreed that whichever of them became the rabbi would take the Servant into his house. On the way they were accosted by a villager who had been among their father's hasidim. When he heard of his master's death, he wanted to hand the note of request he had with him to them because they were Rabbi Mendel's sons, but they did not wish to take it, since neither of them had yet been ordained rabbi. So the younger son gently told the man to give the note to Rabbi Hirsh and the man did so in the simplicity of his heart. They were amazed and somewhat confounded to see Rabbi Hirsh take the note with a matter of fact air. When they came to Rabbi Naftali, he greeted Rabbi Hirsh with the title of rabbi and gave him the place of honor.

They say that a group of hasidim wanted to elect as their rabbi Nathan Yehudah, Rabbi Mendel's eldest son, but he not only refused, but went away to foreign parts for a considerable period of time.

The Renewed Soul

Rabbi Hirsh once said to his hasidim:

"When a man rises in the morning and sees that God has returned his soul to him and that he has become a new creature, he should turn singer and sing to God. My holy master

Rabbi Menahem Mendel had a hasid who whenever he came to the words in the Morning Prayer: 'My God, the soul you have placed in me is pure,' danced and broke into a song of praise."

The Perfection of the Torah

A woman once came to Rabbi Hirsh, her eyes streaming with tears, and complained that she had been the victim of a miscarriage of justice in the rabbinical court. The zaddik summoned the judges and said: "Show me the source from which you derived your verdict, for it seems to me that there has been some error." Together they looked up the passage in the book Breastplate of Judgment on which the verdict had been based, and discovered that there had indeed been a misinterpretation.

One of the judges asked the rabbi how he had known beforehand that there had been an error. He answered: "It is written: 'The law of the Lord is perfect, restoring the soul.' Had the verdict been in accordance with the true law, the woman could never have wept as she did."

The Quintessence of the Torah

Before his death Rabbi Hirsh of Rymanov repeated over and over the words in the song of Moses: "A God of faithfulness and without iniquity." Then he said: "The quintessence of the holy Torah is to know that He is a God of faithfulness and that therefore there can be no iniquity. You may ask: 'If this is so, then why the whole Torah? It would have been enough for God to say that one verse at Sinai!' The answer is: No one can grasp this one truth until he has learned and fulfilled the whole Torah."

FROM THE SCHOOL OF

RABBI SHELOMO OF KARLIN

URI OF STRELISK

With a Quorum of Ten Pulpits

When, after visiting with his teacher Rabbi Shelomo of Karlin, Rabbi Uri returned to Lwow, he did not have a quorum of ten needed for community prayer, but prayed alone during an entire year. One day while he was studying the Book of Splendor, he came to a passage in praise of those who listen to the reading of the Torah and decided from then on to go to the House of Prayer every sabbath to hear the Torah read. But the first sabbath he listened he noticed that they were not reading what was really written in the Torah! So he did not go the following week. But soon after this he again found a passage in the Book of Splendor in praise of those who pray together with the community. He assembled ten men to pray with him and said to himself: "Even if God commanded me to pray with a quorum of ten pulpits, I would pray with them."

Acceptable Offering

Rabbi Uri said:
"It is written: 'And Abel brought, also he . . . ' He brought his own 'he,' his own self. Only when a man offers himself as well, is his offering acceptable."

Before Going to Pray

Every morning before going to pray Rabbi Uri saw to his house, and said his last goodbye to his wife and children.

The Secret Prayer

This is how Rabbi Uri expounded the words of the prayer: "May He who knows that which is hidden accept our call for help and listen to our cry."
"We know very well how we ought to pray; and still we cry for help in the need of the moment. The soul wishes us to cry out in spiritual need, but we are not able to express what the

soul means. And so we pray that God may accept our call for help, but also that he, who knows that which is hidden, may hear the silent cry of the soul."

To Walk Hidden with God

Rabbi Uri said:

"It is written: 'And to walk hidden with thy God.' Know that angels stand. Ceaselessly they stand, each on his own rung, but we move, we move from rung to rung. For angels are not garmented in flesh; they cannot remain hidden while they perform their service, and no matter on what rung they stand, they are always manifest. But man on this earth is clothed in flesh and can hide within this body of his. And so hidden from sight, he can move from rung to rung."

There and Here

Rabbi Uri taught:

"We read in the psalm: 'If I ascend up into heaven, Thou art there; if I make my bed in the nether world, here Thou art.' When I consider myself great and think I can touch the sky, I discover that God is the faraway There, and the higher I reach, the farther away he is. But if I make my bed in the depths, if I bow my soul down to the nether world, he is here with me."

Open Thou Mine Eyes

Once at table Rabbi Uri said the words of the psalm with great fervor: "Open Thou mine eyes, that I may behold wondrous things out of Thy law," and expounded them in this way:

"We know that God created a great light, that man might be able to look from one end of the world to the other and no curtain might separate the sight of the eyes from that which is seen. But then God hid this light. That is why David pleads: 'Open Thou mine eyes.' For it is really not the eye, with its white and its pupil, that produces sight; the eye has sight because the power of God lends sight to the eye. But a curtain prevents the eye from seeing that which is distant in the same way as it sees that which is near. David pleaded that this curtain be removed, that he might behold the wonder of all

146

that is. For, he says, 'out of Thy law,' that is, according to Thy law I see that no separation is intended."

Where?

Rabbi Uri once said to the hasidim who had come together in Strelisk: "You journey to me, and where do I journey? I journey and journey continually to that place where I can cling to God."

The Wish

A zaddik who was visiting Rabbi Uri asked him: "Why is it that none of your hasidim is rich?"

"I shall show you why," answered the rabbi of Strelisk. "Call in any one of the people who are in the anteroom." His visitor did so.

"This is a season of grace," said Rabbi Uri to the hasid who had entered. "Whatever wish you utter now shall be granted to you."

"If I may make a wish," said the man in a voice both shy and burning, "I wish that every morning I may be able to say the prayer 'Blessed be He who spake and the world came into being' just like our rabbi says it."

Generation after Generation

Rabbi Uri said:

"One does not help only one's own generation. Generation after generation David pours enthusiasm into somber souls; generation after generation Samson arms weak souls with the strength of heroes."

Each His Own

Rabbi Uri said:

"David could compose the psalms, and what can I do? I can recite the psalms."

Letters and Souls

Rabbi Uri said:

"The myriads of letters in the Torah correspond to the myriads of souls in Israel. If one single letter is left out of the Torah, it becomes unfit for use; if one single soul is left out of the union of Israel, the Divine Presence will not rest upon it.

Like the letters, so the souls must unite and form a union. But why is it forbidden for one letter in the Torah to touch its neighbor? Because every soul in Israel must have hours when it is alone with its Maker."

The Growing Tree

Rabbi Uri taught:

"Man is like a tree. If you stand in front of a tree and watch it incessantly to see how it grows and to see how much it has grown, you will see nothing at all. But tend to it at all times, prune the runners, and keep the vermin from it, and— all in good time—it will come into its growth. It is the same with man: all that is necessary is for him to overcome his obstacles, and he will thrive and grow. But it is not right to examine him every hour to see how much has been added to his growth."

Into Freedom

Tradition has it that until Rabbi Uri recited the Benediction of Separation at the close of the sabbath, and separated the sabbath from the weekday, the keys of hell were in his hand, and souls who had been freed from torment for the duration of the holy day of rest could fly about in the world unhindered.

The Sign

For a number of hours Rabbi Uri lay unconscious in the agony of death. His favorite disciple, Rabbi Yehudah Zevi, opened the door from time to time, looked at the dying man, and closed the door again. At last he entered the room and went up to the bed. The next moment the hasidim who had followed him in saw their master stretch out one last time, and die. Later, when they asked Rabbi Yehudah how he had known that death was imminent, he replied: "It is written: 'For man shall not see Me and live.' I saw that he saw."

Testimony of the Disciple

The rabbi of Kalev once asked Rabbi Yehudah Zevi to tell him words of the teachings which he had heard from his teacher, Rabbi Uri. "The teachings of my teacher," said Rabbi

Yehudah Zevi, "are like manna that enters the body but does not leave it." But when the rabbi of Kalev would not stop pressing him, Rabbi Yehudah Zevi tore open the coat over his breast and cried: "Look into my heart! There you will learn what my teacher is."

YEHUDAH ZEVI OF STRETYN AND HIS
SON ABRAHAM OF STRETYN

Men Can Meet

In the course of a journey, Rabbi Yehudah Zevi of Stretyn learned that Rabbi Shimon of Yaroslav was traveling the same road from the opposite direction. He got out of his carriage and went to meet him. Now Rabbi Shimon had heard of Rabbi Yehudah Zevi's coming, got out of his carriage, and went toward him. They greeted each other like brothers.

Then Rabbi Yehudah Zevi said: "Now I understand the meaning of the popular saying: 'Men can meet, but mountains never.' When one man considers himself just a human being, pure and simple, and the other does so too, they can meet. But if the one considers himself a lofty mountain, and the other thinks the same, then they cannot meet."

A Pregnancy

Rabbi Yehudah Zevi said:

"When a man grows aware of a new way in which to serve God, he should carry it around with him secretly and without uttering it for nine months, as though he were pregnant with it, and let others know of it only at the end of that time, as though it were a birth."

The Lord Is God

Rabbi Yehudah Zevi said:

"It is written: 'Unto thee it was shown that thou mightest know that the Lord, He is God; there is none else beside Him.' He who is learned knows that there is really no distinction between the name YHVH (which is translated as 'the Lord'), that is, the attribute of mercy, and the name Elohim (which is translated as 'God'), that is, the attribute of rigor. He knows that in reality everything is good. That is the secret meaning of the people's cry after Elijah had overcome the prophets of Baal: 'YHVH is Elohim!' "

Messiah the Son of Joseph

A hasid told this story:

"Once Rabbi Yehudah Zevi said to us at table: 'Today Messiah the son of Joseph will be born in Hungary, and he will become one of the hidden zaddikim. And if God lets me live long enough, I shall go there and see him.'

"Eighteen years later the rabbi traveled to the city of Pest and took me with him along with other hasidim. We stayed in Pest for several weeks and not one of us disciples knew why we had come.

"One day a youth appeared at the inn. He wore a short coat and his face was as beautiful as an angel's. Without asking permission he went straight into the rabbi's room and closed the door behind him. I remembered those words I had heard long ago, kept near the door, and waited to greet him as he came out and ask his blessing. But when hours later he did come out, the rabbi accompanied him to the gate, and when I ran out into the little street, he had vanished. Even now after so many years, my heart still beats with the living impulse I received from him as he went by."

The Suffering He Took Over

During the last three years of his life Rabbi Yehudah Zevi was afflicted with a terrible disease which caused painful ulcers to break out all over his body. The doctors said that from what they knew of human fortitude it was impossible for a man to bear such pain. When one of the rabbi's close friends asked him about this, he said: "When I was young and one who was sick came to me, I could pray with all the force of my soul that his suffering might be taken from him. Later the strength of my prayer flagged and all I could do was to take the suffering upon myself. And so now I bear it."

Drugs

A learned but ungenerous man said to Rabbi Abraham of Stretyn: "They say that you give people mysterious drugs and that your drugs are effective. Give me one that I may attain to the fear of God."

"I don't know any drug for the fear of God," said Rabbi Abraham. "But if you like I can give you one for the love of God."

"That's even better!" cried the other. "Just you give it to me."

"It is the love of one's fellow men," answered the zaddik.

The Unity of Senses

Rabbi Hayyim of Zans was surprised when Rabbi Abraham of Stretyn, who was visiting him, failed to put sugar in his coffee. When he questioned him about it, Rabbi Abraham said: "It is said: 'There is no unity in my bones because of my sin.' Why is there a division between the powers of the limbs of man that are all wrought out of the same matter? Why can eyes only see and ears only hear? Because of the sin of the first man they are not in harmony. But whoever sets himself right to the very root of his soul, to Adam's sin, will bring unity to his body. And such a man can taste sweetness even with his eyes."

MORDECAI OF LEKHOVITZ
AND HIS DESCENDANTS

The Chain

Rabbi Mordecai of Lekhovitz said to his disciples:

"The zaddik cannot say any words of the teachings unless he first links his soul to the soul of his dead teacher or to that of his teacher's teacher. Only then is link joined to link, and the teachings flow from Moses to Joshua, from Joshua to the elders, and so on to the zaddik's own teacher, and from his teacher to him."

The Nature of Prayer

Rabbi Moshe of Kobryn related:

"My teacher, Rabbi Mordecai of Lekhovitz, taught me how to pray. He instructed me as follows: 'He who utters the word "Lord" and in doing so prepares to say "of the world," is not speaking as he should. At the moment he is saying "Lord," he must only think of offering himself up to the Lord, so that even if his soul should leave him with the "Lord," and he were not able to add the word "world," it would be enough for him that he had been able to say "Lord." '

"This is the essence of prayer."

In Your Kingdom

An emissary from the Land of Israel, a devout and honest man, feared that great honors would be conferred upon him (for at that time such was the custom with regard to emissaries) and that he might feel satisfaction thereat. So he prayed to God if that happened, to send him stomach cramps, for the bodily pain would make him forget all about the honors. His prayer was granted. When he arrived in Lekhovitz—it was on a Friday—Rabbi Mordecai received him with great honors. Soon after, the emissary was in such pain that he had to lie down and was unable to sit at the zaddik's table. But from his bed he could hear the hasidim in the next room singing, "They shall rejoice in Your kingdom," the zaddik leading the chorus.

The emissary jumped up. His pains had left him. Just as he was, without his coat and shoes, wearing only the skullcap on his head, he ran into the room and danced around the table. "Praised be the Lord," he cried, keeping time with the singing, "who has brought me to the right place. I heard it: 'They shall rejoice in Your kingdom.' Not in a wife and children, not in sheep and cattle, but in Your kingdom! Praise be the Lord that I have come to the right place. But in Your kingdom! But in Your kingdom!"

The Hole in the Lung

Rabbi Mordecai of Lekhovitz once said to himself:

"We have heard of a bird that sings his praise of God with such fervor that his body bursts. But I pray and yet I remain whole and sound. So what good are my prayers?" After a time the great fervor of his praying tore a hole in his lung. The doctors in the town of Lwow gave him up, but he said to God: "I did not mean to say only one prayer in that way; I want to go on praying." Then God helped him and he recovered. When he happened to be in Lwow again, and a crowd of hasidim surrounded his house, a doctor passed by and asked who had arrived. "The rabbi of Lekhovitz," they answered. "Is he still alive?" cried the doctor. "Then he certainly must be living without a lung."

Miracles

The rabbi of Kobryn said: "We paid no attention to the miracles our teachers worked, and when sometimes a miracle did not come to pass, he gained in our eyes."

Against Worrying

Rabbi Mordecai of Lekhovitz said:

"We must not worry. Only one worry is permissible: a man should worry about nothing but worry."

Why the Rejoicing?

This is what Rabbi Mordecai once said in connection with the verse in the psalm: "Rejoice the soul of Thy servant."

"Why the rejoicing?" said he. " 'For unto Thee, O Lord, do I lift my soul'—it is by rejoicing that I can lift my soul to You."

A Blessing

Once when Rabbi Mordecai attended the circumcision of the son of his friend Rabbi Asher of Stolyn, and they brought him the boy afterward that he might bless him, he said: "May you not fool God, may you not fool yourself, and may you not fool people."

A Sign for Cain

This is how Rabbi Mordecai expounded the verse: "And the Lord set a sign for Cain, lest any finding him should smite him."

"God gave Cain, the penitent, a sign of strength and holiness, so that no accident he met with should beat his spirit down and disturb him in his work of repentance."

Wholesome Insolence

A learned old man who was hostile to the hasidic way once asked Rabbi Mordecai of Lekhovitz: "Tell me why it is that so long as a young man learns in the House of Study and has nothing to do with the oddities of hasidim, he is well behaved and has good manners, but as soon as he joins the hasidim he grows insolent."

The zaddik replied: "Haven't you heard about that learned old fellow who has been taking a great deal of time and trouble with mankind from time immemorial? King Solomon called him an old king, and the fact that he learns along with all those who learn proves his learning. Now when this learned old fellow comes to a timid young man who has nothing but good manners with which to meet people, and tries to tempt him to follow him in his ways, the youth does not dare turn him out. But the hasid, the insolent hasid, seizes the old fellow in both his arms, presses him close to himself till his ribs crack, and kicks him out of the door."

The Verse Within

Once when Rabbi Mordecai was in the great town of Minsk expounding the Torah to a number of men hostile to his way, they laughed at him. "What you say does not explain the verse in the least!" they cried.

"Do you really think," he replied, "that I was trying to explain the verse in the book? That doesn't need explanation! I want to explain the verse that is within me."

For the Joy of Others

The mitnagdim were making fun of the rabbi of Lekhovitz on another occasion. But when they laughed he did nothing but smile and say: "God has not created a single creature that does not give joy to others. So I too have been created for the joy of others, for those who are near to my heart because my nearness is pleasing to them, and for you because you mock me." The mitnagdim listened and grew silent and gloomy.

Hasid and Mitnagid

A hasid of the zaddik of Lekhovitz had a business partner who was a mitnagid. The hasid kept urging him to go to the rabbi with him, but the mitnagid was obstinate in his refusal. Finally, however, when they happened to be in Lekhovitz on business, he let himself be persuaded and agreed to go to the zaddik's for the sabbath meal.

In the course of the meal the hasid saw his friend's face light up with joy. Later he asked him about it. "When the zaddik ate, he looked as holy as the high priest making the offering!" was the reply. After a while the hasid went to the rabbi, much troubled in spirit, and wanted to know why the other had seen something on his very first visit which he, the rabbi's close friend, had not.

"The mitnagid must see, the hasid must believe," answered Rabbi Mordecai.

Fraud

Rabbi Mordecai of Lekhovitz busied himself collecting money for the Land of Israel, and he himself gave large amounts for this cause. At all times—when he rose from his bed in the morning, before Morning Prayer, after Morning Prayer, before studying, after studying, before dining and after dining, and so on until evening he put aside gifts for the Land of Israel. When a sum of money had accumulated he sent it to Rabbi Abraham Kalisker who at that time was the collector for the Land of Israel, and he appended a slip of paper which bore the names of the donors. But since Rabbi Mordecai himself had contributed considerable sums and did not wish anyone to know how large a share of the money was due to him, he added something of what he had given under the name of every other donor listed on the slip.

When the list came to Rabbi Abraham's hand, he looked at it, smiled, shook his head, and pointed to one item after another, saying: "The rabbi of Lekhovitz has something of his own in this! And here there's something more of the rabbi of Lekhovitz!"

Before Thee

Once when Rabbi Mordecai was saying the verse from the psalm: "But I was brutish and ignorant; I was as a beast before Thee," he interrupted himself and cried: "Lord of the world, I want to be ignorant, I want to be brutish, if only I can be before Thee."

In His Father's Footsteps

When Rabbi Noah, Rabbi Mordecai's son, assumed the succession after his father's death, his disciples noticed that there were a number of ways in which he conducted himself differently from his father, and asked him about this.

"I do just as my father did," he replied. "He did not imitate, and I do not imitate."

Against Hypocrisy

Rabbi Noah of Lekhovitz said:

"He who works in the service of God deceitfully—what good does it do him? God cannot be fooled, and if you succeed in fooling the people, it will turn out wrong in the end. Whoever tries to fool others only fools himself, and keeps on being a fool."

157

"I Believe"

Once when Rabbi Noah was in his room, he heard how one of his disciples began to recite the Principles of Faith in the House of Study next door, but stopping immediately after the words "I believe with perfect faith" whispered to himself: "I don't understand that!" and then once more: "I don't understand that." The zaddik left his room and went to the House of Study.

"What is it you do not understand?" he asked.

"I don't understand what it's all about," said the man. "I say 'I believe.' If I really do believe, then how can I possibly sin? But if I do not really believe, why am I telling lies?"

"It means," answered the rabbi, "that the words 'I believe' are a prayer, meaning 'oh, that I may believe!'" Then the hasid was suffused with a glow from within. "That is right!" he cried. "That is right! Oh, that I may believe, Lord of the world, oh, that I may believe!"

Light

"And God said: 'Let there be light.'"

Rabbi Shelomo Hayyim of Kaidanov, a grandson of Rabbi Mordecai of Lekhovitz, read this verse thus: "And he said: 'God, let there be light!'" When a man prays with true fervor, "God, let there be light," then he shall see the light.

A Jew

Before he died Rabbi Shelomo Hayyim said to his sons: "You are not to think that your father was a zaddik, a 'rebbe,' a 'good Jew.' But all the same I haven't been a hypocrite. I did try to be a Jew."

MOSHE OF KOBRYN

The Fish in the Water

Rabbi Moshe of Kobryn told this story:
"When I was a boy I was once playing with other children on the first day of the month of Elul. Then my elder sister said: 'How can you play today at the beginning of the month of preparation for the great judgment, when even the fish in the water tremble?'

"When I heard this I began to tremble and could not stop for hours. And even now as it comes back to me, I feel as if I were a fish in water on the first day of the month of Elul, and like the fish I tremble before the judgment of the world."

Charity

Rabbi Moshe of Kobryn was the son of villagers who labored hard to earn a meager livelihood. When he was a boy there was a famine in Lithuania. Poor men left the cities with their wives and children and swarmed all over the countryside in search of food. Every day throngs of hungry people passed through the village in which Moshe's parents lived. His mother ground grain with a hand mill and each morning she baked bread and distributed it among them.

One day, more people came than usual and there was not enough bread to go around. But the oven was still hot and the bowls were full of dough. So she quickly took some of the dough, kneaded it and formed loaves, and slipped them into the oven. Meanwhile the hungry people complained because they had to wait, and a few insolent fellows among them even railed and cursed. At that, Rabbi Moshe's mother burst into tears. "Do not cry, mother," said the boy. "Let them curse. Just do your work, and fulfil the commandment of God. If they praised you and showered blessings on you, it would not perhaps be fulfilled so well."

To Be a Soldier

The rabbi of Kobryn told this story:

"When I was young I once spent Purim with my teacher Rabbi Mordecai of Lekhovitz. In the middle of the meal he cried: 'Today is the day of gifts, the hour for giving has come. Whoever reaches out his hand, will get from me whatever strength in the service of God he desires for himself.' His disciples asked for a variety of spiritual gifts. Each got what he wanted and kept it.

"Finally the rabbi inquired: 'Well, Moshe, and what do you want?'

"I fought down my shyness and replied: 'I don't want any gratuitous gift. I want to be a common soldier and serve until I deserve what I get.' "

One Thing after Another

The rabbi of Kobryn told this story:

"When my teacher instructed me in one way to serve, I did not want to hear anything more from him until I had done what he had taught me. Not until then did I open up my ears again."

The Faithful Follower

Rabbi Mordecai of Lekhovitz was a disciple of Rabbi Shelomo of Karlin. When this rabbi died, his disciples Rabbi Mordecai and Rabbi Asher of Stolyn divided the communities of his hasidim between them. But they could not come to an agreement about Kobryn, which each wanted to include in his own area. Rabbi Mordecai suggested a solution. "I have a hasid in Kobryn," he said, "Rabbi Moshe. I give you a year to get him to visit you. If he does, you shall have Kobryn. During this year you may do anything you like to attract him to you and I shall do everything I can to drive him from me."

And so it came to pass. The next time Rabbi Moshe went to Lekhovitz, his teacher did not greet him. But Moshe neither questioned nor doubted; he was just as devoted to Rabbi Mordecai as before. And even though Rabbi Asher called on him, put himself out to be agreeable, and promised him all kinds of good things in this and the coming world, Moshe remained faithful. And so Kobryn fell to his teacher's share.

Angels and Humans

The rabbi of Kobryn once looked at the Heavens and cried: "Angel, little angel! It is no great trick to be an angel up there in the sky! You don't have to eat and drink, beget children and earn money. Just you come down to earth and worry about eating and drinking, about raising children and earning money, and we shall see if you keep on being an angel. If you succeed, you may boast—but not now!"

An Answer

The rabbi of Kobryn liked to tell the story of the answer General Gowin gave to Czar Nicholas. The general was very old and had served fifty years. At maneuvers which the Czar attended the general headed one of the armies.

Nicholas rode down the first row and addressed the general: "Well, Gowin, I see you are up and doing. Is your blood still hot?"

Said Gowin: "Not my blood, your majesty. The service is still hot in me."

Books

Once he said:

"If it were within my power, I should hide everything written by the zaddikim. For when a man has too much knowledge, his wisdom is apt to be greater than his deeds."

The End of the Matter

The rabbi of Kobryn taught:

"At the close of Ecclesiastes we read: 'The end of the matter, all having been heard: fear God!' Now whatever matter you come to the end of, you will always hear this one maxim, 'Fear God!' and this one is the whole. There is not a single thing in all the world that does not show you a way to fear God and to serve him. All is commandment."

Up and Down

Rabbi Moshe of Kobryn taught:

"When you walk over a freshly ploughed field, furrows alternate with ridges. The way in the service of God is like that. Now you go up, now you go down, now the Evil Urge gets a hold on you, now you get a hold on him. Just you see to it that it is you who deal the last blow!"

For the King

"And if one of you should suddenly fall from the heights he has reached," said the rabbi of Kobryn to his hasidim, "and plunge into the abyss, let him not give way to despair! Let him take the yoke of the Kingdom of Heaven upon him anew, and begin the fight all over again.

"When the Saxons in our region were fighting the Russians, a Russian soldier got one of them in his power. 'Cry for mercy,' he shouted, 'and I'll let you go!'

" 'Nothing doing,' the Saxon panted in his face. 'It would be a disgrace to my king.'

"The Russian bellowed back: 'Cry mercy or I'll knock off your head.' But as the steel cut the artery in his throat, the Saxon repeated: 'It would be a disgrace to my king.' "

Simply to Act

Before drawing water for the baking of the unleavened bread, the rabbi of Kobryn said to those standing around him: "The king teaches his men all manner of military thrusts and feints, but when they are in the thick of the fight, they throw all they have learned overboard and simply shoot. In respect to the drawing of water there are also many mysteries to be learned, but when it comes to the action itself all I know is what I am bidden to do."

The Dress That Did Not Fit

The wife of a high-ranking officer had told a tailor to make her an expensive dress. But it turned out too tight and he was thrown out of the house in disgrace. The tailor went to the rabbi of Kobryn and begged him to tell him what to do so as not to lose all his customers among the gentry.

"Go back," said the zaddik, "and offer to make the dress over. Then rip it up and sew the pieces together again just as they are."

The man did as he was told. Timidly and humbly he made over the dress he had botched in his proud assurance, and it turned out perfect.

This is a story Rabbi Moshe was fond of telling himself.

The Soul and the Evil Urge

The rabbi of Kobryn taught:

The soul says to the Evil Urge what Abraham said to Lot: " . . . If thou wilt take the left hand, then I will go to the right; or if thou take the right hand, then I will go to the left." The soul says: "When you try to lead me left, I will not heed you and go the right. But should you by any chance advise me to go right in your company, I'd prefer to go left."

Bitter, Not Bad

The rabbi of Kobryn taught:

"When a man suffers, he ought not to say: 'That's bad! That's bad!' Nothing that God imposes on man is bad. But it is all right to say: 'That's bitter!' For among medicines there are some that are made with bitter herbs."

Not By Bread Only

In the course of the sabbath meal Rabbi Moshe once took a piece of bread in his hand and said to his hasidim:

"It is written: 'Man doth not live by bread only, but by every thing that proceedeth out of the mouth of the Lord doth man live.' The life of man is not sustained by the stuff of bread but by the sparks of divine life that are within it. He is here. All exists because of his life-giving life, and when he withdraws from anything, it crumbles away to nothing."

By Whose Word

One of the rabbi of Kobryn's hasidim was employed in public works. One morning while he was attending to his business, he was overcome by a worry. He did not know what to do. Finally he let everything go, returned to town and without stopping at his own house went straight to the zaddik, who was just about to have breakfast. A dish of barley had been set before the zaddik and he was saying the blessing over it, ending: "by whose word all things exist."

The zaddik did not look at his hasid who had just crossed the threshold, and he did not offer to shake hands with him. So the man stood to one side and waited for an opportunity to present his problem. Finally the rabbi said to him: "Zalman, I thought you were like your father, but now I see you are not like him. Your father once came to me with a whole load of troubles. As he entered, I was saying the blessing, ending 'by whose word all things exist,' just like today. When I had ended I saw that your father was preparing to leave. 'Abramele,' I asked, 'didn't you have something on your mind?'

" 'No,' said he, and took leave of me.

"Do you understand? When a Jew hears that everything exists because of the word of God—what is there left to ask? For this is the answer to all his questions and worries."

And Rabbi Moshe gave the hasid his hand in greeting. For a while the hasid was silent, then he bade his master farewell and went back to his work comforted.

Where Is Man?

The time for the sabbath meal had come and many young men were standing around the table of the rabbi of Kobryn. He fixed his eyes on one of them who had often been at his house and asked the servant: "Who is that?" The servant was surprised, but gave the visitor's name. "I do not know him," said Rabbi Moshe. The servant gave the names of the young man's father and father-in-law, and when this too failed to jog the rabbi's memory, the servant told him when the young man had come to Kobryn and how he had heard the rabbi's teachings.

At this the zaddik seemed to remember, and he addressed

the subject of his inquiries who was standing before him in great distress: "Now I know why I did not recognize you. Where a man sends his thoughts, there he is himself, and since your thoughts were very far away, all I saw was a lump of flesh."

Do Not Crowd

Once on a Hanukkah evening the people crowded around to see the rabbi of Kobryn light the candles. But he said: "It is written: 'The people saw, they tottered, they stood afar off.' When you jostle and crowd, you are very far off."

The Flame Goes Out

A hasid complained to the rabbi of Kobryn that every time he set out to see him, his heart was aflame with fervor and he thought he would fly straight to Heaven the moment he stood before his teacher; yet every time he saw him face to face, the flame went out, and then his heart felt more shriveled and cold than at home.

The rabbi said: "Remember what David says in the psalm: 'My soul thirsteth for God,' and further on, 'So have I looked for Thee in the sanctuary.' David implores God to let him feel the same fervor in the holy sanctuary that he felt when he was 'in a dry and weary land where no water was.' For first the all-merciful God wakens a man to holiness, but once he is kindled to act the flame is taken from him, so that he may act for himself and of himself attain to the state of perfect awakening."

Satan's Ruse

"In olden times," so said the rabbi of Kobryn, "when Satan wanted to prevent a hasid from going to the zaddik, he assumed the shape of his father, or his mother, or his wife, and tried his utmost to persuade him to give up his plan. But when he saw that resistance only strengthened the hasid in his faithfulness, he changed his tactics. He made his peace with the man he was dealing with, grew very friendly, and said, all gentleness and docility: 'You have converted me. Just you go to your rabbi, but permit me to join you; just you pray in your own way, and let me pray along with you; just you learn whatever you can, and I shall help you learn.'

"And so the time comes when Satan says: 'Just you sit down in the zaddik's seat, and I shall sit beside you. We two shall stay together!' "

Accepting the World

One of Rabbi Moshe's hasidim was very poor. He complained to the zaddik that his wretched circumstances were an obstacle to learning and praying.

"In this day and age," said Rabbi Moshe, "the greatest devotion, greater than learning and praying, consists in accepting the world exactly as it happens to be."

The Original Meaning

This is what Rabbi Moshe said to an author who put questions to him concerning the Kabbalah, the secret teachings, and the kavvanot, the mystical concentrations, which are directed toward superhuman effects. "You must keep in mind that the word Kabbalah is derived from *kabbel:* to accept; and the word kavvanah from *kavven:* to direct. For the ultimate significance of all the wisdom of the Kabbalah is to accept the yoke of the Kingdom of God, and the ultimate significance of all the art of the kavvanot is to direct one's heart to God. When a man says: 'The Lord is my God,' meaning: 'He is mine and I am His,' must not his soul go forth from his body?" The moment the rabbi said this, he fell into a deep faint.

A Free Gift

After Rabbi Yitzhak of Vorki's death one of his hasidim went to Rabbi Moshe of Kobryn. "What do you hope to get from me, here in Lithuania," asked the rabbi, "that you could not get just as much of, or even more, from any zaddik in Poland?"

"My teacher," the man replied, "often said that is was a sacred duty to learn to know the rabbi of Kobryn because he spoke the truth that is in his heart. And so I decided to go to you and hoped you might teach me how to attain to truth."

"Truth," said the rabbi of Kobryn, "is not something that can

166

be attained. God looks at a man who has devoted his entire life to attaining the truth—and suddenly he gives him a free gift of it. That is why it is written: 'You will give truth to Jacob.'"

He took a pinch of snuff between two fingers and scattered it on the floor. "Look, even less than this!" Again he took some snuff—only a few shreds of tobacco. "And it can be even less, if only it is the truth!"

True Fear of God

"Had I the true fear of God," said the rabbi of Kobryn, "I should run through the streets and shout: 'You are sinning against the Torah in which is written: Ye shall be holy.'"

The Peg and the Crown

The rabbi of Kobryn said:

"He who is a leader in Israel must not think that the Lord of the world chose him because he is a great man. If the king chose to hang his crown on a wooden peg in the wall, would the peg boast that its beauty drew the king's gaze to it?"

For the Sake of the Others

On the eve of New Year's Day, before the Afternoon Prayer, the rabbi of Kobryn once laid his head on all the notes of request which were spread out before him, and said:

"Lord of the world, 'Thou knowest my folly, and my trespasses are not hid from Thee.' But what shall I do about all these people? They think I really am something! And so I beg of you: 'Let not them that wait for Thee be ashamed through me!'"

Self-Conquest

Once on the eve of the New Year, when Rabbi Moshe went up to the reader's desk to pray, he began to tremble in every limb. He clung to the pulpit, but the pulpit too swayed back and forth. The zaddik could keep his balance only by bending way back. He looked as though he were driving his trembling inward. Only then did he stand firmly in his place and begin to pray.

The Reader

Before praying on New Year's Day, Rabbi Moshe of Kobryn said:

"Once a king was angered at his rebellious people and sat in judgment upon them. No one dared come before him and plead for mercy. But among the throng was the man who had led the revolt. He knew that his head was forfeit, and came forward and pleaded with the king. So, during the Days of Awe, the reader stands before the Ark and prays for the congregation."

He Called to Them

On New Year's Day before the blowing of the ram's horn, the rabbi of Kobryn used to call out:

"Little brothers, do not depend upon me! Every one had better take his own part!"

The Offering

Once on a sabbath Rabbi Moshe of Kobryn was standing before the Ark and praying the Additional Prayer, which is a substitute for the offerings of sabbaths and feast days. When he said the words: "Lead us into our land and there we shall prepare unto thee the offerings that are obligatory for us," he fell to the floor in a faint. They had great difficulty in reviving him, and he finished the prayer.

That evening, Rabbi Moshe spoke again at his own table: "There in our land we shall bring the special offering for this sabbath, for here we have no sanctuary and no service by sacrifices." And he kindled at the words and cried aloud: "Lord of the world, we, we, we ourselves shall bring ourselves to you in place of the offering!"

Then all understood why in the House of Prayer he had fallen to the floor as if all life had left him.

The Fool

The rabbi of Kobryn was asked: "Why is it that a cantor is always called a fool?"

"You know," he replied, "that the world of music verges on that of the turning to God. When the cantor sings he is in the world of music and quite close to that other. How can he manage to keep from leaping over into it and giving himself up to the true turning? Is there any foolishness as foolish as that?"

Exchange of Strength

Rabbi Moshe taught:
When a Jew is about to say: "Blessed art thou, O Lord our God, king of the world," and prepares to utter the first word, the word "blessed," he shall do so with all his strength, so that he will have no strength left to say "art thou." And this is the meaning of the verse in the Scriptures: "But they that wait for the Lord shall exchange their strength." What we are really saying is: "Our Father in Heaven, I am giving you all the strength that is within me in that very first word; now will you, in exchange, give me an abundance of new strength, so that I can go on with my prayer."

Into the Word

Rabbi Moshe of Kobryn said:
"When you utter a word before God, then enter into that word with every one of your limbs."
One of his listeners asked: "How can a big human being possibly enter into a little word?"
"Anyone who thinks himself bigger than the word," said the zaddik, "is not the kind of person we are talking about."

The One Who Knows Not How to Ask

When the rabbi of Kobryn came to that part in the Passover Haggadah which tells of the four sons whose father instructs them in the meaning of the Seder, and what is said about the youngest: "And with the one who knows not how to ask— you must open," he always paused, sighed, and said to God: "And the one, alas! who does not know how to pray—open his heart so that he may be able to pray."

One, Who Knows One?

This is what Rabbi Moshe of Kobryn said concerning the first question in the game of riddles which is sung at the close of

169

the Passover Haggadah: "One, who knows One? One, I know One."

" 'One, who knows One?' Who can know the One who is sheer oneness? For do not even the seraphim ask: 'Where is the place of His glory?' One, and I know it in spite of everything! For, as the sage says: 'God, where can I find you? And where can I not find you!' And the seraphim too reply: 'The whole earth is full of His glory.' I know the One who is sheer oneness by his works within me."

The Ladder

Rabbi Moshe taught:
It is written: "And he dreamed, and behold a ladder set up on the earth." That "he" is every man. Every man must know: I am clay, I am one of countless shards of clay, but "the top of it reached to heaven"—my soul reaches to Heaven; "and behold the angels of God ascending and descending on it"— even the ascent and descent of the angels depend upon my deeds.

Everywhere

The rabbi of Kobryn taught:
God says to man, as he said to Moses: "Put off thy shoes from thy feet"—put off the habitual which encloses your foot, and you will know that the place on which you are now standing is holy ground. For there is no rung of human life on which we cannot find the holiness of God everywhere and at all times.

He Cometh!

The rabbi of Kobryn taught:
In the Midrash we read that when Moses proclaimed to the people that God would deliver them from servitude, they said to him: "How can we be delivered, for the whole land of Egypt is full of our idol worship!" But he answered them: "Because God wants to deliver you, he does not heed your idol worship. As it is written: 'Hark! my beloved! Behold he cometh, leaping upon the mountains, skipping upon the hills!' " And that is the way it is now. When a man bethinks himself and yearns to be delivered from his evil ways, the Evil Urge

whispers to him: "How can you hope for deliverance! Have you not wasted all your days on trivial matters!" But the zaddikim say: "Because God wants to deliver you he will not heed what has been, he will leap across all and everything and deliver you."

For the Sake of God

The rabbi of Kobryn taught:

It is written: "And Moses reported the words of the people unto the Lord." In obedience to God's command Moses had brought Israel the message that they were to be a "kingdom of priests and a holy nation," and the people had replied: "All that the Lord has spoken, we will do." This means: It is not to attain a high rung that we desire to serve God, but only because he has spoken to us. Their answer pleased Moses, and he reported it to God in their name and his own.

Not to Fear Death

When the hasidim sat around the rabbi of Kobryn's table at the Feast of Weeks, he said to them: "It is written that at Mount Sinai the people said to Moses: 'Speak thou with us and we will hear; but let no God speak with us, lest we die.' How is it possible that in their greatest hour Israel refused to hear the voice of God for fear of death that is nothing but a wresting of the soul from its husk to cling to the light of life!"

Over and over again and more and more earnestly the zaddik repeated his question. The third time he uttered it, he fainted away and lay motionless a while. It took them a long time to revive him, but then he straightened up in his chair and concluded his teaching: " ' . . . lest we die.' For it was very hard for them to give up serving God on earth."

The Most Humble

The rabbi of Kobryn was asked: "How is it possible that Dathan and Abiram reproached Moses with wanting to make himself a prince over them? For does not the Torah testify that he was the most humble of all men?"

The rabbi expounded: "When Moses sat in the zaddik's chair,

he pronounced judgment with great force. That is why they thought he wanted to make himself a prince over them. But deep in his heart he was the most humble of men. How different are the people who go their way, head bowed to the earth, and term themselves humble. That is a worthless sort of humility. True humility is hidden in the heart."

Words Not Taken to Heart

Once after the rabbi of Kobryn had "said Torah" at the sabbath meal, he said to the hasidim seated around his table: "I see that all the words I have spoken have not found a single man who took them into his heart. And if you ask me how I know this, since I am neither a prophet myself nor the son of a prophet, let me tell you. Words that come from the heart go to the heart in all their truth. But if they find no heart that will receive them, then God shows mercy to the man who spoke them: He does not let them err about in space, but they all return to the heart from which they were spoken. That is what has happened to me. I felt something like a thrust—and they all thronged back into my heart."

* * *

Some time after Rabbi Moshe's death, a friend said: "If there had been someone to whom he could have talked, he would still be alive."

Rest

Once when he was old, he was seated at the sabbath meal and anyone could see that he was very weak. His trusted servant urged him to go and take a rest. "Fool," cried the rabbi, "the only rest I know is when I sit together with Israel. I have no other rest."

"If I Knew"

Rabbi Moshe once said:
"If I knew for sure that I had helped a single one of my hasidim to serve God, I should have nothing to worry me."
Another time he said:
"If I knew I had said 'Amen' just once in the way it ought to be said, I should have nothing to worry me."

And on still another occasion he said:

"If I knew that after my death it would be said in Heaven that a Jew was coming, I should have nothing to worry me at all."

The End

On the Great Sabbath not many days before he died, Rabbi Moshe of Kobryn repeated the words of the psalm over and over again: "Praise the Lord, O my soul!" Then he added softly: "Soul of mine, you will praise the Lord in every world, no matter in what world you are. But this is what I beg of God: 'I will praise the Lord while I live'—as long as I still live here, I want to be able to praise him."

On the last day of Passover he talked at table a long time before grace was said. Then he concluded: "Now I have nothing more to say. Let us say grace."

On the following night he lay down on his deathbed, and he died a week later.

Most Important

Soon after the death of Rabbi Moshe, Rabbi Mendel of Kotzk asked one of his disciples:

"What was most important to your teacher?"

The disciple thought and then replied:

"Whatever he happened to be doing at the moment."

MOSHE AND ELEAZAR OF KOZNITZ

For the Light

Rabbi Moshe, the son of the maggid of Koznitz, said:
"It is written: 'Pure olive oil beaten for the light.' We are to
be beaten and bruised, but in order to glow with light."

The Window and the Curtain

When young Rabbi Eleazar of Koznitz, Rabbi Moshe's son,
was a guest in the house of Rabbi Naftali of Roptchitz, he
once cast a surprised glance at the window, where the curtains
had been drawn. When his host asked him the cause of his
surprise, he said: "If you want people to look in, then why
the curtains? And if you do not want them to, why the
window?"

"And what explanation have you found for this?" asked
Rabbi Naftali.

"When you want someone you love to look in," said the young
rabbi, "you draw aside the curtain."

HAYYIM MEIR YEHIEL OF MOGIELNICA AND
YISAKHAR OF WOLBORZ

Justification

Rabbi Hayyim Meir Yehiel told this story:

"My mother, peace be with her, lost one child after another in early infancy. Finally she gave birth to a child they named Moshe, and he looked as though he might survive. The first time he sat at the table of his grandfather the holy maggid, for the third sabbath meal, was when he was seven years old. On that day the passage in the Scriptures had been read which deals with how God commanded Moses to speak to the rock 'that it give forth its water' and Moses smote the rock and 'water came forth abundantly.' While they were at the meal, the boy Moshe suddenly leaped on the table and cried: 'The Torah speaks of the sin of Moses—but was it sin for him to smite the rock? Did not God himself say to him: "Take the rod!"'

"And he spoke on and on and gave a logical justification for Moses our teacher. Then he got down from the table and said to his mother: 'Mother, my head aches.' He went to his room, lay down on his bed, and died. Later, the zaddikim of that generation said that the soul of our teacher Moses had been in the boy and that he had been born only to justify Moses, our teacher.

"When he died, my mother implored her father, the holy maggid, to help her so that she might rear a son to manhood. He answered her: 'My daughter, when you lie with your husband your soul soars high in ecstasy and that is why the children you conceive do not get enough of the stuff of earth. You must bring your soul down to earth and then you will conceive a son who will live.' My mother absorbed this counsel with all her heart and soon afterward she conceived me.

"The night before I was born she dreamed that she was led into a great hall, where old men wearing crowns and white robes were seated at a long table listening to a boy, to her son Moshe, who sat at the head of the board. She wanted to run up to him and embrace him, but he called to her: 'Do not touch me!' Then he blessed her for the hour of birth."

Not without the Garment of Flesh

Rabbi Hayyim Meir Yehiel told this story:

"When I was five years old I said to my grandfather, the holy maggid: 'Grandfather, you go to a rabbi, and my father goes to a rabbi. I am the only one who doesn't go to a rabbi; I want to go to a rabbi too.' I began to cry.

"Said my grandfather to me: 'But I too am a rabbi.'

"Said I to him: 'Then why do you go to a rabbi?'

"Said he: 'What makes you think I go to a rabbi?'

"Said I: 'Because at night I see an old man with you, and you are seated before him as a servant before his master—so he must be your rabbi.'

" 'My child,' said he, 'that is the Baal Shem Tov, may his merits shield us. When you are older you will also be able to study with him.'

"Said I: 'No, I don't want a dead rabbi.'

"And I think the same to this very day. For I do not want the rungs of the spirit without the garment of the flesh. When learning from a rabbi, the disciple must resemble his teacher at least in one thing—in having a garment of flesh. That is the mystery of the Divine Presence in exile."

Only on My Own

Rabbi Hayyim Meir Yehiel, the grandson of the maggid of Koznitz, told this incident.

"When I was a boy of eleven, my grandfather summoned me and said: 'Come to me at dawn and I shall teach you the Kabbalah.' I did not do as he said, but from that time on I studied alone at dawn and did my service, for I did not want anything I could not get on my own.

"After a time my grandfather again summoned me and said: 'First I thought you did not like getting up early. But now I have found out that you are up early, and nevertheless you do not come to me.' But he had grasped the fact that I wanted to study on my own, for he went on to say: 'Well, just make a point of being there every morning when I pray, and I shall see to it that you receive holy insight.'

"But I did not even want to get this without working for it myself, and so I was present only at the beginning and end of the prayer. Time passed, and then one night I had a vision. My teacher, the rabbi of Apt, blessed be his memory, appeared to me and brought me phylacteries from paradise. When I had bound one of the phylacteries to my forehead I sensed a holy insight."

The Choice of a Soul

Rabbi Hayyim Meir Yehiel once said to his hasidim:

"I know a man who as a boy was removed to the upper worlds on the night he became Bar Mitzvah, and there they allowed him to choose a soul to his own liking. And so he selected a great soul. But it did not reach any high rung after all, and he remained a little man."

The hasidim realized that he had been speaking of himself.

The Secret of the Counting

The rabbi of Mogielnica once said to his hasidim: "I shall explain to you the secret of the counting of the fifty days between Passover and the Feast of Weeks. First it is dark, then it grows very light, but after that it grows dark again, and then, from day to day, from step to step, more and more light appears until it is all light again, and the receiving of the Torah, for which we have prepared ourselves, comes to pass."

Against Pious Thoughts

On a certain Purim when the rabbi of Mogielnica was reading the scroll of Esther, a young man stood near by and said to him when the reading was over: "I fear I did not listen closely enough and perhaps skipped over one word or another while I was silently reciting the scroll with you."

Later the rabbi said to his friends: "There's your superpious man! All he cares about is doing exactly what is prescribed. But he whose soul is directed toward doing the will of God within the commandment, and clings wholly to God's will, may very possibly fail to do something of what is prescribed, but it does not trouble him. For it is written: 'In thy love for her wilt thou err constantly.' "

No Contradictions

The rabbi of Mogielnica said:
"It is well known that the sayings of our sages which seem to contradict one another are all 'words of the living God.' Each of them decided according to the depth of his root in Heaven, and up there all their words are truth, for in the upper worlds there are no contradictions. There all opposites, such as prohibition and permission, guilt and guiltlessness, are one unified whole. The distinction between prohibition and permission appears only in their actions on earth."

There Is a Difference

Rabbi Hayyim of Mogielnica was about to go on a journey, but because he was so old and weak he could not manage to get into the carriage. Some of the hasidim who were present went in search of a stool. But when Rabbi Yisakhar saw his teacher standing and waiting he lay down on the ground. The zaddik set foot on his back and got into the carriage.
Later, the disciples discussed the incident. One of them said: "What is there so remarkable about it? I am ready to lie under the rabbi's feet for two hours!"
On Friday evening before the zaddik came to the meal, the youth lay down under the table. His master noticed it at once. "Now, now," he said, "come out from under that table!"

Marriage

Rabbi Yisakhar of Wolborz recounted:
"After my wedding a friend and I were studying the marital laws in the House of Study, when our teacher, Rabbi Hayyim of Mogielnica, came in and gave us a document which, he said, would explain itself. He left immediately. The document was a marriage contract in which we did not notice anything that required explanation. We asked the rabbi's son about it.

181

" 'Don't you see,' said he, 'that there is a drawing of two clasping hands on the sheet? That's what he was referring to.' "Later his father confirmed him and interpreted the symbol. 'You can see by the sleeves,' he explained, 'that the hands are those of the groom and the bride. The groom gives his hand to the bride and says: "I betroth thee unto Me for ever"—one hand shall nevermore be withdrawn from the other—"in righteousness and in justice"—now a pat and now a slap—"in lovingkindness and in compassion"—now a tidbit and now a good drink—but we shall remain together "for ever"; we dare not lose our tempers. That is how a Jew should be with the Lord of the world—he mustn't lose his temper!' "

In the World of Confusion

They tell this story:

To Rabbi Yisakhar of Wolborz there came a dead man whom he had once known when he was alive and prominent in his community, and begged the rabbi's help, saying that his wife had died some time ago and now he needed money to arrange for his marriage with another.

"Don't you know," the zaddik asked him, "that you are no longer among the living, that you are in the world of confusion?"

When the man refused to believe him, he lifted the tails of the dead man's coat and showed him that he was dressed in his shroud.

Later Rabbi Yisakhar's son asked: "Well, if that is so—perhaps I too am in the world of confusion?"

"Once you know that there is such a thing as that world," answered his father, "you are not in it."

FROM THE SCHOOL OF

THE RABBI OF LUBLIN

DAVID OF LELOV

The New Suit

Little David's father was a poor man. During the first months of an exceptionally severe winter he could not buy his son a warm suit of clothes. At long last he managed to scrape together the money. When David arrived at the school in his new suit, he saw a younger boy shivering in rags, and immediately changed clothes with him.

As soon as David reached home he went to his mother and told her what had happened. "Put on your old suit," she said, "and go back to school. If your father comes home and finds out what you have done he will be angry and beat you."

"But mother," answered the boy, "it is better for him to beat me and work off his anger."

The Name of God

Rabbi David of Lelov once heard a simple man who was praying say the name of God after every verse. The reason he did this was that there are two dots one above the other at the close of each verse. The man took each to be the tiny letter Yud or Yod, and since the name of God is sometimes abbreviated in the form of two Yuds, he thought that what he saw at the end of every verse was the name of God.

The zaddik instructed him: "Wherever you find two Jews [Yuds] side by side and on a par, there is the name of God. But whenever it looks to you as if one Jew [Yud] were standing above the other, then they are not Jews [Yuds] and it is not the name of God."

Concerning Those Who Ply a Trade

Rabbi Yitzhak of Vorki told this story:

"Once when I was traveling with Rabbi David Lelov, of blessed memory, we arrived in the little town of Elkish about an hour past midnight. Rabbi David did not want to wake

anyone, so we went to Rabbi Berish, the baker. He was standing at his oven and doing his work. When we entered I saw
his face cloud over because we had found him working.

" 'Oh,' said Rabbi David, 'if only God let me earn my bread
by the work of my hands! The truth of the matter is that everyone in Israel has an inner urge he himself does not know of.
What he wants is to work for his fellow men. Everyone who
plies a trade, the cobbler, the tailor, or the baker, takes money
in return for his work only that he may live and continue
to work for his fellow men.' While Rabbi David was speaking,
I saw the baker's face clear and grow brighter and brighter."

The Mistake

Rabbi Yitzhak of Vorki told this story:
"Once when I was on the road with my holy teacher Rabbi
David of Lelov, and we stopped over in a town far from our
home, a woman suddenly fell upon him in the street and
began to beat him. She thought he was her husband who had
abandoned her many years ago. After a few moments, she
saw her error and burst into a flood of tears.

" 'Stop crying,' Rabbi David said to her. 'You were not striking
me, but your husband.' And he added in a low tone: 'How
often we strike someone because we take him for another!' "

Peace-Making

Rabbi David and his disciple Yitzhak, later the rabbi of Vorki,
were once on their way to a place Rabbi David had been
asked to come to in order to make peace between two men
who had a long-standing quarrel. On the sabbath he acted
as the reader of the prayers. The two adversaries were present.
After the close of the sabbath he ordered the horses harnessed
for the journey home.

"But the rabbi has not carried out what he came for," said
his disciple.

"You are mistaken," said Rabbi David. "When in the course
of my prayer I said: 'He who maketh peace in his high places,
may he make peace for us,' the peace was made." And it was
really so.

With the Children

Whenever Rabbi David of Lelov came to a Jewish town he gathered all the children around him and gave each a little whistle. Then he packed them into the big wagon he used for traveling, and drove them all over town. The children whistled with might and main the entire time, and the entire time Rabbi David's face was wreathed in smiles.

With Animals

Once Rabbi David went to Lublin with his disciple Rabbi Yitzhak, in order to spend the New Year with his teacher, the Seer, as he did year after year. On New Year's Day, before the blowing of the ram's horn, the Seer looked around and noticed that Rabbi David was not there. Yitzhak immediately ran to the inn to look for him. He found Rabbi David standing in front of the gate to the house, holding out his cap full of barley to the horses, which their driver in his hurry to get to the House of Prayer had left behind unfed.

When Rabbi David, having finished feeding the horses, came to the House of Prayer, the Seer said: "That was fine blowing of the ram's horn Rabbi David treated us to!"

* * *

One Friday afternoon Rabbi David was on a journey, when suddenly the horse stopped and refused to go on. The driver beat the horse, but the zaddik objected.

"Rabbi," cried the driver, "the sun will soon be setting and the sabbath is almost here."

"You are quite right," answered Rabbi David, "but what you have to do is to make the animal understand you. Otherwise, it will some day summon you to court in Heaven, and that will not be to your honor."

Concerning Joseph's Brothers

The rabbi of Lelov said to his hasidim:

"A man cannot be redeemed until he recognizes the flaws in his soul and tries to mend them. A nation cannot be redeemed until it recognizes the flaws in its soul and tries to mend them. Whoever permits no recognition of his flaws, be it man or nation, permits no redemption. We can be redeemed to the extent to which we recognize ourselves.

"When Jacob's sons said to Joseph: 'We are upright men,' he answered: 'That is it that I spoke unto you saying: Ye are spies.' But later, when they confessed the truth with their lips and with their hearts and said to one another: 'We are verily guilty concerning our brother,' the first gleam of their redemption dawned. Overcome with compassion, Joseph turned aside and wept."

MOSHE TEITELBAUM

The Enemy

In his youth Rabbi Moshe Teitelbaum had been an enemy of the hasidic teachings, for he regarded them as rank heresy. Once he was staying with his friend Rabbi Joseph Asher, who was also opposed to these innovators. At just about this time, the prayer-book of the holy Rabbi Isaac Luria had appeared in print. When the volume was brought to the two friends, Rabbi Moshe snatched the heavy tome from the messenger, and threw it on the floor. But Rabbi Joseph Asher picked it up and said: "After all, it is a prayer-book, and we must not treat it disrespectfully."

When the rabbi of Lublin was told of the incident, he said: "Rabbi Moshe will become a hasid; Rabbi Joseph Asher will remain an opponent of the hasidic way. For he who can burn with enmity can also burn with love for God, but he who is coldly hostile will always find the way closed." And so it was.

Fear

In the notes Rabbi Moshe Teitelbaum made on the dreams he had in his youth we find the following.

"I was looking out of the window on the eve of the New Year and there were the people running to the House of Prayer, and I saw that they were driven by the fear of the Day of Judgment. And I said to myself: 'God be thanked, I have been doing the right thing all through the year! I have studied right and prayed right, so I do not have to be afraid.' And then my dreams showed me all my good works. I looked and looked: They were torn, ragged, ruined! And at that instant I woke up. Overcome with fear I ran to the House of Prayer along with the rest."

Paradise

In Rabbi Moshe Teitelbaum's notes on his dreams there is an entry which reads: "I have been in the paradise of the Tannaim." He had also kept a sheet with the words: "The angels will immerse you, and you shall suffer no harm." In his dream he stood near a mountain and wanted to get into the paradise of the Tannaim. But he was told that first he had to immerse himself in Miriam's Well. And at that very instant he looked into the deep water and shuddered. But angels laid hold of him and immersed him and carried him up from the depths. Then he entered the paradise of the Tannaim. There he saw one of the masters sitting with a fur cap on his head and studying the tractate called "The First Gate." There the path stopped. Rabbi Moshe was surprised. "That can't be paradise!" he cried. "Listen, child," said the angels, "you seem to think that the Tannaim are in paradise, but that's not so: paradise is in the Tannaim."

Mourning and Joy

When Rabbi Moshe Teitelbaum became a disciple of the Seer of Lublin, he studied the hasidic way of life for a time and liked it well. But once a question rose in his heart. He noticed that they were always joyful, that they performed every labor with joy, walked and rested with joy and prayed with sublime joy. Then he remembered the words in the Path of Life: "Every God-fearing man must mourn and lament the destruction of the Temple." The next time he was on the way to the rabbi of Lublin he was filled with doubts but he curbed them and said to God: "Lord, you know all my thoughts, and know that it is my purpose not to permit my eyes to regard the ways of good men as wrong. So be with me, and help me when I come to my master, to propound my question. For our sages say: 'If a man comes to be cleansed, they will assist him.' The word 'they' is used, not 'he.' For the 'they' refers to human beings." In this way he prayed and communed with God all the way to Lublin.

The moment he crossed the Seer's threshold, the master said to him: "Why is your face clouded today? It does, indeed, say in the Path of Life that every God-fearing man should mourn and lament the destruction of the Temple. But believe me, we too break into lamentation for Jerusalem at midnight, and we moan and weep, and yet it is all done in a spirit of joy. Do you know the story of the king who was sent into exile? He wandered about for a long time until he found refuge with a friend. This faithful friend shed tears whenever he remembered that the king had been driven out of his realm. But at the same time he rejoiced that the king was lodging in his house. Now, you see, dear friend, that the exiled Divine Presence is lodging with us. I really should not reveal this thing, for we are bidden to keep silence on matters concerning God, but our sages have said: 'If a man comes to be cleansed, they will assist him.' The word 'they' is used, not 'he.' For the 'they' refers to human beings."

Waiting

Rabbi Moshe Teitelbaum was always waiting for the coming of the Messiah.

Whenever he heard a noise in the street, he asked in trembling tones: "Has the messenger come?"

Before going to sleep he would lay out his sabbath clothes near the bed and lean his pilgrim's staff against them. A watchman had orders to wake the rabbi at the very first sign he saw.

Once someone wanted to sell Rabbi Moshe a fine house right next to the House of Prayer. "What would I do with it?" he cried. "Soon the Messiah will come and I shall go to Jerusalem."

The great zaddikim of his era said that a spark from the soul of Jeremiah had been reborn in him. When anyone wondered at the greatness of his sorrow on the day commemorating the destruction of the Temple, he said: "Why should you be astonished? 'I am the man that hath seen affliction,' but God will let me see the restoration as well."

Even when he was very old, it never occurred to him that he could possibly die before the coming of the Messiah.

* * *

Once while he was walking in the procession around the pulpit on the seventh day of the Feast of Booths, the day of the Great Prayer for Salvation, he prayed: "Lord of the world, grant us the coming of the end. And do not think that I am concerned

191

about my own welfare! I agree that I shall not be liberated and redeemed; I am ready to be as the stone hurled from the sling, and to suffer every anguish—for the one and only purpose that your Divine Presence may suffer no more."

*   *   *

When he was eighty-two, he prayed on the eve of the Day of Atonement before "All Vows": "Lord of the world, you know that I am a wicked sinner, but you also know that I intend to speak the truth. I do not lie and so I shall say only what is so. Had I, Moshe, the son of Hannah, known that my hair would turn gray before the Messiah came, I would very probably not have stood it. But you, Lord of the world, have made a fool of me day after day, until I turned gray. By my life, it is indeed a great trick for the Almighty to make a fool of an old fool! I implore you, Lord of the world, let it come now! Not for our sake, but for your own, that your Name may be sanctified amongst the many!"

*   *   *

Before his death he said: "I am thinking about my holy teachers, whose soul is in the uppermost paradise. Why do they keep silence? Why do they not shake all the worlds to bring the Messiah down to earth?" And after a little he continued: "In the realm of delight they have most likely been so deluged with joy that they have forgotten the earth, and to them it seems as if the Messiah had already come." And presently he added: "Even if they try to do the same to me—I shall not abandon my people."

NAFTALI OF ROPTCHITZ

The Watchman

In Roptchitz, the town where Rabbi Naftali lived, it was the custom for the rich people whose houses stood isolated or at the far end of the town to hire men to watch over their property by night. Late one evening when Rabbi Naftali was skirting the woods which circled the city, he met such a watchman walking up and down. "For whom are you working?" he asked. The man told him and then inquired in his turn: "And whom are you working for, Rabbi?"

The words struck the zaddik like a shaft. "I am not working for anybody just yet," he barely managed to say. Then he walked up and down beside the man for a long time. "Will you be my servant?" he finally asked. "I should like to," the man replied, "but what would be my duties?"

"To remind me," said Rabbi Naftali.

The Morning Prayer

"There are zaddikim," said Rabbi Naftali, "who pray that those in need of help may come to them and find help through their prayers. But the rabbi of Roptchitz gets up early in the morning and prays that all those in need of help may find it in their own homes, not have to go to Roptchitz, and not be deluded into thinking that the rabbi has helped them."

A Wish

Once, after the Additional Prayer on the Day of Atonement, the rabbi of Roptchitz said: "I wish that I could be reborn as a cow, that a Jew might come to me in the morning to take some of my milk to refresh himself before beginning the service of God."

Leader and Generation

Rabbi Naftali was once talking about the story of the Midrash which tells that God showed Moses all the generations to come, generation after generation with its preachers, generation after generation with its judges.

"Why," asked one of his disciples, "is the generation mentioned first and the leader afterward? Should he not take precedence?"

"You know," said the rabbi, "that the radiance of Moses' face was like that of the sun, of Joshua's like that of the moon, and so the faces of the successive leaders grew paler and paler. If God had inadvertently shown to Moses, Naftali, the school assistant [for so he liked to call himself], as a rabbi, Moses would have cried out: 'Is that supposed to be a rabbi!' and fainted with the shock. That is why God first showed him the generation and then the leader befitting it."

The Foolish Request

The rabbi of Roptchitz told the following incident:

"During the siege of Sebastopol Czar Nicholas was once riding along one of the walls when an enemy archer took aim at him. A Russian soldier who observed this from afar screamed and startled the emperor's horse so that it swerved to the side and the arrow missed its target. The Czar told the man to ask any favor he pleased. 'Our sergeant is so brutal,' the soldier faltered. 'He is always beating me. If only I could serve under another sergeant!'

" 'Fool,' cried Nicholas, 'be a sergeant yourself!'

"We are like that: we pray for the petty needs of the hour and do not know how to pray for our redemption."

The Twin Loaves

Two youths who were deeply devoted to each other used to go to Rabbi Naftali together to sit at his table. When he distributed the bread, for such was his custom, he always gave the two friends twin loaves clinging each to each. Once they were vexed with each other. They did not know how this feeling had entered their hearts and could not overcome it. Soon after when they again went to Roptchitz and were seated at the rabbi's table on the eve of the sabbath, he took the twin loaves, cut them apart, and gave one to each of the youths. On their way home from the meal they were overcome with emotion and both cried out in the same breath: "We are at fault, we are at fault!" They went to an inn, ordered schnapps and drank a toast to each other. The next day at the midday meal of the sabbath Rabbi Naftali again put twin loaves into the hands of the friends.

Conflagration

Young Rabbi Feyvish, a disciple of the rabbi of Roptchitz, recited the Lamentations every midnight as if Jerusalem the city of God had been destroyed that very day. Time after time he was overwhelmed with an infinite sorrow.

Late one evening the rabbi of Roptchitz asked the hasidim who were with him to follow him into the House of Study. "I shall show you," he said, "the meaning of the prophet's words: 'Arise, cry out in the night!'" In the semidarkness of the House of Study they found young Feyvish lying on a bench in a deep sleep. For a while they stood in front of him and wondered why the zaddik had taken them here. Suddenly the youth slipped to the floor, tore open his shirt collar, and cried: "Mother, I am burning up!" Just then the clock struck twelve.

Later on Feyvish left the rabbi of Roptchitz and became the disciple of the rabbi of Apt. His first teacher was much grieved about this. "With all my strength," he said, "I tried to keep down the fire. With the rabbi of Apt he will be a burnt-offering in the conflagration of his heart." Soon after this Rabbi Feyvish died in the House of Prayer during the saying of the prayer: "The breath of all that lives shall bless your name."

The Teacher

Rabbi Naftali of Roptchitz received a man who came with a long list of sins in his hand. He said that he had already been to another zaddik, but that he had imposed so heavy a penance upon him that he was physically unable to endure it. The rabbi cut him short. "And what wrong did our Father do to you," he cried in a terrible voice, "that you have betrayed him?" These words struck the man down. He lost consciousness and fell.

Several hasidim from Hungary who were standing by began

to laugh. Rabbi Naftali turned on them angrily. "I have all but slain a human soul," he cried, "and you laugh!"

"Forgive us," they said. "When our teacher Rabbi Eisik of Kalev lay on his deathbed, he gave us a sign: 'If you find a man who can take the insides out of a sinner, cleanse them, and put them back again that he may live, that is the man you shall take for your rabbi.' That was why we laughed. We have found a new master and we shall keep him until the coming of the Messiah; then we shall return to our old teacher." Then the zaddik laughed with them. He raised the penitent sinner from the floor. " 'Thine iniquity is taken away, and thy sin expiated,' " he said. "Go in peace; keep to the way of God, and he will help you."

The Penitent Who Felt Ashamed

A sinner who wanted to atone came to the rabbi of Roptchitz to learn what penance he should do. He was ashamed to confess all his sins to the zaddik and yet he had to disclose each and every one, for otherwise the rabbi could not have told him the proper form of atonement. So he said that one of his friends had done such and such a thing, but had been too ashamed to come in person and had commissioned him to go in his stead and find out for him the purification for every one of his sins.

Rabbi Naftali looked smilingly into the man's sly and tense face. "Your friend," said he, "is a fool. He could easily have come to me himself and pretended to represent someone who was ashamed to come in his own person."

The Arrogant Ascetic

When Rabbi Naftali was young, there was a man in his native city who fasted and kept vigils until he considered himself quite close to perfection, and his heart swelled. Rabbi Naftali, who knew very well what was going on within that man, once happened to be in the House of Study when a boy grazed the man with his elbow while he was sunk in meditation. The rabbi rebuked the boy: "How dare you disturb this man! Don't you know that he has been fasting for four and twenty hours?"

"Rather say from one sabbath to the next," the ascetic corrected his statement. And with that, what was hidden became manifest.

The Other Half

Once on the Great Sabbath the rabbi of Roptchitz came home from the House of Prayer with weary steps. "What made you so tired?" asked his wife. "It was the sermon," he replied. "I had to speak of the poor and their many needs for the coming Passover, for unleavened bread and wine and everything else is terribly high this year."

"And what did you accomplish with your sermon?" his wife went on to ask.

"Half of what is necessary," he answered. "You see, the poor are now ready to take. As for the other half, whether the rich are ready to give—I don't know about that yet."

Do Not Stop!

On the Day of Rejoicing in the Law, the rabbi of Ulanov, who was a dear friend of the rabbi of Roptchitz, lay dying. In Roptchitz the hasidim had just begun the great round dance in the court of the zaddik's house. He was standing at the window and looking down at them with a smile, when suddenly he raised his hand. Instantly they stopped and gazed up at him with faltering breath. For a while he kept silent and seemed as someone who has been overcome by bad news. Then he signed to the hasidim with his hand and cried: "When one of the generals falls in battle, do the companies scatter and take to flight? The fight goes on! Rejoice and dance!" Later it became known that the rabbi of Ulanov had died that very hour.

SHELOMO LEIB OF LENTSHNO

Refractory Eyes

"When I was a boy," said Rabbi Shelomo Leib of Lentshno, "I adjured all the parts of my body to do nothing save what was the will of God. And they all consented; all except my eyes. So I said I would not open my eyes, and kept lying down. When my mother asked me why I did not get up, I refused to tell, so she beat me with a stick. Then I asked my eyes whether they were now ready to take the oath. But they still held out. Finally my mother beat me so hard that they took pity on me and said 'yes.' So then I could get up."

Fearless

Rabbi Zevi Elimelekh of Dynov was asked how it was that he had always remained true to his friend Rabbi Shemolo Leib of Lentshno, even though he belonged to another school. He answered: "How could I be against him! When the two of us were studying with Rabbi Mendel in Rymanov, everyone there was so overcome with fear that not even the greatest dared raise his eyebrows. But he, Shelomo Leib, took off his shoes and danced on the table in his stocking feet, right in front of the rabbi, who sat there, and watched, and never uttered a word."

In the Image of God

The Yehudi once told his friend Rabbi Kalman of Cracow that among his disciples there was one in whose face one could still see the full image of God. Kalman took a candle and went to the House of Study where the disciples slept. He studied every face intently, but did not find what he was seeking.

"I guess you didn't look behind the stove," said the Yehudi when his friend told him of his vain search; and he accompanied him back. Behind the stove they found young Shelomo

Leib. Rabbi Kalman looked at him for a very long time by the light of his candle. "It is true," he said then. "It is true."

A Wanderer and Fugitive

After studying in Lublin and Rymanov for a time, Rabbi Shelomo Leib attached himself to the Yehudi, who said to him: "The most effective penance is to become a wanderer and fugitive." So Rabbi Shelomo decided in his soul to become a fugitive and wanderer.

Many years later a hasid who lived in Lentshno visited Rabbi Mendel of Kotzk. The rabbi asked him: "Did you see the rabbi of Lentshno?"

"I took leave of him before coming here," answered the hasid. "And was he cheerful?" asked the rabbi of Kotzk. "Yes," replied the hasid. "That's the way it is," the rabbi of Kotzk said sorrowfully. "He who is first a wanderer and fugitive becomes cheerful afterward."

The Four Hundred

Rabbi Yitzhak of Vorki once asked Rabbi Shelomo Leib of Lentshno: "Why do your hasidim look so broken in spirit and depressed?"

He replied: "Don't you know that my men are part of the four hundred who went into exile with David, and of whom it is written: 'And everyone that was in distress, and everyone that was in debt, and everyone that was discontented. . . .'"

The Perfect Swimmer

When the rabbi of Lentshno's son was a boy he once saw Rabbi Yitzhak of Vorki praying. Full of amazement he came running to his father and asked how it was possible for such a zaddik to pray quietly and simply, without giving any sign of ecstasy.

"A poor swimmer," answered his father, "has to thrash around in order to stay up in the water. The perfect swimmer rests on the tide and it carries him."

YISAKHAR BAER OF RADOSHITZ

Two Ways

A grandson of the rabbi of Radoshitz told this:

"In his youth Rabbi Yisakhar Baer had been a disciple of Rabbi Moshe Leib of Sasov. The rabbi of Sasov used to take him along on his trips to ransom prisoners. Once they were on the Vistula, when a storm broke out and almost capsized the boat. The rabbi of Sasov rose and cried: 'We are going to our Father!' and clamped his hands as wedding guests do during the bridal dance. They were saved.

"Some time after this they went to Warsaw to see the governor. When they arrived at his palace they saw that it was surrounded by armed guards who refused to admit anyone without a written permit. Rabbi Moshe Leib asked my grandfather: 'What shall I tell them?' He replied: 'Say to them in their own language: Puszczaj!' That means 'Let pass' and also 'Let go!'

"Rabbi Moshe Leib, who was almost a giant in stature, went up to one of the guards and roared the word 'Puszczaj' at him. The man retreated in alarm and let the two proceed. We do not know just what happened after that, but the rabbi of Sasov must have roared 'Puszczaj' to the governor as well, because all the prisoners on whose behalf they had come were released."

In the Bowl

Rabbi Yisakhar Baer was very poor in his youth. One year he had to fast after as well as before the Day of Atonement, and when the Feast of Booths drew near he did not have the wherewithal to celebrate it. So he stayed in the House of Study after prayer, for he knew that there was no food in his house. But his wife had sold a piece of jewelry she still had, without telling him about it, and had bought holiday loaves and potatoes and candles for the sum she received.

Toward evening when the rabbi came home and entered the

booth, he found a festive table awaiting him, and was filled with joy. He washed his hands, seated himself, and began to eat the potatoes with great gusto, for he had gone hungry for days.

But when Rabbi Yisakhar Baer grew aware of how preoccupied he was with eating, he stopped. "Berel," he said to himself, "you are not sitting in the festive booth; why, you are sitting right in the bowl!" And he did not take another bite.

The Terror of the Ritual Bath

This story is told:

Once young Yishakhar was so very poor that he had eaten nothing for a number of days, for it went against his grain to confide his trouble to others. So one evening when he felt that he could not keep alive much longer, he said to himself that he had better take one more ritual bath before he grew too weak. In those days the bath in Radoshitz lay sixty or seventy steps below the level of the ground. He undressed down to his shirt and started on his way. As he descended the stairs he heard a noise as though someone were striking his hand on water, but he went on. The noise grew louder and louder and it was clear that there were many hands beating on water. Yishakhar Baer paused a moment and then resumed his way. A gust of wind extinguished his lantern. In the darkness he heard a hideous clamor down below. He noticed creatures rising out of the depths to block his path. Quickly he threw off his shirt and jumped into the water. It grew very quiet. All he heard was one more sound as though someone were saying: "Lost," and snapping his fingers. Yisakhar Baer immersed himself again and again. Then he climbed up the stairs, dressed and went home. In front of his house stood a wagon loaded with sacks of flour and other food. "Are you Rabbi Yisakhar Baer?" asked the driver. "I was told to deliver these goods to you."

Now a few hours earlier on that very day, a farm wagon had driven up to the house of a liquor merchant, a hasid who lived near the town. In the wagon was a tall, very old man. As the merchant came to the door to greet him, he looked at him piercingly with his rather nearsighted eyes, and asked: "Where is the rabbi of this place?"

"We have no rabbi here," answered the distiller.

"Don't you know any extraordinary man in the town of Radoshitz?" the old man went on to ask. "Any 'fine Jew'?"

"There is no 'fine man' here," the hasid assured him. "We have nothing extraordinary of any description, unless you would consider the man who teaches our children something extraordinary. He certainly is a singular fellow, what you might call a 'pious' man. What we call him is just Berel, the idler."

At that the old man straightened up in the wagon so that he looked even taller than he was, and fairly snorted: "What's that? You call him an idler? He's no idler, he's a great man! He shakes the world the way an ordinary person might shake a tree in the woods." Then he called to his driver: "Back to Lublin!" and on the instant the wagon with the two men vanished.

Suddenly the hasid realized that the tall man he had seen was the rabbi of Lublin, for someone had once given him a description of the Seer of Lublin. But the next moment he thought: "Why, the rabbi of Lublin died two years ago!" Then he loaded a wagon with sacks of flour and other food and sent it to Radoshitz.

His First Healing

Once when young Yisakhar Baer was on his way to Pzhysha to see his teacher the Yehudi, and was about to cross a hill which lies before the town, he heard screams and sobs from the valley below. There could be no doubt that the sounds came from his master's house. He ran down in great bewilderment. The moment the Yehudi caught sight of Yisakhar Baer, he told him with tears streaming down his cheeks that his son was ill and on the verge of death. "We don't know what to do next," he said. "But here you are, just in the nick of time. Take the child, and I know you will make him well."

Yisakhar Baer listened in great dismay. He had never had anything to do with such matters, nor ever felt any extra-

ordinary powers within himself. But he took up the child,
put him down in his cradle again, and rocked him, and rock-
ing, he poured his pleading soul out before God. In an hour
the boy was out of danger.

Peasant Wisdom

Rabbi Yisakhar Baer once met an old peasant from the village
of Oleshnye who had known him when he was young, but
was not aware of his rise in the world. "Berel," the peasant
called to him, "what's new with you?"
"And what's new with you?" asked the rabbi.
"Well, Berel, what shall I tell you," answered the other. "What
you don't get by your own work you don't have."
From that time on whenever Rabbi Baer spoke of the proper
way to conduct one's life, he added: "And the old man of
Oleshnye said: 'What you don't get by your own work you
don't have.'"

The Confession

Once when Rabbi Yisakhar Baer was very ill, he said to himself: "It is usual for a sick man to confess his sins. Now what
shall I confess? Shall I say: 'I have sinned'? But a man in
the condition I am in now cannot lie, and I have not sinned.
Or shall I say: 'I have done too little in the service of God'?
But I did whatever I possibly could. There is one thing though
that I can confess: My feeling toward God was not clear and
not pure enough, not wholly turned to him and him alone. I
can take on myself the task of making it clearer and purer.
For in this there are no bounds to improvement, since our
feeling is based on our grasp of the magnitude of God, of
boundless God. And so that is the task I shall take on myself.
If God helps me recover, I shall try to make my feeling for
him clearer, purer and more wholly turned to him."
He recovered and lived for another twenty years.

The Imitator

The rabbi of Radoshitz had a disciple who could imitate his
teacher's way of pronouncing the sabbath eve Benediction of
Sanctification so perfectly that whoever heard him from a

distance thought it was the rabbi himself. Once when he happened to be in Radoshitz, the zaddik summoned him. "I am told," said he, "that you can utter the Benediction of Sanctification in exact imitation of my voice and gestures. Do it for me!"

"If the rabbi will promise not to be annoyed," said his disciple, "I shall be glad to do it."

"You need have no fears," said the zaddik.

The disciple pronounced the blessing over the wine just like the rabbi, and made exactly the same gestures. But when he came to a certain passage, he paused, grew motionless, and then finished the Benediction as best he could.

When his disciple had ended, the zaddik asked him: "Why didn't you go on?"

"Rabbi," answered his disciple, "when you come to that passage, you offer yourself up, and I am under no obligation to do that."

Strange Assistance

Rabbi Moshe of Lelov's daughter, a granddaughter of Rabbi David of Lelov who had been the Yehudi's friend and protector, was childless. Time after time she beset her father with requests to pray for her. Finally he told her that only the rabbi of Radoshitz could assist her in this matter. She immediately made preparation for the journey and traveled to Radoshitz in the company of her mother-in-law, who was also the daughter of a distinguished zaddik. When she had told Rabbi Yisakhar Baer her trouble, he turned on her and berated her as one scolds a spoiled child: "What's all this about wanting children, you impudent baggage! Out with you!"

The young woman, who had been delicately reared and never heard a rough word, fled, dissolved in tears. "Now I shall cry and cry till I die," she said to herself. But her mother-in-law went to the rabbi and asked him why he had shamed the poor woman as he did, whether she had by any chance committed some sin.

"Wish her good luck," answered the rabbi. "Everything is right with her now. There was no other way than to stir her to the very depths." The woman returned to him and he gave her his blessing. Soon after she came home she conceived a son.

I and You

The rabbi of Radoshitz was asked: "How are we to interpret the passage in the Talmud where Rabbi Simeon ben Yohai says to his son: 'My son, you and I are enough for the world'?" He replied: "In the Tosefta we read: 'The meaning which underlies the creation of the world is that the creature says: You are our God, and the Holy One, blessed be he, says: I am the Lord your God.' This 'you' and this 'I' are enough for the world."

God's Prayer

This question was put to the rabbi of Radoshitz: "There is one sentence in the Talmud which we do not understand. We read: 'Whence do you deduce that God himself prays? It says: And I shall bring them to my holy mountain, and make them joyful in the house of prayer. It does not say "their prayer" but "my prayer." And it follows from this that God himself prays.'

"How shall we interpret this? Is the 'but' supposed to exclude the prayers of man?"

He answered: "Not at all. God takes pleasure in the prayer of righteous men. And more than that: It is he who wakens those prayers within them and gives them the strength to pray. And so man's prayer is God's prayer."

The Light behind the Window

On a certain Passover before the Seder celebration, Rabbi Yisakhar Baer called his guest the rabbi of Mogielnica, a grandson of the maggid of Koznitz, to the window, and pointed to something outside. "Do you see, Rav of Mogielnica?" he said. "Do you see?"

After the feast was over the rabbi of Mogielnica danced around the table and sang in a low voice: "The holy old man, our brother, has shown me a light. Great is the light he has shown me. But who knows, who knows how many years must pass, how long we still must sleep before it comes to us, before it comes to us."

SHALOM OF BELZ

Transformation

Rabbi Shalom's elder brother once asked him: "How did you happen to attain to such perfection? When we were quite young I learned more quickly than you."

"This is how it happened, brother," the rabbi of Belz replied. "When I became Bar Mitzvah, my grandfather Rabbi Eleazar of Amsterdam, of blessed memory, came to me one night in a vision and gave me another soul in exchange for mine. Ever since that time I have been a different person."

The Light of the Teachings

Young Shalom's first teacher was the rabbi of Lutzk in Sokal. Then he heard about the Seer of Lublin, and the more he heard about him the more his heart burned with longing to hear his Torah. But when he asked his teacher's permission to go to the Seer, it was refused. "If you go to Lublin," he said, "I shall take from you all you have accomplished here."

Shalom did not let this stop him, however, and went to Lublin notwithstanding. When he returned and passed his teacher's house, the rabbi happened to be standing at the window. He called his wife. "Just look," said he, "how the light of the Torah shines out from the face of my disciple!"

The Confession

A hasid relates:

"Once I went to Rabbi Shalom of Belz and told him my trouble: that while I prayed alien thoughts came and confused me, not thoughts about the business of the day but evil and frightening visions; and I begged him to heal my soul. When I had finished he said to me: 'Feel no shame before me, my son. Tell me everything that is disturbing and perplexing you.' I started right in, and told him about every terror and every lust which had attacked me. While I was speaking he kept his eyes closed, but I looked at him and saw how his holy thoughts were laboring to draw those aliens thoughts up from the depths of my soul. When I had ended he said: 'God will help you to keep them away from now on.' And ever since they have never come into my mind."

Tomorrow

It was before the Passover and while the hasidim were drawing water for the baking of the unleavened bread, they called to one another: "Next year in Jerusalem!" Then Rabbi Shalom said: "Why not before next year? With this water which we are now drawing we may be baking unleavened bread in Jerusalem tomorrow on the day before the feast, and may eat it—if the Messiah comes to redeem us."

Adam and Eve

On one of his frequent visits to the rabbi of Belz, Rabbi Hayyim of Zans took his young son Barukh with him. They found Rabbi Shalom and his wife sitting at table in a room with plain board walls. They stayed for a while, and on their way home Rabbi Hayyim asked his son: "What impression did those two make on you—the holy rabbi and his wife?"
"As we entered the room," said the boy, "they seemed to me like Adam and Eve before they sinned."
"That is just how they seemed to me," said his father. "And how did the room in which they were seated look to you?"
"Like paradise," said Barukh.
"That is just how it looked to me," said Rabbi Hayyim.

Why?

When his wife died, Rabbi Shalom said:
"Lord of the world! If I had the strength to wake her, should I not have done so by now? I am simply not able to do it. But you, Lord of the world, you have the strength, and you can do it—why don't you waken Israel?"

HAYYIM OF ZANS AND YEHEZKEL OF SHENYAVA

The Fire

When the town of Brody burned and little Hayyim was taken to Rabbi Moshe Leib's house in Sasov, the zaddik said to him: "Hayyim, tell me what you saw during the fire."

The boy replied: "On the one side I saw Jews putting out the fire, and on the other I saw 'Germans' [the name given to those who had rejected Jewish dress and customs] setting fires. So I asked myself: 'Why are the Jews taking so much trouble putting out the flames? It would be simpler just to drive away the Germans, and there would soon be an end to the fire.' "

Nothing But...

When Rabbi Hayyim was a boy, someone once heard him running back and forth in his room and whispering to himself without stopping: "I mean nothing but You, nothing but You alone."

His Bad Foot

In his youth Rabbi Hayyim Zans was a disciple of the zaddik of Roptchitz. His fervor in praying was so great that he stamped on the floor with both feet. But one foot was lame. Once when the zaddik's wife had watched Hayyim pray, she went to her husband and said: "What a heartless person you are! Why do you let him pound the floor with his bad foot? Tell him to use only his good foot."

"I could do that right enough," answered the zaddik, "if, in praying, he knew every time whether he was using his good or his bad foot."

For the Smallest Spark

A zaddik who bore Rabbi Hayyim of Zans a grudge once said to him: "You climb around in the upper worlds and I accomplish just as much as you when I recite ten psalms."

"It is true that I climb around in those worlds," the rabbi

of Zans replied, "but for the smallest spark of the fear of God I give up everything else."

Teaching and Service

A certain rav, very anxious to discuss sublime subjects with the rabbi of Zans with no one to listen in on their conversation, finally managed to have the zaddik invite him on the drive he always took before the Afternoon Prayer. When the town lay behind them, Rabbi Hayyim asked him what he had on his mind. "The question I should like to put to you," said the rav, "is this: What is the difference between the way of teaching and the way of service?"

The rabbi lit his pipe and blew thick clouds of smoke into the clear air. In between he uttered long low growls like a restless lion. The rav felt very ill at ease and wished he had never put his question.

When they had driven about a mile, the zaddik roused himself and said: "You want to know the difference between the way of teaching and the way of service. I shall tell you: The way of teaching is when a man is always ready to give his soul for the glory of God, and the way of service is when a man is always prepared to fulfil the verse: 'My soul failed me when he spoke.'" He knocked at the window, and this indicated to the coachman that he was to start back home.

To the People

A rather officious man once insisted on presenting a request to Rabbi Hayyim after the Afternoon Prayer. When he refused to take "no" for an answer, the zaddik spoke roughly to him. A friend who was present asked him why he was so angry, and he answered that whoever uttered the Afternoon Prayer was face to face with the World of Emanation; why should he not be angry, coming from that world, to be annoyed with the petty troubles of a petty man.

His friend replied: "Following the passage in the Scriptures which tells of God's first revelation to Moses on Sinai, we read: 'And Moses went down from the mount unto the people.' Rashi's comment on this is: 'This informs us that when Moses

209

left the mount he did not return to his own affairs, but to the people.' How are we to interpret that? What affairs in the desert did our teacher Moses, peace be upon him, renounce in order to go to the people? We must interpret it as follows: When Moses descended from the mountain he was still clinging to the upper worlds, and in them was accomplishing his sublime work of permeating the divine attribute of rigor with that of mercy. Those were the affairs Moses had to attend to. And yet he paused in his great work, disengaged himself from the upper worlds, and turned to the people. He listened to all their petty troubles, stored the heaviness of heart of all Israel within himself, and then bore it upward in prayer."

When Rabbi Hayyim heard this, his anger melted away. He asked someone to call back the man he had shouted at, and gave ear to his request. Almost all that night he listened to the troubles and wishes of the hasidim gathered about him.

His Reason

The rabbi of Zans once said: "I love the poor. And do you know why? It is because God loves them."

What You Get Out of Life

The rabbi of Zans told the following story and accompanied his words with gestures that conjured up a picture.

"People come to me who ride to market every day in the week. One such man approached me and cried: 'My dear rabbi! I haven't gotten anything out of life. All week I get out of one wagon and into another. But when a man stops to think that he is permitted to pray to God himself, he lacks nothing at all in the world.' "

The Apples

A poor woman, an apple vendor whose stand was near Rabbi Hayyim's house, once came to him complaining: "Rabbi, I have no money to buy what I need for the sabbath."

"And what about your apple stand?" asked the zaddik.

"People say my apples are bad," she answered, "and they won't buy."

210

Rabbi Hayyim immediately ran out on the street and called: "Who wants to buy good apples?" A crowd collected around him in no time at all; they handed out coins without looking at them or counting them, and soon all the apples were sold for two and three times what they were worth.

"Now you see," he said to the woman as he turned to go, "your apples were good; all that was the matter was that people just didn't know about it."

The Turkey

Rabbi Hayyim had singled out certain poor people in his town, and gave them money every month. Not merely alms; he gave each what he required to support himself and his family.

On a certain market day a poultry dealer brought an unusually fine turkey to Zans. He took it straight to the rabbi's house and tried to sell it to his wife for the sabbath. But she thought it too dear, and so the man went off with his high-priced bird. A little later the woman found out that one of the men who received his sustenance from her husband had bought the turkey. "Now look at your poor!" she complained to the rabbi. "I wasn't able to buy the bird because the price was too high, but that man went and bought it!" "That shows," said the zaddik, "that he wants a good turkey as well for the sabbath. I didn't know that, but now that I do know it, I must raise the amount I give him every month."

Putting to Shame

A poor schoolteacher once came to visit Rabbi Hayyim of Zans. "I suppose you are preparing for your daughter's wedding," said the zaddik. "I don't know," said the other. Rabbi Hayyim looked at him inquiringly. "I still haven't the money to buy the bridegroom a prayer shawl and a fur cap, as custom demands," said the schoolteacher sadly.

Rabbi Yehezkel, the rabbi's son, who was listening to the conversation, interrupted at this point. "Father," he cried,

211

"just a few days ago I saw this man buying both these things!"
The teacher reddened and left the room in silence.

"What have you done!" said Rabbi Hayyim. "Perhaps he
was not able to pay for what he bought, or perhaps he needs
money to have a dress made for his wife to wear at the wedding,
but does not want to say so. And now you have put a man
to shame."

Rabbi Yehezkel ran into the street, caught up with the schoolteacher, and begged his forgiveness. But the man refused to
forgive him and insisted that the zaddik should judge the matter. Soon they both stood before him.

"Don't forgive him," the old man said to the schoolteacher.
"Don't forgive him until he has paid the entire cost of the
wedding down to the last shoe lace." And so it was done.

True Wisdom

One day the rabbi of Zans was standing at the window and
looking out into the street. Seeing a passer-by, he knocked
on the pane and signed to the man to come into the house.
When the stranger entered the room Rabbi Hayyim asked him:
"Tell me, if you found a purse full of ducats, would you return
it to its owner?"

"Rabbi," said the man, "if I knew the owner I should return
the purse without a moment's delay."

"You are a fool," said the rabbi of Zans. Then he resumed
his position at the window, called another passer-by, and put
the same question to him. "I'm not so foolish as all that,"
said this man. "I am not such a fool as to give up a purse
full of money that comes my way!"

"You're a bad lot," said the rabbi of Zans, and called in a
third man. He replied: "Rabbi, how can I know on what
rung I shall be when I find the purse, or whether I shall
succeed in fending off the Evil Urge? Perhaps it will get the
better of me, and I shall appropriate what belongs to another.
But perhaps God, blessed be he, will help me fight it, and in
that case I shall return what I have found to its rightful owner."

"Those are good words!" cried the zaddik. "You are a true
sage!"

The Story of the General

Once when Rabbi Hayyim was on a journey, great honors were showered upon him. Later he said to his son who had accompanied him: "I shall tell you a story about a general. It is customary for the guards to accord greater honor to a general than to a colonel. Now it once happened that a general was court-martialed because of some wrong he had done and demoted to colonel. When he left the house in which the military court had sat and passed the guards, they did not notice that he no longer wore a general's insignia and saluted him just as always. Only then was he pierced to the heart."

Looking for the Way

In the month of Elul when men prepare their souls for the days of judgment, Rabbi Hayyim was in the habit of telling stories to a tune that moved all his listeners to turn to God. Once he told this story: "A man lost his way in a great forest. After a while another lost his way and chanced on the first. Without knowing what had happened to him, he asked the way out of the woods. 'I don't know,' said the first. 'But I can point out the ways that lead further into the thicket, and after that let us try to find the way together.'

"So, my congregation," the rabbi concluded his story, "let us look for the way together."

In the King's Uniform

The servant of the rabbi of Zans told this story:

"One morning before prayers the rabbi lay down again for a short while because he was suddenly tired. Just then—and later we discovered that it was by mistake, because all practical affairs were usually referred to the zaddik's son, the rabbi of the district—a soldier came to collect taxes. The zaddik was startled when he laid eyes on him. When the soldier had gone he said to me: 'This soldier is a simple peasant, but when he appears in the king's uniform, we fear him. Let us put on the King's uniform, the prayer shawl and the phylacteries, and all the nations will fear the King.' "

The rabbi of Zans used to say: "All zaddikim serve, each in his own way, each according to his rung, and whoever says: 'Only my rabbi is righteous,' loses both worlds."

A Piece of Advice

Rabbi Hayyim had married his son to the daughter of Rabbi Eliezer of Dzikov, who was a son of Rabbi Naftali of Roptchitz. The day after the wedding he visited the father of the bride and said: "Now that we are related, I feel close to you and can tell you what is eating at my heart. Look! My hair and beard have turned white, and I have not yet atoned!"

"O my friend," replied Rabbi Eliezer, "you are thinking only of yourself. How about forgetting yourself and thinking of the world?"

Resignation

The rabbi of Zans used to tell this story about himself:

"In my youth when I was fired with the love of God, I thought I would convert the whole world to God. But soon I discovered that it would be quite enough to convert the people who lived in my town, and I tried for a long time, but did not succeed. Then I realized that my program was still much too ambitious, and I concentrated on the persons in my own household. But I could not convert them either. Finally it dawned on me: I must work upon myself, so that I may give true service to God. But I did not accomplish even this."

The Missing Number

Shortly before his death Rabbi Hayyim said to a man who had come to visit him: "If I had nine true friends whose hearts were one with mine, we should each put a loaf in his knapsack and go out into the field together and walk in the field and pray and pray, until our prayers were granted and redemption came."

In the Pulpit

When Rabbi Yehezkel, the son of the rabbi of Zans, was stopping in the town of Ujhely in Hungary, he had the crier announce that he would preach in the House of Prayer. The entire congregation gathered at the appointed time. The rabbi ascended the pulpit and said: "My friends! Once I preached in this place, and my heart was not wholly directed toward Heaven. But to pray with a divided heart is a great sin. And so I decided to do penance. Now according to the word of our sages, wrong must be expiated where it was done, and so I have again come to this pulpit. And I pray to the Holy One, blessed be he, to forgive me."

Thereupon the whole congregation recognized the power of the word of God; the fear of God entered their hearts, and all accomplished the turning.

His Discourse

When Rabbi Yehezkel was elected rav of the town he was still a young man. The entire congregation expected him to preach a sermon on the first sabbath after his arrival, for such was the custom, but he denied them their wish. At the third sabbath meal the most distinguished men of the town, who were guests at his table, begged him to expound the Torah to them. He called for a Bible, opened to the weekly portion, and read it through from beginning to end. Then he said: "This is the Torah of God. It is holy, and it is not my office to talk about it." He kissed the book and had it put back in its place.

ZEVI HIRSH OF ZHYDATCHOV, YEHUDAH ZEVI OF ROZDOL AND YITZHAK EISIK OF ZHYDATCHOV

From the Depths

Rabbi Hirsh of Zhydatchov told this story:

"On the day before the sabbath they drove me out of the town of Brody and I was in great disgrace. I walked on and on without stopping and when I got home toward evening, just before the beginning of the sabbath, I went to the House of Prayer in my workaday clothes and could only just manage to say the words of the prayer. But in the morning before I prayed I spoke to God, saying: 'Lord of the world, you see the humiliation of those who have been humiliated, and you see my crushed heart. Give me light so that I can pray to you.' Then suddenly my heart caught fire. My prayer was a flowing flame. Never before had that happened to me, and it will never happen again."

The Double Answer

Rabbi Hirsh once said to his hasidim:

"When a man comes to me and asks me to pray for help in some need of his in this world—one on behalf of a lease, another on behalf of a shop—his soul besieges me at that instant and asks for redemption in the upper world. And it is my duty to reply to both of his entreaties—with a single answer."

It Is Not the Multitude That Does It

Once when Rabbi Hirsh of Zhydatchov entered the House of Prayer, he said to the hasidim who were gathered there: "My sons, it is written: 'A king is not saved by the multitude of a host.' It is of no help to God when a zaddik has a multitude of hasidim."

His Suspicion

The rabbi of Komarno, who was a nephew of Rabbi Hirsh, related this incident.

"It was the Feast of Weeks. Dawn was just breaking when I

216

entered the room of my teacher and uncle, but he did not notice me. He was walking back and forth and I heard him crying out his heart to God. Now at that time four or five hundred people had come to him over the holidays. He said: 'Perhaps Sammael has sent me this multitude to tempt me away from you? Have pity on my poor soul that I may not be exiled from your presence!'"

Every Rabbi Is Good

One sabbath Rabbi Zevi Hirsh interrupted his teachings at the third meal and said:

"There are hasidim who travel to their rabbi and say that save for him there is no rabbi in all the world. That is idol worship. What then should they say? They should say: 'Every rabbi is good for his people, but our rabbi is best for what concerns us.'"

Illuminated

When Rabbi Moshe of Sambor, Rabbi Zevi Hirsh's younger brother, was a youth, he went about in the villages and traded with the peasants. But when he came home and said the Afternoon Prayer he felt as if his whole body were lit by a great light.

He himself tells this story: "I once asked my brother and teacher: 'Why is it: Sometimes when I have been traveling on business and come home and begin to pray, I feel illuminated, almost as though the Divine Presence had come to me?'

"And my brother answered me in his usual clear, direct way: 'Why should you be surprised at that? When a traveler walks in the way of God, then whether he knows it or not all the holy sparks which cling to the herbs of the field and the trees of the forest rush forth and attach themselves to such a man, and this illuminates him with a great light.'"

Not Yet!

When Rabbi Hirsh was on his way to Munkacs, he visited old Rabbi Moshe in Ujhely, and Rabbi Moshe complained to him as he had done so often before that the Messiah had not yet come. "You know," said Rabbi Hirsh, "I stake my whole self for everyone, even the most unfaithful, and probe down to the root of his apostasy where wickedness can be recognized as need and lust. And if I get that far, I can pull him out all right! What do you say: shall we give all those souls up as lost? For wouldn't they be lost if the Messiah came today?"

The Change in the Work

When Rabbi Hirsh returned from his wife's funeral and went up the stairs to his room, he was heard saying to himself: "Up to now I have accomplished holy unification by marriage here below, now I shall try to accomplish unification by marriage up above."

Two weeks later he died.

The Everlasting Foundation

The wife of Rabbi Yehudah Zevi of Rozdol, whose uncle was Rabbi Hirsh, once asked him: "Why don't you say something to your enemies who are out to hurt you, and why do you even do them favors when you could be bringing God's punishment down upon them by prayer?"

He said: "Did you never stop to think why so many people go to the zaddik and bring him gifts, hundreds and thousands of gifts just to one man? It is because every building must have a foundation, and without it the structure cannot stand. Now the structure of the world stands because of the zaddik, as it is written: 'The righteous is the foundation of the world.' And so it is only right that all support him who supports them all. But why should people come to me as well, and bring gifts to me even though I am not a zaddik? I have thought about this and weighed the question. Then it occurred to me that the world requires still another foundation. For it is written: 'He hangeth the world over nothingness,' and the Talmud comments on this: 'The world rests upon him who, in the hour of conflict, reduces himself to nothing, and does not say anything against those who hate him.' So you see, it is because people need nothingness in addition to the zaddik that they support me."

The Greatest Lust

A learned man once said to the rabbi of Rozdol: "It seems to me that the condition of being a zaddik is the greatest of all lusts."

"That's how it is," the rabbi replied, "but to attain to it, you first have to get the better of all the lesser lusts."

Remembering and Forgetting

On New Year's Day Rabbi Yehudah Zevi of Rozdol said:

"Today we have prayed: 'For thou art he who remembereth from eternity all forgotten things.' What is the meaning of this? That God remembers only what man forgets. When someone does a good deed and it slips his mind and he does not remember having done anything good at all, then God remembers his service. But when a man's heart swells with pride and he says to himself: 'How well I spoke! How well I learned!' then nothing of all of this persists in the eyes of God. When a man falls into sin and later dwells upon it and repents, God will forget that sin. But he remembers sins which are lightly thrust aside."

The Cord of Grace

Rabbi Yitzhak Eisik of Zhydatchov, Rabbi Hirsh's nephew, was an only son. Once when he was little more than a boy, his father asked him: "How do you interpret the words of our sages: 'Whoever occupies himself with the Torah by night, around him God strings a cord of grace by day.' Do we not always rise at midnight to occupy ourselves with the Torah, and are we not in need and trouble by day notwithstanding? So where does the cord of grace come in?"

The boy answered: "Father, the fact that we rise midnight after midnight, and occupy ourselves with the Torah, without heeding our troubles—that in itself is the cord of grace."

Three Signs

On one of his visits to Rabbi Zevi Hirsh, Rabbi Shalom of Kaminka took his son, young Yehoshua, to Zhydatchov with him. At the midday meal the boy saw a youth with heavy black curls enter the room. In one hand he carried a pitcher of water, in the other a bowl, and a towel was slung over his shoulder. He went from one person to the next all around the table with a joy that shone from his face and animated his whole body, and waited on them until they had all washed their hands. "Father," asked Yehoshua, "who is that dark youth?" "Take a good look at him," answered Rabbi Shalom. "He will be a prince in Israel."

Many years later, when Rabbi Hirsh had died and his younger brother Yitzhak Eisik, that same "dark youth," had become rabbi of Zhydatchov, and hasidim were streaming to him from all over, his fame reached Rabbi Yehoshua, who had become his father's successor in Kaminka. "I'll go to him," he decided, "and watch him to find out whether his way is right, and whether I should become his disciple. And I shall think up three signs I must have for this: first he must come to greet me when I arrive, second he must invite me to eat with him, third he must guess one of my thoughts."

Rabbi Yehoshua set out for Zhydatchov, but as he approached the town he suddenly felt feverish and when he arrived he had to be carried from his carriage and put to bed. When Rabbi Yitzhak heard of this he visited Rabbi Yehoshua and said he would surely be well that very day, and so he should have supper with him. Later, when Rabbi Yehoshua, who really had gotten over his fever, was seated at Rabbi Yitzhak's table, his host said to him smilingly: "Well, rav of Kaminka, and if a man is not able to guess another's thoughts, does that mean he isn't a rabbi?"

Rabbi Yehoshua became one of Rabbi Yitzhak's favorite disciples.

Give and Take

Rabbi Yitzhak Eisik said:
"The motto of life is 'Give and take.' Everyone must be both a giver and a receiver. He who is not both is as a barren tree."

Through the Darkness

Rabbi Yitzhak Eisik never exhibited any violent emotion in praying. He prayed in a gentle and holy voice, but his words trembled through every heart in the House of Prayer.

Once on the Feast of Weeks when he spoke the song of praise which precedes the reading of the Torah, one of his disciples who had known the Seer of Lublin was so deeply stirred that he lost the use of his eyes. He did not regain his sight until the zaddik stopped speaking. After prayers he told his teacher what had happened, and Rabbi Yitzhak Eisik explained it to him, saying: "That was because your soul which was caught up in the word went through the 'darkness, cloud, and thick darkness' of Mount Sinai."

A Breath

A disciple of Rabbi Yítzhak Eisik told this story:
"In the beginning when I came to hear our master speak but was not yet able to understand him, I opened my mouth wide, so that at least his holy breath might enter into me."

Moralizing

Rabbi Yitzhak Eisik of Zhydatchov was once host to Rabbi Zalman Leib of Sziget in Hungary, who brought with him a number of his hasidim, among them several farm and vine-yard owners, who were beginning to behave somewhat like the so-called "enlightened" group. Rabbi Zalman begged his host to admonish them. "Admonishing is not the custom here," replied the zaddik. "When I face my congregation on the sabbath and say the prayer: 'All shall thank thee and all shall praise thee,' those are our words of admonition. If they fail to rouse a man to the turning, moralizing will not do any good."
On the following day while Rabbi Yitzhak, standing in front of the Ark, was saying, "All shall thank thee," the rabbi from Hungary happened to look at those of his people who were worrying him, and he saw that they were weeping.

The Exile Festival

Rabbi Yitzhak Eisik wanted to go to the Holy Land and settle there. His sons and his friends tried to shake his resolve and did not succeed. But then something very strange happened.
On the evening before the second day of Passover, the zaddik entered the House of Prayer in the prayer shawl he wore on

weekdays. After the Prayer of Benedictions, he stood silent instead of beginning on the festival psalms, and his congregation waited in astonishment, for the like had never happened before. After a time he began to recite the psalms and he spoke with the same sublime animation as always.

Later, in the course of the meal, he said: "Today during the Evening Prayer I was wholly deprived of the power to think, and not only that: I felt I was wearing my everyday prayer shawl. I did not know what God had done to me, but finally it was revealed to me: Because I wanted to go to the Land of Israel, I no longer had any connection with the holiness of the second day of the festival which is observed only in the countries outside Palestine, and I remained in the weekday. When I realized this I thought over everything very thoroughly and decided not to give up this holiness, but rather to renounce settling in the Holy Land. Not until then was the power of thought restored to me."

But even though Rabbi Yitzhak had renounced his intention of going to the Land of Israel, he was there at all times with his eyes and his heart. He had a House of Prayer built in the holy city of Safed, and it was named for him. From then on he used to say that it was through it that his prayers rose to Heaven. He also said that every day after the Morning Prayer he made an excursion to the Holy Land. And when some passage in the Book of Splendor would not reveal itself to his understanding, he would lean his head on the box into which one puts donations for the Holy Land in the name of Rabbi Meir, the worker of miracles (a box he always kept on his table), and would repeat the saying of our sages: "The air of the Land of Israel makes wise," and instantly the gates of light swung open to him.

They Traveled Together

A hasid wished to go to the Land of Israel and went to Rabbi Yitzhak to ask his advice in the matter. The zaddik said: "Wait a while. You and I will go to the Land of Israel together." The hasid thought that Rabbi Yitzhak intended traveling there and waited to hear from him. But the message he received was news of the zaddik's death. When he heard this he said: "Then I must prepare for the journey." He immersed himself in the ritual bath, bade them call the Holy Brotherhood, and confessed his sins. Then he wrote his last will and testament and lay down. A few days later he died.

Free

During the last year of his life Rabbi Eisik of Zhydatchov often lifted his hands toward the window that gave on the street and said to himself: "Take a look at it—take a look at the coarse world!"

On the morning of the day of his death—he died toward evening—he put on his prayer shawl and phylacteries as always. But when he had uttered the first benediction of the Morning Prayer, he ordered his prayer shawl and phylacteries taken off, and said: "Today I am free of prayer shawl and phylacteries and commandments, and I shall soon be free of the world."

YAAKOV YITZHAK OF PZHYSHA (THE YEHUDI)*
AND HIS DESCENDANTS

The Peacemaker

Yaakov Yitzhak's father sometimes received visits from his brother, who lived off the main road in a little town where he worked for small pay as a servant in the House of Prayer. In reality, he was one of the thirty-six hidden zaddikim who, according to tradition, uphold the world. Whenever he came to see his brother, the two went walking in the fields beyond the town and spoke of the mysteries of the Torah. Once they took the boy with them and he walked behind his elders. They came to a meadow in which sheep were grazing. Suddenly they noticed that the animals had started a fight about their share in the pasture. The bellwethers were making for each other with lowered horns and neither shepherd nor dog was in sight. Instantly the boy sprang forward, assumed control of the meadow, and ordered his realm. He separated the opponents and made peace between them. In a trice every sheep and every lamb had been allotted what it required. But now a number of the creatures seemed in no hurry to eat, but pressed close to the boy, who scratched their coats and talked to them. "Brother," said the servant in the House of Prayer, "that boy will some day be a shepherd of the flock."

The Road to Perfection

Once the Yehudi was asked to examine thirteen-year-old Hanokh, later the rabbi of Alexander, in the Talmud. It took the boy an hour to think over the passage which had been assigned to him before he could expound it. When he had done, the zaddik cupped his hand around Hanokh's cheek and said: "When I was thirteen I plumbed passages more difficult than this in no time at all, and when I was eighteen, I had

*"Yehudi" means a Jew; see "Anger Placates a Foe," "The Festival of the Exile" and "Elijah" in this chapter.

the reputation of being a great scholar in the Torah. But one day it dawned on me that man cannot attain to perfection by learning alone. I understood what is told of our father Abraham; that he explored the sun, the moon, and the stars, and did not find God, and how in this very not-finding the presence of God was revealed to him. For three months I mulled over this realization. Then I explored until I too reached the truth of not-finding."

The Smith

When Rabbi Yaakov Yitzhak was young and had board and lodging in the house of his father-in-law, his next-door neighbor was a smith. The smith got up very early in the morning and struck hammer on anvil until the sound roared like thunder in the ears of the sleeping youth. Yaakov Yitzhak woke up and thought: "If this man tears himself away from sleep so early for worldly work and worldly profit, shall I not be able to do the same for the service of the eternal God?"

The following morning he rose before the smith, who, as he entered his smithy, heard the young man reading in a low tone. This irritated him: "There he is at work already, and he doesn't need to! I certainly won't let a fellow like that get ahead of me!" On the following night he got up before the Yehudi. But the young rabbi took up the challenge and won the race. In later years he used to say: "Whatever I have attained I owe first and foremost to a smith."

What He Learned in Lublin

When the rav of Leipnik, who was opposed to the hasidic way, became acquainted with young Yitzhak and his learning, he asked him: "What do you want of the rabbi of Lublin? What can you learn from him? What have you learned from him?" The Yehudi replied: "Even if there were nothing else, I certainly learned one thing from my teacher, the holy rabbi of Lublin: when I get into bed, I fall asleep on the instant."

The Angel's Lot

The Yehudi told this story:
"A hasid died and was faced with the judgment of Heaven.

He had powerful advocates and it seemed that the verdict would be favorable, when a great angel appeared and accused him of a wrongdoing. 'Why did you do this?' he was asked, and all he could think of as an excuse was: 'My wife talked me into it.' Then the angel laughed aloud and said: 'That is indeed a peculiar kind of vindication! He could not resist the voice of a woman!' Sentence was passed: the man was punished for the wrong he had done, the angel was to be tested by entering an earthly body and becoming some woman's husband."

When the hasidim heard the end of this story, they decided that the rabbi had been talking about himself.

Answering Back

The Yehudi's wife often subjected him to long quarrelsome speeches. He always listened to what she had to say, but remained silent and accepted it cheerfully. Once however when her nagging was a good deal worse than usual, he answered her back. Later his disciple Rabbi Bunam asked him: "In what way is this day different from others?" The Yehudi answered him: "I saw that her soul was about to leave her body for rage because I did not let her scolding annoy me. And so I said a trifling word, that she might feel that her words troubled me and draw strength from this feeling."

Anger Placates a Foe

There were people who never tired of slandering the Yehudi to his teacher, the rabbi of Lublin. They asserted he was trying to usurp the rabbi's place. Among them was the rabbi of Lublin's wife. When she died quite suddenly, her husband sent for the Yehudi and said to him: "That's your work!"

"God forbid!"

"Well, what did you do when you heard that she was maligning you?"

"I recited the psalms."

"And you call that doing nothing?"

"What should I have done?"

"Got angry," said the rabbi of Lublin.

"Rabbi," said the Yehudi, "look into my eyes, and through

my eyes into my heart, and examine it to see if it is possible for me to become angry."

The Seer looked into the eyes of his disciple. "It is true," he said. " 'The Jew' doesn't know how to be angry."

Making Up

Once when the Yehudi was seated at the table of the maggid of Koznitz on the second day of the Feast of Weeks, his host said to him: "It troubles me that on this second day of the festival, which is observed only in the countries outside Palestine, I have a greater sense of holiness and light than on the first, which is the only one kept in the Land of Israel. Can you, holy Jew, tell me, why it is that the day celebrated in exile seems holier to my heart than the single great day celebrated in our homeland?"

The Yehudi replied: "When a man has quarreled with his wife and they make up, their love is greater than before."

"You have given me new life," said the maggid, and kissed him on the forehead.

Elijah

This story is told:

The Yehudi used to put on a peasant's smock and a cap with a visor such as peasants wear, and ride to market with his servant, who had also donned this kind of dress, to look for Elijah wandering through the world in the guise of a peasant.

On one such occasion he met a villager leading a mare by the rein. The Yehudi took his servant by the arm and cried: "There he is!" The stranger flashed his anger full in the Yehudi's face. "Jew!" he cried. "If you know, why let your tongue wag!" And he vanished on the instant.

Some say that it was from this time on that people called the rabbi of Pzhysha just Yehudi, the "Jew," and nothing else.

A Temptation

Once the Yehudi was walking up and down the street. For hours he talked about apparently idle and worldly matters with the plain people, but in reality he was accomplishing marvelous unifications in the upper worlds. Then the Evil Urge came and whispered to him: "See how great and splendid is the power of your soul!" But he replied: "What do you want to make me conceited about? I am sure that everybody does what I do, only that I notice it as little in them as they do in me."

Can and Want To

Once when the Yehudi was walking cross-country, he happened on a hay wagon which had turned over. "Help me raise it up!" said the driver. The rabbi tried but he could not budge it. "I can't," he finally said. The peasant looked at him sternly. "You can all right," said he, "but you don't want to."

On the evening of that day the Yehudi went to his disciples: "I was told today: We can raise up the Name of God, but we don't want to."

Silence and Speech

A man had taken upon himself the discipline of silence and for three years had spoken no words save those of the Torah and of prayer. Finally the Yehudi sent for him. "Young man," he said, "how is it that I do not see a single word of yours in the world of truth?"

"Rabbi," said the other to justify himself, "why should I indulge in the vanity of speech? Is it not better just to learn and to pray?"

"If you do that," said the Yehudi, "not a word of your own reaches the world of truth. He who only learns and prays is murdering the word of his own soul. What do you mean by 'vanity of speech'? Whatever you have to say can be vanity or it can be truth. And now I am going to have a pipe and some tobacco brought for you to smoke tonight. Come to me after the Evening Prayer and I shall teach you how to talk."

They sat together the whole night. When morning came, the young man's apprenticeship was over.

Speech

The Yehudi and Peretz his disciple were crossing a meadow. Cattle put out to pasture there were lowing, and where it was watered by a stream a flock of geese rose from the water with a great cackling and beating of wings. "If only one could understand what all of them are saying!" cried Peretz.

"When you get to the point of understanding the very core of what you yourself are saying," said the rabbi, "you will understand the language of all creatures."

Not What Goes in at the Mouth...

The Yehudi once told his disciple Rabbi Bunam to go on a journey. Bunam did not ask any questions but left the town with a number of other hasidim and just followed the highway. Toward noon they came to a village and stopped at an inn. The innkeeper was so pleased with his pious guests that he invited them to have dinner with him. Rabbi Bunam sat down in the main room, while the others went in and out and asked all sorts of questions concerning the meat which was to be served them: whether the animal was unblemished, what the butcher was like, and just how carefully the meat had been salted. At that a man dressed in rags spoke up. He had been sitting behind the stove and still had his staff in his hand. "O you hasidim," he said, "you make a big to-do about what you put into your mouths being clean, but you don't worry half as much about the purity of what comes out of your mouths!"

Rabbi Bunam was about to reply, but the wayfarer had already disappeared—for this is Elijah's habit. Then the rabbi understood why his teacher had sent him on this journey.

Honoring One's Parents

The Yehudi was studying the Talmud with his disciples. A certain passage puzzled him and he fell silent and became absorbed in thinking about it. Among his disciples was a boy whose father had died soon after he was born. Since he knew that such interruptions on the part of his teacher were apt to last quite a while, he hurried home because he was very hungry. Just as he started on his way back to the House of Study, his mother called to him and asked him to carry a heavy bundle of hay down from the loft for her. But he did not turn back to the house because he feared to be late. Then suddenly he thought better of it. "The purpose of learning is doing," he told himself, ran back, and obeyed his mother. Then he went on to the House of Study.

The instant the boy crossed the threshold, the Yehudi roused himself from his meditations, rose to his full height, and said joyfully to him: "I am sure you must have honored your mother this hour. We know that Abayyi was the only one of the masters of the Talmud who knew neither his father nor his mother, and that because of this his soul from time to time slips into the body of those who keep the commandment of honoring their parents, which it was not vouchsafed him to do. Well, Abayyi just appeared to me and expounded that difficult passage."

Holy Despair

This is what the Yehudi said concerning the verse in the psalm: "How long shall I take counsel in my soul, having sorrow in my heart by day?"

"So long as I take counsel in my soul, there must needs be sorrow in my heart by day. It is only when I realize that no counsel can help me, and no longer take counsel and know of no help save that which comes from God—it is only then that help is accorded me." And then he added: "This is the mystic meaning of the ritual bath."

Expounding the Scriptures

Rabbi Bunam once came into his teacher the Yehudi's room. He looked up from his book like one who is interrupting, but not loath to interrupt, his work, and said almost playfully: "Say a verse from the Torah and I will expound it to you." Bunam said the first verse that occurred to him: "And Moses spoke in the ears of all the assembly of Israel the words of this song until they were consummated."

"Until they were consummated," the Yehudi repeated and turned back to his book. The interview was at an end.

Rabbi Bunam left the room full of great happiness. Fifteen-year-old Hanokh, who had been in the room with him, asked him how he could be so happy since he had not received the promised interpretation.

"Just think a bit!" said Bunam. Then the other understood too: again and again Moses had spoken his song to the children of Israel, until he had made them consummated and perfect.

Abraham and His Guests

This is what the Yehudi said concerning the verse in the Scriptures that tells about Abraham being visited by angels: "And he stood over them and they did eat."

"Why is this said in the Scriptures? It is not customary for the host who does not eat with his guests to stand over them while they eat. Now this is what is meant by these words in the Scriptures: The angels have their virtues and flaws, and men have their virtues and flaws. The virtue of angels is that they cannot deteriorate, and their flaw is that they cannot improve. Man's flaw is that he can deteriorate, and his virtue that he can improve. But a man who practices hospitality in the true sense of the word, acquires the virtues of his guests. Thus Abraham acquired the virtue of angels, that of not being able to deteriorate. And so he was over and above them."

The Right Child

After a sabbath meal at which many fathers of families were present, the Yehudi said: "You people! If any one of you is asked why he toils so on earth, he replies: 'To bring up my son to study and serve God.' And after the son is grown up, he forgets why his father toiled on earth, and toils in his turn, and if you ask him why, he will say: 'I must bring up my son to be studious and do good works.' And so it goes on, you people, from generation to generation. But when shall we get to see the right child?"

Unmixed

The Yehudi used to say:

"The main thing is not to mix the good with the bad. A hair of goodness is enough if only it has not the slightest trace of admixture."

The Stork

The Yehudi was asked: "In the Talmud it says that the stork is called *hasidah* in Hebrew, that is, the devout or the loving one, because he gives so much love to his mate and his young. Then why is he classed in the Scriptures with the unclean birds?"

He answered: "Because he gives love only to his own."

Our Test

The Yehudi said:

"Everything can be tested in some particular way to discover whether it is any good. And what is the test for the man of Israel? It is the love of Israel. When he sees the love of Israel growing in his soul day after day, he knows that he is ascending in the service of God."

The Most Valuable

The Yehudi used to say:

"I should be glad to give up my share in this and the coming world for a single ounce of Jewishness."

The Most Difficult

The Yehudi once said:

"It's no great trick to be a worker of miracles, a man who has reached a certain spiritual rung can shift Heaven and earth—but to be a Jew, that's difficult!"

Deterioration

One night the Yehudi and his disciple Rabbi Bunam shared a room. Contrary to his habit, the Yehudi did not fall asleep, but kept thinking and sighing.

Rabbi Bunam asked: "Why are you sighing?"

The Yehudi replied: "I can't stop thinking about how the judges came after Moses, the prophets after the judges, then the Men of the Great Assembly, then the Tannaim and Amoraim, and so on to the moralists, and when they too deteriorated and false moralists multiplied, the zaddikim appeared. I am sighing because I see that they too will deteriorate. What will Israel do then?"

He Who Went Before

When young Peretz lay dying, the Yehudi sat by his disciple's bed and said to him: "Peretz, your time is not come."

The other answered: "Rabbi, I know that, but have I permission to say something?"

"Speak," said the Yehudi.

"I saw," said Peretz, "that the rabbi will soon have to leave this earth, and I do not want to stay here without you."

The Yehudi died a few weeks after him.

Ultimate Insight

Sometimes the Yehudi said that every New Year's Day gave him fresh insight into the service of God, and then everything he had done in the past year seemed insignificant compared to the new, and thus he went from one crossing to the next, on an endless way. But once toward the end of a year when he was reading the Book of the Angel Raziel, it was revealed to him that he would die soon after New Year's Day. He went to his teacher, the Seer of Lublin, and told him this. "Stay with us over New Year's," said the Seer, "and you will be spared." But the Yehudi bade him farewell and returned to his own house.

The day the Yehudi died, Rabbi Kalman was walking with Rabbi Shemuel in a distant part of the country. Rabbi Kalman said: "There is a certain unification which can be accomplished on this day, but only in the Land of Israel. Whoever accomplishes it in any other place must die on the selfsame day. That was what happened to Moses, our master, peace be with him."

The Watch He Took Apart

Rabbi Yerahmiel, the Yehudi's eldest son, who was a watchmaker before he became a rabbi, once told this story to the congregation assembled in the House of Study:

"When I had learned the watchmaker's trade, I lived with my father-in-law, and he too knew quite a bit about watches. Once I wanted to go to a great zaddik and had no money for the journey. Then I told my father-in-law that if he gave me ten gulden, I would repair his watch which had been out of order for a long time, and which he had not been able to repair himself. He agreed. So I took the whole watch apart to see what was wrong with it. And then I saw that there was nothing wrong with it at all, except that one hair spring

233

was the least bit bent. I straightened it out, and the watch was as good and true as when it left the hand of its maker."

When Rabbi Yerahmiel had ended his story, the entire congregation wept.

Playing with a Watch

A hasid of Rabbi Pinhas of Kinsk, a grandson of Rabbi Yerahmiel, once came into the master's room and found him lying down and playing with his watch. He was surprised because it was almost noon and the rabbi had not yet prayed. Just then Rabbi Yerahmiel said to the hasid: "You are surprised at what I am doing? But do you really know what I am doing? I am learning how to leave the world."

After the Close of the Sabbath

One Friday on his return from the ritual bath, Rabbi Yehoshua Asher, the Yehudi's second son, asked his sons not to come to his house for the sabbath meal as they usually did, but to go to bed early, so that they might be able to stay with him a long time the night after the close of the sabbath. They did not however do as he said, and appeared at his table that evening as always. After the meal he said to them: "Do not visit me tomorrow during the day as you usually do, and see to it that you rest after midday meal." But again they failed to heed his words and appeared at their father's table as always. At the third sabbath meal the rabbi bade his eldest son cut the bread in his place, and when he was reluctant to do this, his father said: "You must learn to cut bread for Israel and to accord them abundance of blessings."

After they had eaten, said the Evening Prayer, and recited the Benediction of Separation, the rabbi ate the meal of escort of the sabbath with all those dear to him, and again he bade his eldest son cut the bread. After the meal he said to his sons: "I beg you not to go away but to do me the favor of staying with me." A little later he ordered clean underwear brought to his room. His wife was surprised that he wished this at so unusual an hour, but she gave the servant the garments, and the rabbi put them on. Then he told the servant to light candles in the House of Study and in all the rooms. At first his wife objected, but when she heard that the rabbi really wished it, she fetched the candles. Shortly after this, the rabbi had the doors thrown open and sent for his sons and his close friends who were waiting in the House of Study and in the entrance to the house.

The rabbi was in his bed. He then asked to have his pipe handed to him. He puffed at it slowly and calmly for a little and put it down on the chair. Then he drew the covers up over his face. All they could hear, just barely hear, was a sigh, and he had passed away.

Not to Seek the Righteous

A man who had done something wrong and was suffering from the consequences of his action asked the maggid of Trisk to advise him in this matter. But he sternly refused to have anything to do with it. "It is proper to ask advice *before* acting, not afterward," said he.

Then the man turned to Rabbi Yaakov Zevi of Parysov, a son of Rabbi Yehoshua Asher. "You must be helped," Rabbi Yaakov Zevi said. "We must not be set on seeking the righteous, but on imploring mercy for sinners. Abraham sought the righteous, and so he did not succeed in what he undertook. But Moses prayed: 'Pardon, I pray Thee, the iniquity of this people,' and God answered him: 'I have pardoned according to Thy word.' "

Where to Find God

A merchant once came to Rabbi Meir Shalom, a son of Rabbi Yehoshua Asher, and complained of another merchant who had opened his shop right next door to him. "You seem to think," said the zaddik, "that it is your shop that supports you, and are setting your heart upon it instead of on God who is your support. But perhaps you do not know where God lives? It is written: 'Love thy neighbor as thyself: I am the Lord.' This means: 'You shall want for your neighbor what he needs, just as you do for yourself—and therein you will find the Lord.' "

A grandson of Rabbi Nehemiah, the Yehudi's third son, told this story:

"When my grandfather was returning from Sadagora where he had been visiting with the rabbi of Rizhyn, he began to doze in the carriage which he was driving with one of his hasidim. A man with a great sack on his back passed them on the road. When he was about a hundred ells away he turned and called to my grandfather who was wakened by the sound: 'Nehemiah, is that you?' My grandfather leaned out of the carriage. 'Little Nehemiah,' the man continued, 'you're bound for Poland? Then give my greetings to the holy rabbi of Radoshitz, give my greetings to the holy rabbi of Mogielnica and give my greetings to your holy brother, Rabbi Yerahmiel!' Then he walked on. But all the persons to whom he had sent his greetings were dead. Soon after he reached home my grandfather died."

PZHYSHA AND ITS DAUGHTER SCHOOLS

SIMHA BUNAM OF PZHYSHA

Verses for Chess

When Rabbi Bunam was young and a trader in lumber, he
liked to play chess with persons of rather dubious reputation.
Whenever he made a move he did it with inner fervor as
serene as if he were intent on some holy rite, and from time
to time he accompanied his actions by a jesting verse which
he half spoke, half sang. For instance: "Be careful when
you move at chess, or you'll end up with one pawn less." The
verses always suited the stage of the game, but the tone in
which they were said was such that his audience felt impelled
to listen. They realized more and more that the verses had to
do with their very lives. They did not want to admit it, they
resisted, they yielded. Their hearts were possessed with the
great turning.

The Wrong Move

Once Rabbi Bunam was playing chess with a man he was
particularly anxious to turn from his evil way. He made a
wrong move, and now it was the move of his opponent, who
put him in a difficult position. Rabbi Bunam begged to be
allowed to take back his move and the man consented. But
when the same thing happened again, the other refused to
give in to him a second time. "I let it pass once," he said,
"but this time it must count."
"Woe to the man," the zaddik cried, "who has crept so deep
into evil that prayer can no longer help him turn!" His fellow
player stared at him silent and motionless, his soul on fire.

Worldly Talk

Rabbi Bunam took his lumber down the Vistula to Danzig
where he intended to sell it. But in between he studied with
the holy Yehudi.
Once he came to the Yehudi straight from Danzig. "Did you

239

hear any news there?" the holy Yehudi asked him. Bunam at once began to tell him all manner of things. Yerahmiel, the son of the Yehudi, was annoyed to see them wasting his father's time with idle worldly talk. But later when the guest had left, Rabbi the Yehudi said to his son "Do you know that what he told me reached from under the great abyss up to the throne of glory?"

The Walls

On a business trip to Leipzig, Rabbi Bunam, together with a number of merchants who had accompanied him, stopped at the house of a Jew in order to say the Afternoon Prayer. But the moment he entered he realized that he had come to an ill-smelling house; never had he prayed in such a room. He gave the others a sign and they left. The rabbi turned to go to the next house. But after a few steps he stopped. "We must go back!" he cried. "The walls are summoning me to judgment because I scorned and put them to shame."

Do They Deny God?

When Rabbi Bunam was in Danzig he sat down at table every Saturday with the "Germans"—that was how those Jews who had given up the Torah and Jewish ways were called—and spoke about the Torah. But the "Germans" only made fun of his strange talk. Indignantly his son Rabbi Abraham Moshe begged him to stop talking about the Torah to unbelievers who only mocked it.

"What can I do?" said Rabbi Bunam. "When the time comes and the word wakens within me—how can I restrain it? All the same though—next sabbath when I am getting ready to talk, step on my foot under the table to remind me to keep quiet." And so his son did on the following sabbath when they were again seated at table.

But Rabbi Bunam reproved him: "No! These people here are not unbelievers! I just heard one of them who has a bad headache cry out: 'Hear, O Israel!' Now Pharaoh really was an unbeliever, for when he was suffering under the blows of God he declared that he did not know Him."

The Program and the Play

In the days when Rabbi Bunam still traded in lumber, a number of merchants in Danzig asked him why he who was so well versed in the sacred writings went to visit zaddikim; what could they tell him that he could not learn from his books just as well? He answered them, but they did not understand him. In the evening they invited him to go to the play with them, but he refused. When they returned from the theater they told him they had seen many wonderful things. "I know all about those wonderful things," said he. "I have read the program."

"But from that," they said, "you cannot possibly know what we have seen with our own eyes."

"That's just how it is," he said, "with the books and the zaddikim."

In a Brothel

A lumber merchant once asked Rabbi Bunam to take his son, who was to attend to some business for him, to Danzig, and begged him to keep an eye on the youth.

One evening Rabbi Bunam could not find him at the inn. He left immediately and walked along the street until he came to a house where he heard someone playing the piano and singing. He went in. When he entered, the song had just come to an end, and he saw the lumber merchant's son leave the room. "Sing your best selection," he said to the girl who had been singing, and gave her a gulden. She sang, the door of the room opened, and the youth returned.

Rabbi Bunam went up to him and said in a casual tone, "Oh, so there you are. They have been asking for you. How about coming right back with me?" When they reached the inn, Rabbi Bunam played cards with the youth for a while and then they went to bed. The next evening he went to the theater with him. But when they returned Rabbi Bunam began to recite psalms and spoke with great force until he had extricated the youth completely from the power of materiality, and brought him to the point of perfect turning.

Years later the zaddik once told his friends: "That time in the

brothel I learned that the Divine Presence can descend anywhere and if, in a certain place, there is only a single being
who receives it, that being receives all of its blessing."

In the Public Park

One evening when Rabbi Bunam was in Danzig he went to the
public gardens. They were lit with many lights, and young men
and girls were strolling about in bright-colored dress. "These
lights are the candles of the Day of Atonement," he said to
himself. "And these garments are the shrouds of those who
pray."

Charity

When Rabbi Bunam still traded in lumber and went to Danzig
every year to the market, he stopped on the way in a little
town where he intended to spend the sabbath and there heard
of a devout and learned man who lived in great poverty. Rabbi
Bunam invited himself to the man's house as his sabbath guest,
had furnishings, dishes, and food taken to the empty house and
even managed to persuade him to accept suitable clothing.
When the sabbath was over, Rabbi Bunam, in parting, pre-
sented his host with a considerable sum of money. But the
latter refused to accept it, saying that he had already received
more than enough.

"The rest," said Rabbi Bunam, "I did not give you, but myself,
in order to heal the wound of pity which your wretchedness
dealt me; only now can I fulfil the commandment of charity.
That is why it is written: 'Thou shalt surely give him, and
thy heart shall not be grieved when thou givest unto him.'
He who cannot endure the sight of poverty must allay it until
the grievance of his heart is overcome; only then can he really
give to his fellow man."

The Pharmacist

Later, Rabbi Bunam became a pharmacist in Pzhysha. But at
night he studied with Rabbi Yaakov Yitzhak, the holy Yehudi.
When the rabbi had difficulty in healing a soul in the course
of his work with his hasidim, he used to say: "Call the pharmacist; he will help me."

The Guitar

Rabbi Yehezkel of Koznitz told a disciple of Rabbi Bunam:
"When your teacher was a pharmacist in Pzhysha we saw a
great deal of each other. One time I would go to him, the next
he would come to me. One evening when I entered his pharmacy
I saw an instrument lying on a bench, the kind whose strings
you pluck with your fingers. Just then a peasant woman came
to have a prescription filled. With one hand Rabbi Bunam
made up the medicine, with the other he fingered the strings.
When the woman had left I said to him: "Rabbi Bunam, that
is unholy conduct!" Said he: "Rabbi Yehezkel, you are no
real hasid!"
I went home and in my heart I bore him a grudge. But that
night my grandfather appeared to me, boxed my ears, and
shouted: "Don't spy on that man, he shines into all the halls
of Heaven."

The Decision

When his teacher the holy Yehudi died, Rabbi Bunam remained
in the town of Pzhysha. Once when his wife was sitting at the
window, she saw a carriage full of people stop in front of
their house. She ran to her husband and cried: "Bunam, a
whole carriage-load of hasidim has come to you!"
"What are you thinking of," he said. "You know that that's
not my business." But an hour later, when they had all left,
he said to her: "There's no helping it. I cannot hold out
against it any longer. The moment they came in, I knew the
needs and wishes of every one of them."

The Shepherd

After the death of Yehudi, for a time his disciples did not
know whom to choose for their master. They asked Rabbi
Bunam to advise them.
He said: "A shepherd was pasturing his sheep near the edge
of a meadow. He grew very tired, lay down on the ground,
and fell asleep. Such a thing had never happened to him before. At midnight he awoke. There was a full moon high in
the Heavens, and the night was cool and clear. The shepherd
drank some water from the brook and felt better. But at the

same time he remembered his sheep and his heart skipped a beat. He looked around and saw his beasts lying a few steps off, one crowded up against the next, as if they were in the fold. He counted them and not one was missing. He cried: 'Dear God, how can I repay you! Entrust your sheep to me and I shall guard them like the apple of my eye.' Find such a shepherd and make him your rabbi."

Rabbi Abele Neustaedter, who long before had instructed the Yehudi in the Kabbalah, and whom many among those present regarded as his former disciple's successor, rose from his chair and seated Rabbi Bunam in his place.

The Expensive Doctor

When Rabbi Bunam became the successor of his teacher the Yehudi, many young men came to him and forgot their homes and callings. This caused their fathers great annoyance and Rabbi Bunam was more harshly persecuted than any of the zaddikim of his generation. Once a young man's father-in-law came after him, had his carriage wait at the rabbi's door, rushed into the house, and shouted from the threshold: "You corrupt our best sons until they throw up everything and waste years here with you. And then you say that you are teaching them the fear of God! Teaching the fear of God! We don't need you for that. We have plenty of books for that purpose and they can find more in them than they can get from you."

Rabbi Bunam waited until the man ran out of words. Then he said: "You know that I used to be a pharmacist. In those days I observed that a doctor who visited all the sick without being called and without asking money for his services met with less confidence and respect for his orders than another who charged big fees. The pain and the trouble they suffer from their fathers and fathers-in-law is the fee these sick souls must pay who come to me, and they believe in the doctor who proves such a fearful expense to them."

The Cloak

A disciple of Rabbi Bunam was asked: "What is so wonderful about your teacher that you make such a great to-do over him?"

244

He replied: "Elijah found Elisha when he was ploughing the field with his oxen. You must not think of Elisha as a prophet, but as a real farmer who calls to his team: 'Giddap! Giddap!' Then the master came and cast his cloak over him and instantly Elisha's soul burned bright as a flame. He slaughtered his beasts, he broke his plough.

" 'What have I done to you?' asked Elijah.

" 'Oh,' Elisha cried, 'What you have done to me!'

"He left his father and mother and ran after his teacher, and no one could tear him away from Elijah. That is how it is when Rabbi Bunam takes one of his disciples by the hand. No matter how simple a man he is, life begins to stir within him so strongly that he yearns to offer himself up on the altar to God."

The Treasure

Rabbi Bunam used to tell young men who came to him for the first time the story of Rabbi Eisik, son of Rabbi Yekel in Cracow. After many years of great poverty which had never shaken his faith in God, he dreamed someone bade him look for a treasure in Prague, under the bridge which leads to the king's palace. When the dream recurred a third time, Rabbi Eisik prepared for the journey and set out for Prague. But the bridge was guarded day and night and he did not dare to start digging. Nevertheless he went to the bridge every morning and kept walking around it until evening.

Finally the captain of the guards, who had been watching him, asked in a kindly way whether he was looking for something or waiting for somebody. Rabbi Eisik told him of the dream which had brought him here from a faraway country. The captain laughed: "And so to please the dream, you poor fellow wore out your shoes to come here! As for having faith in dreams, if I had had it, I should have had to get going when a dream once told me to go to Cracow and dig for treasure under the stove in the room of a Jew—Eisik, son of Yekel, that was the name! Eisik, son of Yekel! I can just imagine what it would be like, how I should have to try every house over there, where one half of the Jews are named Eisik, and the other Yekel!" And he laughed again. Rabbi Eisik bowed, traveled home, dug up the treasure from under the stove, and built the House of Prayer which is called "Reb Eisik's Shul."

"Take this story to heart," Rabbi Bunam used to add, "and make what it says your own: There is something you cannot find anywhere in the world, not even at the zaddik's, and there is, nevertheless, a place where you can find it."

The Watchman Who Brooded

Rabbi Bunam once said: "It sometimes happens that a man becomes sinful and he himself does not know how it came about, for there was not a single moment when all his thoughts were not on guard." And he told this parable:

A great nobleman once had a race horse in his stable. He valued it more than anything he possessed and had it well guarded. The door of the stable was bolted and a watchman was always posted in front of it. One night the owner felt restless. He went to the stable. There sat the watchman and was obviously brooding over something with great effort. "What are you brooding about?" asked the master.

"I am wondering," said the man, "where the clay goes to when you drive a nail into the wall."

"Just you go on thinking about it," said the master. He returned to the house and went to bed. But he was unable to sleep and after a while he could not stand it, and went back to the stable. Again he found the watchman brooding in front of the door. "What are you thinking about now?" asked his master.

"I am wondering," he said, "where the batter goes to when you bake a doughnut."

"Just you go on thinking about that," said his master approvingly. Again he retired and again he could not stay in bed and went to the stable a third time. The watchman was sitting in his place and brooding. "What is going through your head now?" asked the master.

"I am just wondering," said the watchman. "There is the door

246

and it is bolted. Here am I, sitting in front of it and watching: and yet the horse has been stolen. How is that possible?"

The Three Prisoners

After the death of Rabbi Uri of Strelisk, who was called the Seraph, one of his hasidim came to Rabbi Bunam and wanted to become his disciple. Rabbi Bunam asked: "What was your teacher's way of instructing you to serve?"

"His way," said the hasid, "was to plant humility in our hearts. That was why everyone who came to him, whether he was a nobleman or a scholar, had first to fill two large buckets at the well in the market place, or to do some other hard and menial labor in the street."

Rabbi Bunam said: "I shall tell you a story. Three men, two of them wise and one foolish, were once put in a dungeon black as night, and every day food and eating utensils were lowered down to them. The darkness and the misery of imprisonment had deprived the fool of his last bit of sense, so that he no longer knew how to use the utensils he could not see. One of his companions showed him, but the next day he had forgotten again, and so his wise companion had to teach him continually.

"But the third prisoner sat in silence and did not bother about the fool. Once the second prisoner asked him why he never offered his help.

" 'Look!' said the other. 'You take infinite trouble and yet you never reach the goal, because every day destroys your work. But I sit here and try to think out how I can manage to bore a hole in the wall so that light and sun can enter, and all three of us can see everything.' "

Saved

Rabbi Bunam told this story:

"Rabbi Eleazar of Amsterdam was at sea on a journey to the Holy Land, when, on the eve of New Year's Day, a storm almost sank the ship. Before dawn Rabbi Eleazar told all his people to go on deck and blow the ram's horn at the first ray of light. When they had done this, the storm died down."

"But do not think," Rabbi Bunam added, "that Rabbi Eleazar intended to save the ship. On the contrary, he was quite certain it would go down, but before dying with his people he wanted to fulfil a holy commandment, that of blowing the ram's horn. Had he been out to save the ship through a miracle, he would not have succeeded."

The Story He Told

Rabbi Bunam said:

"Once when I was on the road near Warsaw, I felt that I had to tell a certain story. But this story was of a worldly nature and I knew that it would only rouse laughter among the many people who had gathered about me. The Evil Urge tried very hard to dissuade me, saying that I should lose all those people because once they heard this story they would no longer consider me a rabbi. But I said to my heart: 'Why should you be concerned about the secret ways of God?' And I remembered the words of Rabbi Pinhas of Koretz: 'All joys hail from paradise, and jests too, provided they are uttered in true joy.' And so in my heart of hearts I renounced my rabbi's office and told the story. The gathering burst out laughing. And those who up to this point had been distant from me attached themselves to me."

All and Each

Rabbi Bunam once said:

"On a sabbath, when my room is full of people, it is difficult for me to 'say Torah.' For each person requires his own Torah, and each wishes to find his own perfection. And so what I give to all I withhold from each."

Ears and Mouth

Once when Rabbi Bunam was "saying Torah" at his table, everyone crowded so close up to him that the servant shouted at them to stop.

"Let them be," the zaddik said to him. "Believe me, just as

they bend their ears toward me to hear what I am saying,
I too bend down my ears to hear what my mouth is saying."

A Bit of Sand

Rabbi Bunam was once walking outside the city with some
of his disciples. He bent, picked up a speck of sand, looked at
it, and put it back exactly where he had found it. "He who
does not believe," he said, "that God wants this bit of sand
to lie in this particular place, does not believe at all."

The Beginning of Teaching

Rabbi Bunam began his teaching with the words:
"We thank you, who are blessed and are the source of blessing, and are manifest and hidden." Then he said: "The man of
feeling must feel His divinity as he feels the place on which
he stands. And just as he cannot imagine himself without such
a place, so in all simplicity he ought to become aware of Him
who is the Place of the world, the manifest locus comprising
the world; but at the same time, he must know that it is He
who is the hidden life which fills the world."

The Taste of Bread

Rabbi Bunam once said at the third sabbath meal:
"It is written: 'Taste and see that the Lord is good.' What you
taste in bread is not its true taste. Only the zaddikim who have
purified all their limbs taste the true taste of the bread, as
God created it. They taste and see that the Lord is good."

All Bones

When Rabbi Bunam's enemies asked him why he delayed praying every morning, he replied: "Man has bones which sleep
on even after he is awake. But it is written: 'All my bones
shall say: Lord, who is like unto Thee?' That is why man
must wait to pray until all his bones are awake."

Two Pockets

Rabbi Bunam said to his disciples:
"Everyone must have two pockets, so that he can reach into

the one or the other, according to his needs. In his right pocket are to be the words: 'For my sake was the world created,' and in his left: 'I am earth and ashes.' "

Two Doors

Rabbi Bunam said:
"Man is always passing through two doors: out of this world and into the next, and out and in again."

The Wedding Ring

Rabbi Bunam taught:
"Like one who has made all the preparations for the wedding and forgotten to buy the wedding ring, so is he who has toiled a whole life long and forgotten to hallow himself—in the end he wrings his hands and devours himself in remorse."

The Scarf

Rabbi Bunam's favorite disciple had lost his scarf and looked all over for it with great zeal. His companions laughed at him. "He is right," said the zaddik, "to treasure a thing which has served him. Just so after death the soul visits the body that has sunk and leans above it."

Gifts

Rabbi Bunam said to his hasidim:
"He among you who is concerned with nothing but love is a philanderer; he among you who is nothing but devout is a thief; he among you who is nothing but clever is an unbeliever. Only he who has all these three gifts together can serve God as he should."

The Mead

Rabbi Bunam was informed that his disciples gathered at feasts of friendship. So he told his disciples this story:
"A man desired a good livelihood and so he asked around to find out what he should do. He was advised to learn how to make mead, since people like to drink mead. So he went to another city and had an experienced mead brewer teach him the principles of this trade. Then he returned home. And first of all—for such was the custom—he arranged a mead feast

and invited a great many people who, he thought, would spread the fame of his mead. But when the mead was brought to the table and the guests tasted it, they made wry faces, for it was bitter and undrinkable.

"The man returned to his instructor and angrily demanded the return of the money he had paid. The brewer asked him whether he had used the right amount of all the ingredients, and the man answered yes to every question in a furious voice. Finally the brewer said: 'And of course you put the honey in all right?'

" 'Honey!' said the man. 'No, I never thought of that!'

" 'You fool,' cried the master brewer, 'do you have to be told that too?'

"And that's the way it is with you," Rabbi Bunam concluded his story. "A feast is all very well, but along with it there must be a full measure of hasidic honey."

Master and Disciple

Rabbi Hanokh told this story:

"For a whole year I felt a longing to go to my master Rabbi Bunam and talk with him. But every time I entered the house, I felt I wasn't man enough. Once though, when I was walking across a field and weeping, I knew that I must run to the rabbi without delay. He asked: 'Why are you weeping?'

"I answered: 'I am after all alive in this world, a being created with all the senses and all the limbs, but I do not know what it is I was created for and what I am good for in this world.'

" 'Little fool,' he replied, 'that's the same question I have carried around with me all my life. You will come and eat the evening meal with me today.' "

Self-Confidence

Rabbi Hanokh told this story:

"In the house of my teacher Rabbi Bunam, it was customary for all his hasidim to assemble on the eve of the Day of Atonement, and to recall themselves to him. Once when I had settled the accounts of my soul, I was ashamed to have him see me. But I decided to go with the others, to remind him of me, and then leave hurriedly. And that is what I did. The moment he saw me getting ready to go, however, he called me to him. It flattered my vanity that the rabbi wanted to look upon me. But the very moment I felt flattered at heart, he said to me: 'Now there is no longer any need for it.' "

A Saying of the Fathers

A disciple told this story:
"My master Rabbi Simha Bunam once drew my head toward him with his holy hand until his lips touched the inside of my ear. Three times he whispered to me the words from the Sayings of the Fathers: 'Be not like servants who minister to their master on condition that they receive a reward.' My brain seemed to split with the holy and awesome breath of his mouth."

Blow!

Once when Rabbi Bunam honored a man in his House of Prayer by asking him to blow the ram's horn, and the fellow began to make lengthy preparations to concentrate on the meaning of the sounds, the zaddik cried out: "Fool, go ahead and blow!"

To Clutch at Life

Rabbi Bunam said:
"On New Year's the world begins anew, and before it begins anew, it comes to a close. Just as before dying, all the powers of the body clutch hard at life, so man at the turn of the year ought to clutch at life with all his might and main."

In Exile

On New Year's Day, when he had returned from the service, Rabbi Bunam told this story to the hasidim who had gathered in his house:
A king's son rebelled against his father and was banished from the sight of his face. After a time, the king was moved to pity his son's fate and bade him be sought out. It was long before one of the messengers found him, far from home. He was at a village inn, dancing barefoot and in a torn shirt in the midst of drunken peasants.
The courtier bowed and said: "Your father has sent me to

ask you what you desire. Whatever it may be, he is prepared to grant your wish."

The prince began to weep. "Oh," said he, "if only I had some warm clothing and a pair of stout shoes!"

"See," added Rabbi Bunam, "that is how we whine for the small needs of the hour and forget that the Divine Presence is in exile!"

I Am Prayer

This is what Rabbi Bunam said concerning the verse in the psalm: "And I am prayer."

"It is as if a poor man, who has not eaten in three days and whose clothes are in rags, should appear before the king. Is there any need for him to say what he wants? That is how David faced God—he was the prayer."

The Butcher on the Sabbath

Rabbi Bunam once said:

"How I envy the butcher who weighs out meat for the sabbath all day Friday, and before evening goes from house to house to collect his money. And then he hears the call that the sabbath is being welcomed in the House of Prayer and he runs there as fast as his legs will carry him, so that he too can welcome the sabbath, and hurries home to pronounce the blessing, and sighs and says: 'Praise be to God who has given us the sabbath as a day of rest.'

"Oh, if I could only savor the sabbath as he does!"

The Sign of Pardon

"In this day and age, when there are no prophets," Rabbi Bunam once said to his disciples, "how can we tell when a sin we have committed has been pardoned?"

His disciples gave various answers, but none of them pleased the rabbi. "We can tell," he said, "by the fact that we no longer commit that sin."

The Exception

Rabbi Bunam once said:

"Yes, I know how to bring all sinners to the point of turning— all except the liars!"

Result of Mortification of the Flesh

A man once told Rabbi Bunam: "Time and again I have mortified my flesh and done all I should, and yet Elijah has not appeared to me."

In reply the zaddik told him this story: "The holy Baal Shem
Tov once went on a long journey. He hired a team, seated
himself in the carriage, and uttered one of the holy Names.
Immediately the road leaped to meet the straining horses and
hardly had they begun to trot when they had reached the
first inn, not knowing what had happened to them. At this
stop they were usually fed, but they had scarcely calmed
down when the second inn rushed past them. Finally it occurred
to the beasts that they must have become men and so would
not receive food until evening, in the town where they were
to spend the night. But when evening came and the carriage
failed to stop, but raced on from town to town, the horses
agreed that the only possible explanation was that they must
have been transformed into angels and no longer required
either food or drink. At that moment the carriage reached its
destination. They were stabled, given their measure of oats,
and they thrust their heads into their feed bags as starved
horses do."

"As long as you are in a like situation," said Rabbi Bunam,
"you would do well to be content."

The Obliging Dream

A man who pursued honors came to Rabbi Bunam and told
him his father had appeared to him in a dream and said: "I
herewith announce to you that you are destined to be a leader."
The zaddik accepted the story in silence. Soon afterward, the
man returned and said that he had the same dream over
again.

"I see," said Rabbi Bunam, "that you are prepared to become
a leader of men. If your father comes to you once more, answer
him that you are ready to lead, but that now he should also
appear to the people whom you are supposed to lead."

Reluctant Honor

Someone said to Rabbi Bunam: "My case certainly proves the falseness of the saying that honor will run after him who flees from her and will flee from him who runs after her. For I ran diligently away from her, but she did not take a single step to catch up with me."

"Evidently she noticed that you were looking back at her," answered the rabbi, "and was no longer attracted by the game."

Sacrificing to Idols

Rabbi Bunam was asked: "What is meant by the expression 'sacrificing to idols'? It is unthinkable that a man should really bring a sacrifice to idols!"

He said: "I shall give you an example. When a devout and righteous man sits at table with others and would like to eat a little more but refrains because of what the people might think of him—that is sacrificing to idols."

The Maze

Rabbi Bunam was told about zaddikim who wore themselves out in the ecstasies of solitary service.

He replied: "A king had a broad maze with many intricate windings built around his palace. Whoever wanted to look upon him had to go through this maze where every step might lead into unending confusion. Those who dared enter because of their great love for the king were of two kinds. The one thought only of fighting their way forward bit by bit, the others left signs at the most puzzling twists and turns to encourage later comers to proceed on their way, without however making the way any easier. The first submitted to the intention in the *orders* of the king; the second trusted in the purpose of his mercy."

I See

One day, after he had gone blind, Rabbi Bunam visited Rabbi Fishel, the fame of whose miracle-cures had spread through the land. "Entrust yourself to my care," said his host. "I shall restore your light."

"That is not necessary," answered Bunam. "I see what I need to see."

Do Not Change Places

Rabbi Bunam once said:

"I should not like to change places with our father Abraham! What good would it do God if Abraham became like blind Bunam, and blind Bunam became like Abraham? Rather than have this happen, I think I shall try to grow a little over and beyond myself."

The Fool and the Sage

Rabbi Bunam once said:

"If I were to set out to give learned and subtle interpretations of the Scriptures, I could say a great many things. But a fool says what he knows, while a sage knows what he says."

The Solitary Tree

Rabbi Bunam once said:

"When I look at the world, it sometimes seems to me that every man is a tree in a wilderness, and that God has no one in his world but him, and that he has no one to turn to, save only God."

The Unredeemed Place

Once Rabbi Bunam was praying at an inn. People jostled and pushed him, but he did not go into his room. Later he said to his disciples: "Sometimes it seems impossible to pray in a certain place and one seeks out another place. But that is not the right thing to do. For the place we have quitted cries out mournfully: 'Why did you refuse to make your devotions here with me? If you met with obstacles, it was a sign that it was up to you to redeem me.' "

The Forbidden Way

The story is told:

Rabbi Bunam once drove out into the country with his disciples. While they were on the way they all fell asleep. Suddenly the disciples woke up. The carriage had come to a standstill in the tangled depths of a wood. Not a path as far as eye could see and no one could understand how they ever got there. They roused the zaddik. He looked around and cried: "Watchman!"

"Who goes?" the answer came from the thicket.

"The pharmacist of Pzhysha."

Threateningly the voice replied: "This time, but never again!" A road opened up, the carriage drove on, the disciples recognized the region, but never had they seen a wood in those parts. They did not dare to look back.

The Great Crime

Rabbi Bunam said to his hasidim:

"The sins which man commits—those are not his great crime. Temptation is powerful and his strength is slight! The great crime of man is that he can turn at every moment, and does not do so."

David and We

Rabbi Bunam was asked: "We confess our sins so many times on the Day of Atonement. Why do we not receive a message of forgiveness? Now David had hardly finished saying: 'I have sinned,' when he was told: 'The Lord has put away thy sin.'"

He replied: "What David said was, 'I have sinned against the Lord,' and what he meant was: 'Do with me according to your will and I shall accept it with love, for you, O Lord, are just.' But when we say 'we have sinned,' we think that it is fitting for God to forgive us, and when immediately after that we add: 'We have betrayed you,' we think that now, after God has forgiven us, it is fitting that he favor us with all manner of good things."

Young Trees

Rabbi Meir of Stabnitz was always opposing Rabbi Bunam and his way. Once he compelled two of his hasidim to swear they would do whatever he asked them to. When they had taken this oath, he charged them to journey to Pzhysha and give the following message to Rabbi Bunam: "How is it possible that you are a rabbi? Can one acquire what one needs to be a rabbi by selling lumber in Danzig?"

The men arrived in Pzhysha with heavy hearts. They begged

Rabbi Bunam to forgive them for the insult they were forced to inflict on him, and repeated the message.

"Tell your teacher," the zaddik answered, "that had I known what was ahead of me when I was young, I should have lived as he did. But it is better that I did not know."

Later he said to his disciples: "Meir has been a man of God from his youth on and does not know how to sin. Then how can he know what is wrong with the people who seek him out? I was in Danzig and in the theaters, and I know what sinning is like—and ever since then I have known how to straighten out a young tree that is growing crooked."

At the Big Wedding

In Ostila, at the wedding of a grandson of the great rabbi of Apt where more than two hundred zaddikim in white robes had assembled, Rabbi Bunam's opponents preferred all manner of false charges against him and his hasidim, and tried to have all of them excommunicated. Several disciples of Rabbi Bunam defended their cause with great strength and passion, and one of them even leaped upon the table, tore open his shirt so that his breast was bared, and called to the rabbi of Apt: "Look into my heart, and you will see what my master is!"

Finally the rabbi of Apt, who was the chairman, said: "The son of my friend the holy Yehudi, of blessed memory, is here; let us ask him to tell us the truth about this matter."

Rabbi Yerahmiel, the son of the holy Yehudi, rose. Since, after his father's death, there had been a number of unpleasant incidents between his followers and those of Rabbi Bunam, everyone expected him to express doubts as to the new way. But he said: "My father used to say: 'Bunam is the very tip of my heart.' And once when I thought he was wasting my father's time with worldly talk, my father said to me afterward: 'Do you know that what he told me reaches from under the great abyss up to the throne of glory?' "

Everyone fell silent. Only Rabbi Simeon Deutsch, who had in days gone by maligned the holy Yehudi to his teacher the Seer of Lublin, launched forth into fresh accusations and compared Rabbi Bunam to Sabbatai Zevi, the false Messiah.

Then the old rabbi of Apt rose and thundered at him with his great voice: "Rabbi Simeon, you are a wrangler! If you were in an empty wood, you would pick a quarrel with the very leaves on the trees. We have not forgotten what you did at Lublin! We shall not lend you an ear." After these words, nothing more was said of this matter throughout the wedding.

Eternal Creation

Rabbi Bunam taught:

"This is how we must interpret the first words in the Scriptures: 'In the beginning of God's creation of the heaven and the earth.' For even now, the world is still in a state of creation. When a craftsman makes a tool and it is finished, it does not require him any longer. Not so with the world! Day after day, instant after instant, the world requires the renewal of the powers of the primordial word through which it was created, and if the power of these powers were withdrawn from it for a single moment, it would lapse into tohu bohu."

Curse and Blessing

Someone asked Rabbi Bunam: "Why did God put such a strange curse upon the serpent? Why did he say that it was to eat dust? When God endowed the serpent with the ability to feed on dust, I think it was a blessing rather than a curse, for it can find whatever it needs for life everywhere."

Rabbi Bunam replied: "God told man that he must eat his bread in the sweat of his face, and if he has no bread he can pray to God for help. To woman God said she was to bear her children in pain, and if the hour of birth is very difficult, she can pray to God to ease her pain. Thus both are still bound to God and can find a way to him. But to the serpent which was the source of evil, God gave everything it requires, so that it might never have to ask him for anything at all. Thus at all times, God supplies the wicked with an abundance of riches."

For the Sake of Redemption

Rabbi Bunam expounded:

"It is written: 'And now, lest he put forth his hand, and take also of the tree of life, and eat and live forever.' When human beings committed their first sin, God in the fulness of his mercy permitted them to live in the world of death, so that they might achieve perfect redemption. That is why he decided to prevent them from taking also of the tree of life, for then their spirit would never have fought free of matter and prepared for redemption. So he drove them out of paradise."

The Sacrifice of Isaac

Rabbi Bunam was asked: "Why in the story of the sacrifice of Isaac is it especially stated and related that they went 'both of them together'? For is it not self-evident?"

He replied: "The temptation which Isaac resisted was greater than that of Abraham. Abraham heard the command from the lips of God. When Isaac heard his father say that God himself would provide the lamb for the burnt-offering, he understood— though he heard the command from the lips of man. But Abraham brooded: 'Whence has my son this great strength? It must be the strength of his youth!' Then he fetched forth from within himself the strength of his own youth. Only then did both of them really go together."

Two Kinds of Service

On a sabbath, at table, Rabbi Bunam was explaining the Scriptures.

"It is written: 'And the children of Israel sighed by reason of their service, and they cried, and their cry came up unto God out of their service.' Why is the word 'service' used twice? The first time it refers to the bondage in Egypt, but the second time it refers to the service of God. 'Away from the service of flesh and blood!' That was what they meant when they cried to God for help. 'Through the service of God, up to God.' "

Burdens

Rabbi Bunam expounded:

"It is written: 'I will bring you out from under the burdens of the Egyptians.' Why is the word 'burdens' used here rather than bondage? Because Israel had grown accustomed to bondage. When God saw that they no longer felt what was happening to them, he said: 'I will bring you out from under the burdens of Egypt. Suffering these burdens is not doing you any good; I shall have to redeem you.'"

No More than This

Rabbi Bunam was asked: "It is written: 'And ye shall be unto me a kingdom of priests, and a holy nation. These are the words which thou shalt speak unto the children of Israel.' Our teacher Rashi comments: 'These are the words, no more and no less.' What does he mean by that?"

Rabbi Bunam explained: "Moses was good. He wanted to reveal more to the people, but he was not allowed. For it was God's will that the people make an effort of their own. Moses was to say just these words to them, no more, and no less, so that they might feel: something is hidden here, and we must strive to discover it for ourselves. That is why, further on, we read: 'And he set before them all these words.' No more and no less."

It Is I

Rabbi Bunam was asked: "It is written: 'I am the Lord thy God, who brought thee out of the land of Egypt.' Why does it not read: 'I am the Lord thy God, who created heaven and earth'?"

Rabbi Bunam expounded: "'Heaven and earth!' Then man might have said: 'Heaven—that is too much for me.' So God said to man: 'I am the one who fished you out of the mud. Now you come here and listen to me!'"

We Want Water

Rabbi Bunam expounded:

"It is written that Israel said at Sinai: 'We will do and obey.' Ought it not read: 'I will do and obey,' since every individual was speaking for himself? But it was as if a great throng of people were in prison dying of thirst on a scorching day, and as if suddenly someone came and asked whether they wanted water, and everyone were to answer: 'Yes, we want water!' For every one of them would know how thirsty they all were.

261

So at Sinai they were all thirsting for a drink of the Torah, and each one of them felt the thirst of all, and when the word came to them, each one cried: 'We.' "

Moses and Korah

Rabbi Bunam taught:

"In every generation the soul of Moses and the soul of Korah return. But if once, in days to come, the soul of Korah is willing to subject itself to the soul of Moses, Korah will be redeemed."

True and False Turning

Rabbi Bunam was asked: "Why was the sin of worshipping the golden calf forgiven, though we do not find it said in the Scriptures that the people turned and did penance, and why was the sin of the spies not forgiven, although we read that the people mourned greatly because of it? Do we not know that there is nothing which can resist the turning?"

He replied: "This is the nature of turning: When a man knows he has nothing to hope for and feels like a shard of clay because he has upset the order of life, and how can that which was upset be righted again? Nevertheless, though he has no hope, he prepares to serve God from that time on and does so. That is true turning, and nothing can resist it. That is how it was with the sin of worshipping the golden calf. It was the first sin and the people knew nothing of the power of turning, and so they turned with all their heart. But it was different with the sin of the spies. The people already knew what turning can accomplish, and they thought that if they did penance they would return to their former state; so they did not turn with all their hearts, and their turning accomplished nothing."

The Shepherd Is There

Rabbi Bunam once commented on the verse in the Scriptures: "I saw all Israel scattered upon the mountains, as sheep that have no shepherd."

He said: "This does not mean that the shepherd is not there. The shepherd is always there. But sometimes he hides, and then he is indeed not there for the sheep, because they do not see him."

Against Dejection

Rabbi Bunam expounded:

"In the psalm we read: 'Who healeth the broken in heart . . . '
Why are we told that? For it is a good thing to have a broken
heart, and pleasing to God, as it is written: 'The sacrifices of
God are a broken spirit . . . ' But further on in the psalm we
read: 'And bindeth up their wounds.' God does not entirely
heal those who have broken hearts. He only eases their suffering, lest it torment and deject them. For dejection is not good
and not pleasing to God. A broken heart prepares man for
the service of God, but dejection corrodes service. We must
distinguish as carefully between the two, as between joy and
wantonness; they are so easily confused, and yet are as far
removed from one another as the ends of the earth."

In Water

Rabbi Bunam said:

"It is written in Proverbs: 'As in water face answereth to face,
so the heart of man to man.' Why does the verse read 'in
water' and not 'in a mirror'? Man can see his reflection in
water only when he bends close to it, and the heart of man too
must lean down to the heart of his fellow; then it will see
itself within his heart."

The Gate

This is what Rabbi Bunam said about the words in the psalm:
"Open to me the gates of righteousness": "It is the way of
honest service, that a man will always feel himself to be on
the outside and beg God to open to him the gates of true
service. This is what David meant when he said: 'This is the
gate of the Lord; the righteous shall enter into it.' There is no
gate to the Lord, save prayer such as this."

The Covenant with the Philistines

Rabbi Bunam once had the horses harnessed and drove to
Warsaw with several of his hasidim. When they arrived there
he told the coachman to stop at an inn. They entered and sat
down at a table. At a corner table near theirs sat two porters
who were drinking schnapps and talking about all sorts of

things. After a while the first asked: "Have you already studied the weekly portion of the Torah?"

"Yes," answered the second.

"I too have learned it," said the first, "and I found one thing very hard to understand. It is the passage about our father Abraham and Abimelech, the king of the Philistines, where it says: '. . . and they two made a covenant.' I asked myself: Why say 'they two'? That seems utterly superfluous."

"A good question!" cried the second. "But I wonder what answer you will find to it."

"What I think," said the first, "is that they made a covenant, but still they did not become one; they remained two."

Rabbi Bunam rose, left the inn with his hasidim, and got into the carriage. "Now that we heard what these hidden zaddikim had to tell us," he said, "we can go back home."

World-Peace and Soul-Peace

Rabbi Bunam taught:

"Our sages say: 'Seek peace in your own place.' You cannot find peace anywhere save in your own self. In the psalm we read: 'There is no peace in my bones because of my sin.' When a man has made peace within himself, he will be able to make peace in the whole world."

Concealment

Rabbi Bunam said:

"Before the coming of the Messiah, concealment will be so great that even the zaddikim who walk in white robes will not know their way about, and even they will be confused and flinch in their faith in the Messiah."

* * *

Another time he said:

"Before the coming of the Messiah, there will be summers without heat, and winters without cold, scholars will be without Torah, and hasidim without the hasidic way."

The Test

"The Baal Shem Tov," said Rabbi Bunam, "was wiser than Aher, the great heretic. When Aher heard a voice from Heaven crying: 'Return, O backsliding children—all except Aher,' he gave up everything and left the community. But the Baal Shem —once when he noticed that all his great gifts were suddenly leaving him, he said: 'Well then, I shall serve God as a simple man does. I am a fool, but I have faith,' and he began to pray like a little child. Instantly he was lifted higher than before, for it had only been a test."

The Book of Adam

Rabbi Bunam once said:

"I thought of writing a book. I was going to entitle it 'Adam' and the whole of man was to be in it. But then I thought it over and decided it would be better not to write such a book."

A "Good Jew"

Rabbi Bunam once asked: "Why do they call a zaddik 'a good Jew'?" Jestingly he answered his own question: "If they meant by that that he prays well, they would have to call him 'a good prayer'; if they meant that he learns well, they would have to say 'a good learner.' Now 'a good Jew' thinks well, and drinks well, and everything about him is good."

But to a disciple who had been in Pzhysha only a short time, he said: "You must know why you have come to me. If you think to become 'a good Jew,' you have come in vain. But if you are here in order to become simply a good Jew, you did right."

Abraham and Isaac

Rabbi Bunam explained the tradition that Abraham represented the attribute of mercy, and Isaac that of rigor.

"Abraham's house was wide open on all four sides. He was hospitable to everyone and gave of all the good things he had. Through this he revealed the great Name of God to the world. But when Isaac became rabbi in his stead, he went to a shop, bought iron bolts and locked all the doors. He himself went in to the innermost chamber, isolated himself from men, and devoted himself to the Torah night and day. Fear and trembling seized all his hasidim and all those who came to ask his counsel. In this way he revealed to the world that there is 'rigor.' When, from time to time, a door was opened and people were admitted, everyone who looked on his face instantly accomplished the perfect turning."

Satan's Hasidim

Rabbi Bunam told this story:

"When the Baal Shem Tov made the first hasidim, the Evil Urge was in great straits, for, as he said to his followers, 'now the hasidim of the Baal Shem Tov will set the world ablaze with their holiness.' But then he thought of a way out.

"He disguised himself, pretended to be someone else, and went to two hasidim who lived together in a certain town. 'Your work is praiseworthy,' he said to them. 'But there ought to be at. least ten of you, so that you can pray in a quorum.' He fetched eight of his people and joined them to those two hasidim. And since they had no money to purchase a scroll and other things they needed, he brought them a rich man— also one of his adherents—who provided them with whatever was necessary. He did the same everywhere. When he had finished he said to his hosts: 'Now we no longer need be afraid of anything, for we have the majority, and that is what counts.' "

Repetition

Rabbi Bunam once said to Rabbi Mendel, his disciple: "What do I need so many hasidim like these for? A few who really are hasidim would be enough for me."

"Why did the former zaddikim not do the same?" answered Rabbi Mendel. Long afterward, when his master had been dead for many years and he himself was the rabbi of Kotzk, Rabbi Mendel once said to his disciple Rabbi Hirsh of Tomashov: "What do I need so many hasidim like these for? A few who really are hasidim would be enough for me."

"Why did the former zaddikim not do the same?" answered Rabbi Hirsh.

By Night

Two hours every night, as he lay in bed, Rabbi Bunam would listen to his disciple Mendel, later the rabbi of Kotzk, while he read to him out of the Book of Splendor. Sometimes Rabbi

Bunam fell asleep for a little while, and the reading was interrupted. When he awoke he himself resumed it.

But once when he woke he said to his disciple: "Mendel, I have been thinking it over: Why should I go on living as I do? People keep coming to me and prevent me from serving God. I want to give up my service as a rabbi; I want to devote myself to the service of God." He repeated this again and again. His disciple listened and said nothing.

Finally Rabbi Bunam dozed again. After a few breaths, he sat up and said: "Mendel, no rabbi has been permitted to do so, I am not permitted to do it either."

The Order That Was Rescinded

The Russian government gave orders that the hasidim were no longer to be allowed to visit the zaddikim. Temeril, a noble lady who had provided for Rabbi Bunam in his youth and in whose service he used to sail down the Vistula to take lumber to Danzig, spoke to the governor of Warsaw and succeeded in having the order rescinded.

When Rabbi Bunam was told about it, he said: "Her intentions were good. But it would have been better had she induced the government to build a wall about every zaddik's house, and surround it with Cossacks to allow no one to enter. Then they would let us live on bread and water and do our job."

The Good Enemy

The quarrel that broke out between Rabbi Bunam and Rabbi Meir of Stabnitz lasted for many years. When Rabbi Meir died, a hasid of Rabbi Bunam's came and brought him the good news.

The zaddik jumped up and struck his hands together. "That is meant for me," he cried, "for he was my support." Rabbi Bunam died that same summer.

The Keys

The rabbi of Ger told this story:

"Rabbi Bunam had the keys to all the firmaments. And why not? The man who does not think of himself is the man who is given all the keys. He could have quickened the dead, but he was an honest man and did not take what was not his due."

The Meaning

When Rabbi Bunam lay dying his wife burst into tears. He said: "What are you crying for? My whole life was only that I might learn how to die."

The Secrets of Dying

Rabbi Yudel, who had given faithful service to Rabbi Abraham Moshe, the son of Rabbi Bunam, told this story:

"On the eve of the last sabbath before Rabbi Bunam's death, Rabbi Abraham Moshe told me that he wanted to go to his father. So we went there together and Rabbi Abraham Moshe seated himself at the head of the bed. Then he heard his father saying the Evening Prayer, but immediately afterward he heard him say the Morning Prayer.

"He said: 'Father, now is the time for the Evening Prayer.' But just then his father began to say the Afternoon Prayer.

"When Rabbi Abraham Moshe heard that, he fainted and hit the floor with the back of his head. I ran to him from the opposite corner of the room where I had been standing, and managed to bring him to consciousness. The moment he was conscious he said to me: 'Let us go home,' and we went home.

"When we were back home he told me to say the Benediction of Sanctification in his stead, because he had to go to sleep immediately. He also ordered me not to admit anyone, no matter what happened. He stayed in bed until Tuesday. From time to time I brought him a small glass of wine. That was all he took.

"On Tuesday people came running and reported that Rabbi Bunam was failing rapidly, but I turned them away. Then Rabbi Abraham Moshe's mother, Rabbi Bunam's wife, peace be with her, came to the door and said: 'My son, I beg you to go to your sick father. Do you want people to say that in the hour of his death you did not wish to be with him?'

"'Mother,' he replied, 'believe me, if I could go, I would go, but I cannot.'

"Later I heard that his mother then went to Rabbi Yitzhak of

Vorki, Rabbi Bunam's disciple, and begged him to persuade his friend Rabbi Abraham Moshe to come to his father's death-bed.

"Rabbi Yitzhak answered her: 'If Your Reverence were to order me to climb up on the roof and jump down, I should obey. But in this matter I cannot obey Your Reverence. For Rabbi Abraham and his holy father are concerned with something in which neither angels nor seraphim may interfere, and I cannot meddle in it.'

"But soon after that, at the very moment Rabbi Bunam, may his merit protect us, died, Rabbi Abraham Moshe opened his eyes and said to me: 'Yudel, now there is darkness all over the world.'

"When they carried the bier into the House of Life they went by Rabbi Abraham Moshe's door. He came out and remained standing until they had passed; then he went back in.

"Many years later I was with Rabbi Menahem Mendel of Vorki for the Passover, on the last day of which his father Rabbi Yitzhak of Vorki died. And Rabbi Menahem Mendel ordered me not to let anyone come to him, no matter what happened."

From Now On

After Rabbi Bunam's death, his disciple Yitzhak of Vorki came to his master's son, Abraham Moshe, to speak words of comfort to him. The son lamented: "And who will teach me now?"

"Take courage," said the disciple. "Up to now he has taught you in his coat; from now on, he will teach you without his coat on."

The Craving

On Hanukkah, when Rabbi Abraham Moshe was in the city of Biala with his mother, he said to her: "Mother, I have a craving to die." She answered: "I heard from your father that one has to·learn to die." He answered: "I have learned it." Again she said: "I heard from your father that one has to learn for a very long time, to learn it properly." He answered: "I have learned long enough," and lay down. He died on the seventh day of the feast. Later his mother found out that before going on his journey he had visited his favorite disciples and taken leave of them.

MENAHEM MENDEL OF KOTZK

Two Kinds of Teaching

When Mendel was already the far-famed and much-hated rabbi of Kotzk, he once returned to the little town in which he was born. There he visited the teacher who had taught him his alphabet when he was a child and read the five books of Moses with him. But he did not go to see the teacher who had given him further instruction, and at a chance meeting the man asked his former pupil whether he had any cause to be ashamed of his teacher. Mendel replied: "You taught me things that can be refuted, for according to one interpretation they can mean this, according to another, that. But my first teacher taught me true teachings which cannot be refuted, and they have remained with me as such. That is why I owe him special reverence."

How He Became a Hasid

Rabbi Mendel said:

"I became a hasid because in the town where I lived there was an old man who told stories about zaddikim. He told what he knew, and I heard what I needed."

This Is My God

When Mendel was fifteen he rode to the Seer of Lublin without asking permission of his parents. Soon after, his father came to Lublin to fetch him back. "Why have you left the ways of your fathers," he cried, "and attached yourself to the hasidim!" "In the song sung by the Red Sea," said Mendel, "what we read first is: 'This is my God and I will glorify him,' and only then, 'My father's God and I will exalt him.'"

From Lublin to Pzhysha

When Mendel, together with one of his friends, left Lublin in disappointment and drove to Pzhysha to study with the holy Yehudi, the Seer's disciple, he fell sick on the way. His friend

270

ran to the Yehudi and begged him to remember Mendel in his prayers. "Did you leave Lublin without asking the rabbi's permission?" asked the Yehudi. When he was told that was so, he went to the inn. "As soon as you are well," he said to Mendel, "you must take it upon yourself to return to Lublin and ask the rabbi's permission to leave." Mendel shook his head. "I have never regretted the truth," he said. The Yehudi looked at him long and searchingly. Finally he said: "If you are so sure of your own judgment, you will get well in any case." And so it was.

But when Mendel had recovered and came to him, the Yehudi said: "It is written: 'It is good for a man to bear a yoke in his youth.' " At that the young man felt a readiness to serve truly enter into every limb.

Later on the Seer once asked the Yehudi if he had worthwhile young men about him. "Mendel," he replied, "wants to be worthwhile." Many years later, when Rabbi Mendel of Kotzk was old, he quoted this question and this answer. "At that time," he added, "I did not yet want to be worthwhile. But from the moment the holy Yehudi said it, I did, and I do."

After the Yehudi's Death

Rabbi Mendel told this story to Rabbi Hanokh, his disciple: "When the holy Yehudi lay in bed ill, all the people recited psalms, but I stood by the stove and did not want to recite psalms. Then Rabbi Bunam came up to me and asked: 'Why do you press Heaven so hard?' But I did not understand what he wanted of me. After the Yehudi's death he said to me: 'It is over; the rabbi is no more, but he has left us the fear of God, and where the rabbi's word is, there he himself is.' I said nothing. After that I looked elsewhere for the rabbi's word, but it was not there. And so I went to Rabbi Bunam."

The Offer

The story is also told that when his master had died and Rabbi Mendel was greatly troubled as to who would now be his teacher, the Yehudi appeared to him in a dream and tried to comfort him, saying that he was willing to continue to teach him. "I do not want a teacher from the other world," answered Mendel.

Disgust

Temeril, a lady who lived in Warsaw and was known for her charitable works, visited Rabbi Bunam in Pzhysha and gave him a sum of money to be distributed among worthy poor young men in his House of Study. The zaddik entrusted one of his pupils with this task. When he had just finished allotting the money, Rabbi Mendel arrived in a torn coat with the cotton showing through the ragged lining. "What a pity!" cried the youth who had distributed the funds. "I forgot about you and now I have no more money!"

"Money!" said Rabbi Mendel and spat. For weeks afterward, the youth could not see a coin without feeling his gorge rise within him.

A Conversation

Rabbi Bunam once said to Rabbi Mendel, his disciple: "If I am sentenced to hell—what shall I do?"

Mendel was silent.

After a while Rabbi Bunam said: "This is what I'll do. Our sages say: 'If a disciple is banished, his teachers are banished together with him.' Well then, I shall say: 'Bring me my teachers, the Seer of Lublin and the holy Yehudi!' "

Then Mendel answered: "This cannot of course come up as far as you are concerned," he said, "but knowing it can be of great use to me."

The Secret Burial

Rabbi Mendel was not present when his master Rabbi Bunam died, for just at that time his son was to be married. On his deathbed Rabbi Bunam had bidden Mendel leave him and go to the wedding, and had refused to listen to his objections.

After the wedding Rabbi Mendel learned that his teacher had died and the burial had already taken place. He traveled to Pzhysha, asked for the keys to the room in which his master died, and locked himself in it. After a long time he came out and said to his assembled friends: "Only I and no one else was present at the rabbi's burial."

Why the Castle Was Built

Once when Rabbi Mendel was in the neighborhood of Pilev—that is, Pulavy—he visited the castle of Prince Czartoryski. He went from room to room and finally to the garden, where he stayed for a long time. Just at that time Rabbi Israel, the son of the Seer of Lublin, happened to be taking a trip and was stopping over in Pilev. When he heard that Rabbi Mendel was at the castle of the Czartoryskis, he told this story:

"I passed by here with my father, of blessed memory, when the castle was just being built. My father looked at it and said: 'For whom are they building this castle? For the zaddik who will some day stay there.' Since that zaddik is now in the castle, it is only right that I go there so that I may see him."

The Sabbath

Rabbi Mendel of Kotzk once said to one of his hasidim: "Do you know who I am? There was Rabbi Baer, and there was Rabbi Shmelke; there was Rabbi Elimelekh, there was the rabbi of Lublin, there was the holy Yehudi, and there was Rabbi Bunam. I am the seventh. I am the quintessence of all of them; I am the sabbath."

Concerning His Soul

Rabbi Mendel of Kotzk once said to his son-in-law: "My soul is one of those that hail from the time before the destruction of the Temple. I do not belong among the people of today. And the reason I have come into this world is to draw the distinction between what is holy and what is profane."

The Firmaments

A zaddik who was opposed to the rabbi of Kotzk sent him a message: "I am so great that I reach into the seventh firmament." The rabbi of Kotzk sent back his answer: "I am so small that all the seven firmaments rest upon me."

A Trustworthy Man

A disciple told this story:

"Once when I was standing in the room of my master and teacher, the rabbi of Kotzk, I understood the meaning of what

is written in Proverbs: 'But a trustworthy man who can find?'
This does not mean that you can find only one in a thousand.
It means that a trustworthy man, that is to say a man who can
really be trusted, cannot be found at all, for he is well hidden
—you may stand right in front of him and yet you will not
find him."

Sight and Faith

The rabbi of Kotzk made this comment on certain zaddikim of
his time: "They claim that, during the Feast of Booths, they
saw the Seven Shepherds in their booth as guests. I rely on
my faith. Faith is clearer than sight."

In a Fur Coat

The rabbi of Kotzk once said of a famous rabbi: "That's a
zaddik in a fur coat." His disciples asked him what he meant
by this. "Well," he explained, "one man buys himself a fur
coat in winter, another buys kindling. What is the difference
between them? The first wants to keep only himself warm, the
second wants to give warmth to others too."

Korah's Error

A disciple asked the rabbi of Kotzk what it was that caused
Korah to rebel against Moses and Aaron.
"He had observed," answered the rabbi, "that whenever he stood
up above, among the singing Levites, great gifts of the spirit
descended upon him. And so he thought that if he stood within
the tabernacle with his censer, still greater gifts would accrue to
him. He did not know that the power he had felt came upon
him because Aaron stood in his place and he in his."

In Pacing

A hasid told his son:
"Once when I was in Kotzk on the Day of Rejoicing in the Law,
the rabbi paced around the pulpit with the scroll of the Torah
in his hand, came to where I was standing, and said the verse:
'And in His temple all say: Glory.' Then I felt as though I
were up in the temple of Heaven and heard all the angels cry:
'Glory,' I grew faint and I became a different man."

274

From the Outside

The rabbi of Kotzk was asked how he knew what advice to give the hasidim who came to him in regard to their business affairs, since he certainly was above and beyond all such matters. He replied: "From where can you get the best all-round view of everything?"

It Is Written

When Rabbi Yitzhak Meir, later the rabbi of Ger, was in Kotzk for the first time, he soon noticed that the zaddik's house was neither well-run nor supervised, for something or other was always being stolen. Once he heard Feyvel the servant reproach the rabbi's wife: "Why shouldn't there be stealing, if things aren't locked up but just lie around for the taking!" At that the zaddik's voice rang out from his room: "Feyvel, it is written: 'Thou shalt not steal'!" When Rabbi Yitzhak Meir heard this, he was instantly overwhelmed with the feeling that it was altogether impossible for anyone to steal anything.

After Waking

One morning after prayer the rabbi of Kotzk said: "When I woke up today, it seemed to me that I was not alive. I opened my eyes, looked at my hands, and saw that I could use them. So I washed them. Then I looked at my feet and saw that I could walk with them. So I took a few steps. Now I said the blessing: 'Blessed art thou who quickenest the dead,' and knew that I was alive."

The Lord of the Castle

Rabbi Mendel once spoke to his hasidim about a certain parable in Midrash: How a man passed by a castle and, seeing it on fire and no one trying to put out the blaze, thought that this must be a castle without an owner, until the lord of the castle looked down on him and said: "I am the lord of the castle." When Rabbi Mendel said the words: "I am the lord of the castle," all those around him were struck with great reverence, for they all felt: "The castle is burning, but it has a lord."

God's Back

Concerning the verse in the Scriptures: "And thou shalt see My back; but My face shall not be seen," the rabbi of Kotzk said: "Everything puzzling and confused people see, is called God's back. But no man can see his face, where everything is in harmony."

All Together

The rabbi of Kotzk said:

"It is written: 'The ordinances of the Lord are true, they are righteous altogether.' In this world you see one ordinance decreed for one man, and an apparently contradictory ordinance for another, and you are astonished and cannot understand how both can be righteous. But in the coming world you will see them all together and you will find them altogether righteous."

To What Purpose Was Man Created?

Rabbi Mendel of Kotzk once asked his disciple Rabbi Yaakov of Radzimin: "Yaakov, to what purpose was man created?" He answered: "So that he might perfect his soul."

"Yaakov," said the zaddik, "is that what we learned from our teacher, Rabbi Bunam? No, indeed! Man was created so that he might lift up the Heavens."

The Ladder

Rabbi Mendel of Kotzk said to his disciples: "The souls descended from the realms of Heaven to earth on a ladder. Then it was taken away. Now up there they are calling the souls home. Some do not budge from the spot, for how can one get to Heaven without a ladder? Others leap and fall, and leap again and give up. But there are those who know very well that they cannot make it, but try and try over and over again until God catches hold of them and pulls them up."

Man's Advantage

This is what Rabbi Mendel said about the words in the Scriptures: "This is the law of the burnt-offering":

"Why does God demand sacrifice of man and not of the angels? That of the angels would be purer than that of man could ever be. But what God desires is not the deed but the preparation. The holy angels cannot prepare themselves; they can only do the deed. Preparation is the task of man who is caught in the thicket of tremendous obstacles and must free himself. This is the advantage of the works of man."

Immersion

This is what the rabbi of Kotzk said concerning Rabbi Akiba's saying that "God is the waters of immersion of Israel": "The waters of immersion only purify the soul if one is wholly immersed, so that not a hair is showing. That is how we should be immersed in God."

God's Dwelling

"Where is the dwelling of God?"
This was the question with which the rabbi of Kotzk surprised a number of learned men who happened to be visiting him.
They laughed at him: "What a thing to ask! Is not the whole world full of his glory!"
Then he answered his own question:
"God dwells wherever man lets him in."

Fathers and Sons

A man came to the rabbi of Kotzk and complained of his sons who refused to support him, though he was old and no longer able to earn his own livelihood. "I was always ready to do anything at all for them," he said, "and now they won't have anything to do with me." Silently the rabbi raised his eyes to Heaven. "That's how it is," he said softly. "The father shares in the sorrow of his sons, but the sons do not share in the sorrow of their father."

The Vessel

A disciple of Rabbi Mendel told this story in his old age, shortly before he died:
"I shall tell you the first saying I heard from the rabbi. I heard many after that, but with this first he kindled my heart forever. It was on a sabbath eve after the Benediction of Sanctification. The rabbi sat in his big chair, and his face was transformed as though his soul had left his body and was floating about him. He stretched out his arms with a gesture of great decision,

poured water over our hands, spoke the benediction over the bread, and broke the bread. Then he said:

" 'In the world there are sages, students, and thinkers. They all think of and study the mystery of God. But what can they find out about it? No more than they can grasp from their rung of reason. But the holy children of Israel have a vessel: it is to do God's will and with this vessel they can hold more than is accorded their rung, they can grasp what is accorded on the rung of the ministering angels. That is what is meant by the words spoken at Sinai: "We do, we hear." It is with our doing that we grasp.' "

Giving and Receiving

The rabbi of Kotzk was asked: "Why is the Feast of Weeks designated as 'the time the Torah was given' us, rather than the time we received the Torah?"

He answered: "The giving took place on the day commemorated by this feast, but the receiving takes place at all times. It was given to all equally, but they did not all receive in equal measure."

Upon Thy Heart

Rabbi Mendel of Kotzk said:

" 'And these words which I command thee this day, shall be *upon* thy heart.' The verse does not say: '*in* thy heart.' For there are times when the heart is shut. But the words lie upon the heart, and when the heart opens in holy hours, they sink deep down into it."

No Strange God

They asked the rabbi of Kotzk: "What is new about King David's saying, 'There shall no strange God be in thee'? For was it not specifically stated in the decalogue: 'Thou shalt have no other gods before Me.' "

He replied: "The meaning is this: God ought not to be a stranger to you."

Molten Gods

The rabbi of Kotzk said:

"It is written: 'Thou shalt make thee no molten gods.' When you think God, you should really think of him, and not of a molten god whom you have made in your own image."

278

No Graven Image

The disciples of the rabbi of Kotzk were once discussing why it is written: "Take heed unto yourselves, lest ye forget the covenant of the Lord your God, which He made with you, and make you a graven image, even in the likeness of any thing which the Lord thy God hath bidden thee," and not—as the meaning really demands—"which the Lord thy God hath forbidden thee." The zaddik who had been listening joined in the discussion. "The Torah warns us," said he, "not to make a graven image of any thing the Lord our God has bidden us."

The Hunter

Rabbi Mendel of Kotzk told the story of the hunter whom the prophet Elijah met in the wilderness and asked why he was living there without the Torah and without the commandments. The hunter tried to defend himself. "I never could find the gate that leads to the presence of God," he said.

"You were certainly not born a hunter," said Elijah. "So from whom did you learn to follow this calling?"

"My need taught me," answered the hunter.

Then the prophet said: "And had your need been equally great because you had lost your way far from God, do you think it would have failed to show you the way to Him?"

Fear

The rabbi of Kotzk asked one of his hasidim:

"Have you ever seen a wolf?"

"Yes," he replied.

"And were you afraid of him?"

"Yes."

"But were you aware of the fact that you were afraid?"

"No," answered the hasid. "I was simply afraid."

"That is how it should be with us when we fear God," said the rabbi.

Two Kinds of Fear

The rabbi of Kotzk was asked: "When they stood at Mount Sinai, the people said to Moses: 'Speak thou with us, and we will hear; but let not God speak with us, lest we die.' And

Moses answered: 'Fear not.' He went on to say that God had come 'that His fear may be before you, that ye sin not.' Is not that a contradiction?"

Rabbi Mendel said: " 'Fear not'—that means: This fear of yours, the fear of death, is not the fear God wants of you. He wants you to fear him, he wants you to fear his remoteness, and not to fall into sin which removes you from him."

What Does It Matter to You?

A hasid came to the rabbi of Kotzk. "Rabbi," he complained, "I keep brooding and brooding, and don't seem to be able to stop."

."What do you brood about?" asked the rabbi.

"I keep brooding about whether there really is a judgment and a judge."

"What does it matter to you!"

"Rabbi! If there is no judgment and no judge, then what does all creation mean!"

"What does that matter to you!"

"Rabbi! If there is no judgment and no judge, then what do the words of the Torah mean!"

"What does that matter to you?"

"Rabbi! 'What does it matter to me?' What does the rabbi think? What else could matter to me?"

"Well, if it matters to you as much as all that," said the rabbi of Kotzk, "then you are a good Jew after all—and it is quite all right for a good Jew to brood: nothing can go wrong with him."

Worry

A hasid told the rabbi of Kotzk about his poverty and troubles. "Don't worry," advised the rabbi. "Pray to God with all your heart, and the merciful Lord will have mercy upon you."

"But I don't know how to pray," said the other.

Pity surged up in the rabbi of Kotzk as he looked at him. "Then," he said, "you have indeed a great deal to worry about."

Holiness

It is written: "And ye shall be holy men unto Me."
The rabbi of Kotzk explained: "Ye shall be holy unto me, but as men, ye shall be humanly holy unto me."

Infirmity

A man came to the rabbi of Kotzk and told him his trouble. "People call me a bigot," he said. "What kind of an infirmity are they ascribing to me? Why a bigot? Why not a pious man?"
"A bigot," the rabbi answered him, "converts the main issue in piety into a side issue, and a side issue into the main issue."

Afar Off

This is how Rabbi Mendel expounded the verse from the Scriptures: "Am I a God near at hand . . . and not a God afar off?"
" 'Afar off' refers to the wicked. 'Near at hand' refers to the righteous. God says: 'Do I want him who is already close to me, do I want the righteous? Why, I also want him who is afar off, I want him who is wicked!'"

The "Way" of the Wicked

The rabbi of Kotzk commented on the verse in the Scriptures: "Let the wicked forsake his way."
"Does the wicked man have a way? What he has is a mire, not a way. Now what is meant is this: Let the wicked man leave his 'way,' that is, his illusion of having a way."

The Setting

Rabbi Mendel said:
"The larger and more luminous the jewel, the larger the setting. The greater and more luminous the soul, the greater the 'shell' which surrounds it."

Great Guilt

Rabbi Mendel said:
"He who learns the Torah and is not troubled by it, who sins

and forgives himself, who prays because he prayed yesterday—a very scoundrel is better than he!"

The Week and the Sabbath

Once the rabbi of Kotzk said to Rabbi Yitzhak Meir of Ger:
"I don't know what they want of me! All week everyone does
as he pleases, but come sabbath he puts on his black gown
and girds himself with his black belt, and sets the black fur
hat on his head, and there he is: hand-in-glove with the Bride
of the Sabbath! What I say is: As a man does the week, so
let him do on the sabbath."

Earnestness

The rabbi of Kotzk called to some of his hasidim: "What is
all this talk of praying 'earnestly'! What is the meaning of
to pray 'earnestly'?"
They did not understand what he had in mind.
"Is there anything at all," he said, "that one ought not to do
earnestly?"

No Break

Rabbi Mendel saw to it that his hasidim wore nothing around
the neck while praying, for, he said, there must be no break
between the heart and the brain.

Praying and Eating

Rabbi Mendel was asked: "It is written: 'Ye shall serve the
Lord your God, and he will bless thy bread.' Why is 'ye'
written first, and later 'thy'?"
He explained: "To serve—that means to pray. When a man
prays, and even if he does so alone in his room, he ought
first to unite with all of Israel; thus, in every true prayer, it
is the community that is praying. But when one eats, and even
if it is at a table full of people, each man eats for himself."

Three Principles

Rabbi Mendel of Kotzk once said to his congregation:
"What do I ask of you? Only three things: Not to look fur-

tively outside yourselves, not to look furtively into others, and not to have yourselves in mind."

Comparing One to Another

Someone once told Rabbi Mendel that a certain person was greater than another whom he also mentioned by name. Rabbi Mendel replied: "If I am I because I am I, and you are you because you are you, then I am I, and you are you. But if I am I because you are you, and you are you because I am I, then I am not I, and you are not you."

Idol Worship

The rabbi of Kotzk said:
"When a man makes a reverent face before a face that is no face—that is idol worship!"

The False Peace

Rabbi Mendel of Kotzk and Rabbi Yitzhak of Vorki, who had both been taught by wise Rabbi Bunam, were friends, and their brotherly good will toward each other had never been troubled. But their hasidim had many arguments concerning the teachings and could not reconcile their opinions. Once both zaddikim happened to be in the same city. When they had greeted each other, Rabbi Yitzhak said: "I have news for you. Our disciples have made peace with one another." But at that the rabbi of Kotzk grew angry. His eyes flashed and he cried: "So the power of deception has gained in strength and Satan is about to blot out the truth from the world!"

"What's that you say!" Rabbi Yitzhak stammered.

The rabbi of Kotzk continued: "Remember what the Midrash tells about the hour when God prepared to create man: how the angels formed two factions. Love said: 'Let him be created, for he will do works of love.' Truth said: 'Let him not be created, for he will practice deception.' Justice said: 'Let him be created, for he will do justice.' Peace said: 'Let him not be created, for he will be all controversy.' What did God do? He seized truth and hurled it to earth. Have you ever thought this story over? Is it not strange? Truth, to be sure, lay on the ground and no longer hindered the creation of man. But what did God do with peace, and what answer did he give peace?" The rabbi of Vorki was silent.

"Look!" said the rabbi of Kotzk. "Our sages taught us that controversies in the name of Heaven spring from the root of truth. After truth had fallen to earth, peace understood that a peace without truth is a false peace."

What Cannot Be Imitated

The rabbi of Kotzk said:
"Everything in the world can be imitated except truth. For truth that is imitated is no longer truth."

To Increase Knowledge

This is what the rabbi of Kotzk said about the words of Solomon: "He that increaseth knowledge, increaseth sorrow."
"A man should increase his knowledge, even though by so doing he will inevitably increase his sorrow."

The Sons

A man came to the rabbi of Kotzk and asked how he could make his sons devote themselves to the Torah. The rabbi answered: "If you really want them to do this, then you yourself must spend time over the Torah, and they will do as you do. Otherwise, they will not devote themselves to the Torah but will tell their sons to do it, and so it will go on. For it is written: 'Only take heed to thyself . . . lest thou forget the things which thine eyes saw . . .! Make them known unto thy children and thy children's children.' If you yourself forget the Torah, your sons will also forget it, only urging their sons to know it, and they too will forget the Torah and tell their sons that they should know it, and no one will ever know the Torah."

High Prices

Once when prices in the region of Kotzk were very high, the hasidim who had come for over the sabbath wanted to start home on the following day, but the rabbi kept putting off their departure. His wife was at the stove when he came up to her, his pipe in his mouth. "Mendel," she said, "why detain the hasidim? Prices are high at the inn and they will have to pay so much for their food!"

"Why is food so dear?" he countered. "Because people want to eat all the time. If everyone wanted to learn all the time, learning would be dear and food would be cheap."

Miracles

The rabbi of Kotzk was told of a wonder-worker who was versed in the secret art of making a robot. "That is unimportant," he said. "But does he know the secret art of making a hasid?"

Like a Cooper

Rabbi Mendel of Vorki, the son of Rabbi Yitzhak of Vorki, once came out of the rabbi of Kotzk's room exhausted and covered with sweat. He sat down against the wall of the entrance to rest a little, and said to the hasidim who clustered around him: "Let me tell you: that holy old man examined me limb by limb, from head to toe, the way a cooper examines a cask."

First Prize

Rabbi Yehiel Meir, later the rabbi of Gostynin, who was a poor man, went in to his teacher, the rabbi of Kotzk, with a beaming face and told him he had won the first prize in a lottery. "That wasn't through any fault of mine," said the zaddik. Rabbi Yehiel went home and distributed the money among needy friends.

Different Customs

A hasid of the rabbi of Kotzk and a hasid of the rabbi of Tchernobil were discussing their ways of doing things.

The disciple of the rabbi of Tchernobil said: "We stay awake all night between Thursday and Friday, on Friday we give alms in proportion to what we have, and on the sabbath we recite the entire Book of Psalms."

"And we," said the man from Kotzk, "stay awake every night as long as we can; we give alms whenever we run across a poor man and happen to have money in our pockets, and we do not say the psalms it took David seventy years of hard work to make, all in a row, but according to the needs of the hour."

Thou Shalt Not Steal

Rabbi Yehiel Meir of Gostynin had gone to his teacher in Kotzk for the Feast of Weeks. When he came home, his father-in-law asked him: "Well, did your people over there receive the Torah differently than anywhere else?"

"Certainly!" said his son-in-law.

"What do you mean?" asked the other.

"Well, to give you an instance," said Rabbi Yehiel. "How do you here interpret 'thou shalt not steal'?"

"That we shall not steal from our fellow men," answered his father-in-law. "That's perfectly clear."

"We don't need to be told that any more," said Rabbi Yehiel. "In Kotzk this is interpreted to mean: You shall not steal from yourself."

The Difference

While the quarrel between the hasidim of Kotzk and those of Radoshitz was in full swing, Rabbi Yisakhar Baer of Radoshitz once said to a hasid from Kotzk: "What your teacher believes in is: 'If you can't get over it, you must get under it,' but what I believe in is: 'If you can't get over it, you must get over it anyway.'"

Rabbi Yitzhak Meir of Ger, the disciple and friend of the rabbi of Kotzk, formulated the difference in another way when a hasid of the rabbi of Radoshitz visited him after his master's death. "The world thinks," said he, "that there was hatred and quarreling between Kotzk and Radoshitz. That is a grave mistake. There was only one difference of opinion: in Kotzk they aimed to bring the heart of the Jews closer to their Father in Heaven; in Radoshitz they aimed to bring our Father in Heaven closer to the heart of the Jews."

Between Kotzk and Izbica

Some time after Rabbi Mordecai Joseph of Izbica had broken away from Kotzk and founded a congregation of his own, a hasid who had followed him to Izbica visited Kotzk and went to the rabbi. Rabbi Mendel looked up, gazed at him fixedly, and said loudly: "Who is this?" as though he had never seen him before. When the hasid asked him in great distress: "Rabbi, don't you know me?"—he said: "That can't possibly be you! For the sages say: 'And let the fear of thy master be like the fear of Heaven.' Can there be two Heavens?"

Speak unto the Children of Israel

When a disciple of the rabbi of Lentshno visited the rabbi of Kotzk, his host said to him: "Give my greetings to your teacher. I love him very much. But why does he cry to God to send the Messiah? Why does he not rather cry to Israel to turn to God? It is written: 'Wherefore criest thou unto Me? Speak unto the children of Israel.'"

The Three Pillars

Rabbi Mendel said:
"Three pillars support the world: Torah, service, and good deeds, and as the world approaches its end the two first will shrink, and only good deeds will grow. And then what is written will become truth: 'Zion shall be redeemed with justice.'"

The Hour

The rabbi of Kotzk said:
"Generation after generation has toiled to bring the Messiah, each generation in its own way, and they have not succeeded. One cannot bring the Messiah. Some day when the Jews are all busy with caring for their daily bread, and bewildered in spirit —he will come."

Those Who Cannot Pray

On the eve of the Day of Atonement the rabbi of Kotzk said to one of his hasidim: "Hersh, you shall pray for the Jews who cannot pray, for the Jews in fields and woods, for those who are here and for those who are not here, and not only for the living, but also for the dead. For I tell you the walls are swarming with souls!"

The Sanctuary of Love

The rabbi of Kotzk was asked: "Once there was so much love among the hasidim. Why is this not so in our time?"

He replied: "In Heaven there is a sanctuary of love. The rabbi of Berditchev opened it for mankind, and that is how the hasidim came to love one another so much. But the wicked managed to get in too, and took out love for their trivial loves. Then the zaddik locked up the sanctuary again."

The Corner

It is written: "He setteth an end to darkness."
Whenever he read these words, the rabbi of Kotzk said: "One little corner—God left one little corner in darkness so that we may hide in it!"

Why Write a Book?

Rabbi Mendel's hasidim asked him why he did not write a book. For a while he was silent, then he answered:
"Well, let's say I have written a book. Now who is going to buy it? Our own people will buy it. But when do our people get to read a book, since all through the week they are absorbed in earning their livelihood? They will get to read it on a sabbath. And when will they get to it on a sabbath? First they have to take the ritual bath, then they must learn and pray, and then comes the sabbath meal. But after the sabbath meal is over, they have time to read. Well, suppose one of them stretches out on the sofa, takes the book, and opens it. But he is full and he feels drowsy, so he falls asleep and the book slips to the floor. Now tell me, why should I write a book?"

The Sacred Goat

Rabbi Yitzhak of Vorki was one of the very few who were admitted to Rabbi Mendel during the period when he kept away from the world. Once he visited Kotzk after a long absence, knocked, entered Rabbi Mendel's room and said in greeting: "Peace be with you, Rabbi."
"Why do you say rabbi to me," grumbled the rabbi of Kotzk. "I am no rabbi! Don't you recognize me! I'm the goat! I'm the sacred goat. Don't you remember the story?
"An old Jew once lost his snuffbox made of horn, on his way to the House of Study. He wailed: 'Just as if the dreadful exile weren't enough, this must happen to me! Oh me, oh my, I've

lost my snuffbox made of horn!' And then he came upon the sacred goat. The sacred goat was pacing the earth, and the tips of his black horns touched the stars. When he heard the old Jew lamenting, he leaned down to him, and said: 'Cut a piece from my horns, whatever you need to make a new snuffbox.' The old Jew did this, made a new snuffbox, and filled it with tobacco. Then he went to the House of Study and offered everyone a pinch. They snuffed and snuffed, and everyone who snuffed it cried: 'Oh, what wonderful tobacco! It must be because of the box. Oh, what a wonderful box! Wherever did you get it?' So the old man told them about the good sacred goat. And then one after the other they went out on the street and looked for the sacred goat. The sacred goat was pacing the earth and the tips of his black horns touched the stars. One after another they went up to him and begged permission to cut off a bit of his horns. Time after time the sacred goat leaned down to grant the request. Box after box was made and filled with tobacco. The fame of the boxes spread far and wide. At every step he took the sacred goat met someone who asked for a piece of his horns.

"Now the sacred goat still paces the earth—but he has no horns."

No Glasses

As he grew older, the rabbi of Kotzk suffered pain in his eyes. He was advised to wear glasses for reading, but he refused: "I do not want to get a wall between my eyes and the holy Torah."

Into the Woods

Toward the close of his life the rabbi of Kotzk said: "I always thought I should have only four hundred hasidim, and that I should go into the woods with them and give them manna, and that they would recognize the kingly power of God."

YITZHAK OF VORKI

The Servant Who Neglected His Work

Rabbi Yitzhak of Vorki once rebuked one of his sons because he was neglecting the study of the Torah. When the son, who was already the head of a family, excused himself on the score of his many domestic worries, the rabbi told him this story:

"When I was still working for the charitable lady Temeril as a copyist, I once saw her superintendent beat a servant for neglecting his work. And oddly enough the man swung his scythe even while he was being beaten, and cut the grain with tremendous zeal. Later on I asked him why he had done this. 'You stupid Jew,' said he, 'I was dealt all those blows because I had neglected my work. So what wonder I went at it with might and main!' It is the same with you, my son. All your troubles arise from your neglect of the Torah."

Himself

Once when Rabbi Yitzhak was playing host to certain prominent men of Israel, they discussed the value to a household of an honest and efficient servant. They said that a good servant made for good management and cited Joseph at whose hands everything prospered. Rabbi Yitzhak objected. "I once thought that too," he said. "But then my teacher showed me that everything depends on the master of the house. You see, in my youth my wife gave me a great deal of trouble, and though I myself put up with her as best I could, I was sorry for the servants. So I went to my teacher, Rabbi David of Lelov, and asked him whether I should oppose my wife. All he said was: 'Why do you speak to me? Speak to yourself!' I thought over these words for quite a while before I understood them. But I did understand them when I recalled a certain saying of the Baal Shem Tov: 'There is thought, speech, and action. Thought corresponds to one's wife, speech to one's children, and action to one's servants. Whoever straightens himself out in regard to all three of these will find that everything prospers at his hands.' Then I understood what my teacher had meant: that everything depended on myself."

Dying and Living

As a comment to the words in the psalm: "I shall not die but live," Rabbi Yitzhak said: "In order really to live, a man must give himself to death. But when he has done so, he discovers that he is not to die—but to live."

Adam's Sin

Rabbi Yitzhak was asked: "What do you think was Adam's real sin?"

"Adam's real sin," said he, "was that he worried about the morrow. The serpent set out to reason with him: 'There is no service you can perform, for you cannot distinguish between good and evil and are unable to make a choice. Eat of this fruit and you will be able to distinguish; you will choose the good and receive the reward.' That he gave ear to this—that is where Adam was at fault. He worried that he would not be able to serve, yet at that very hour he had his service: to obey God and to resist the serpent."

The Slanderer

A certain man tried to make Rabbi Yitzhak of Vorki's hasidim rebel against their master by slandering him in every possible way. An uproar ensued. The zaddik was told of the matter. He summoned the man and received him without witnesses. "Fool," he said to him, "why do you tell untruths and lay yourself open to being called a liar? Let me tell you everything bad about myself. Then when you leave here and proclaim that to the world, no argument advanced against you will hold water."

The Offering

On the sabbath on which the weekly portion from the Torah dealing with the Offering is read, Rabbi Yitzhak happened to be visiting the rabbi of Kotzk, who at that time had just begun to live in great seclusion and received only close friends, like the rabbi of Vorki.

"Why," asked Rabbi Yitzhak, "have you gone to such extremes in withdrawing from men?"

Rabbi Mendel replied: "The answer is in the weekly portion we read today: 'That they take for Me an offering'; and that is explained as meaning, 'For Me, that is, for My Name.' When a Jew wishes to take the right way, God's way, then he has no alternative but to make an 'offering.' He must offer up all companionship, not only that of evil men, but also that of good men; for a little further on we read: 'Of every man whose heart maketh him willing.' "

"The answer to what you just said," replied the rabbi of Vorki, "is in today's weekly portion, in the very same verse: 'That they take for Me an offering.' When a Jew wishes to take the right way, God's way, he must take what every man has to offer him. He should accept the companionship of every man and by associating with every man receive from him whatever that man can give him for the way of God. But there is one qualification. From the man whose heart is locked he will receive nothing at all. Only the man 'whose heart maketh him willing' can give."

His Merit

Someone came to Rabbi Yitzhak with a question. "I cannot understand the story the Talmud tells about Rabbi Zera," he said. "It says that when his disciples asked him how he had lived so long, he answered that he had never rejoiced over anyone's misfortune. How can that be a merit?"

The rabbi said: "This is what it means: I could not rejoice in the good fortune life offered me when I heard of someone else's misfortune."

The Alphabet

Rabbi Yitzhak was asked: "Why on the Day of Atonement is the confession of sins arranged in alphabetical order?"

He replied: "If it were otherwise we should not know when to stop beating our breasts. For there is no end to sin, and no end to the awareness of sin, but there *is* an end to the alphabet."

The Heavenly Voice

They asked Rabbi Yitzhak how the following saying of our sages should be interpreted: "You shall do all your host tells you, all save going away." For it seems we certainly ought to obey our host when he bids us go!

The rabbi replied: "Those who believe that the word 'host' here refers to God are right. We should obey him in all things, save when he bids us to go from him. For we know that 'he that is banished is not banished from him.' The truth of the matter is that he who has done much evil must travel a most stormy road in order to turn to God. Heaven announces that his turning is no longer desired and would not be accepted. But if he does not allow this to discourage him, if just then his will breaks through and nevertheless turns to God, then he will be healed. They say that the arch-heretic Elisha ben Abuyah, who was called 'Aher' or 'the Other,' heard a voice calling down from Heaven: 'Return O backsliding children— all except Aher!' Then he broke the last bonds which held him to the Torah and the congregation, and renounced the truth. Should he have refused to believe the voice which addressed itself to him and therefore wanted something of him? That would have been of no avail. Yet grace hangs on a hair: if he had turned, his turning would have been accepted."

The Lost Woman

A widow complained to Rabbi Yitzhak that certain merchants who had employed her husband as copyist refused to pay her a sum of money they still owed him, and had no pity on her in her wretchedness. The zaddik had the merchants brought before him. When they caught sight of the woman they cried out as with one voice: "Are you listening to that lost woman! Her husband has been dead these three years, and half a year ago she bore a bastard!"

"So, she was so poor," said the rabbi, "that she had to lose her self!"

After Thirty Years

A certain man had lived in seclusion for thirty years and devoted himself to the Torah. When he returned to the company of men, he heard about Rabbi Yitzhak of Vorki and decided to go to him. On the way there he pictured to himself the joy and honor with which the zaddik would receive so learned a man who had devoted all his efforts to the Torah for so long a time. When he stood in Rabbi Yitzhak's presence, the rabbi said to him: "You are so learned a man and have devoted all your efforts to the Torah for so long a time—surely you know what God says?" The man grew embarrassed and uncertain. Finally he said hesitantly: "God says we should pray and study." The zaddik laughed. "You do not understand my question," he said. The man left in an unhappy frame of mind.

But he went to the zaddik again and again, and each time Rabbi Yitzhak received him with the same words. Then came the day when he made his farewell.

"What are you taking home with you," asked the zaddik, "since you don't know what God says!" Tears rose in the man's eyes as he said: "Rabbi, that is just why I came to you—to learn something!"

"It is written in Jeremiah," said the zaddik, " 'Can any hide himself in secret places'—that means, anyone who locks himself into his room for thirty years and studies the Torah; 'that I shall not see him?'—that means, I may not want to see such a man; 'saith the Lord'—that is what God says."

Moved to the depths of his being, the man stood there, and for a time he could not speak, he could not even think. Then the spirit moved him. "Rabbi," he sighed, "I should like to ask you a question."

"Speak," said the zaddik. "What is the prescribed thing to do," asked the man, "when scraps of a holy book which has been torn fall to the ground?"

"They should be picked up," said the zaddik, "lest they be destroyed."

The man threw himself on the floor. "Rabbi, rabbi," he cried, "a vessel filled with scraps of the Holy Scriptures lies before you. Do not let them be destroyed!" With both hands the zaddik raised him and seated him at his side. Then he talked to him and helped him with his words.

Hospitality

When Rabbi Yitzhak lived in the town of Kinzk, a very well-to-do man invited him to a banquet. When the zaddik came to the house he saw that the forecourt was lit with large lanterns and the steps covered with rugs. Then he refused to proceed unless his host had the lanterns put out and the rugs removed, or promised to receive even the most unimportant guest with like magnificence from that time on.

"We are bidden to be hospitable," the zaddik said. "And just as we must not differentiate between one ram's horn and another when it comes to blowing the ram's horn, so in his capacity of guest one man is just like another." His host begged him to retract the demand, but in vain. In the end he had to yield, and since he was unable to give the required promise he had the house restored to its everyday appearance.

Commandment and Money

Rabbi Yitzhak once praised an innkeeper who was eager to satisfy every wish of his guests. "How anxious this man is to fulfil the commandment to be hospitable!" he said. "But he takes pay for it," someone remarked. "He accepts money," answered the zaddik, "so that it may be possible for him to fulfil the commandment."

The Zaddikim That Build

Rabbi Yitzhak was asked: "How are we to understand the saying: 'Every zaddik in whose days the Temple is not built is no zaddik at all.' That would mean that all the zaddikim who have lived since the destruction of the Temple were not zaddikim." He explained: "The zaddikim are always building at the upper sanctuary. The zaddik who does not do his share in the building is no zaddik at all."

The Faithful Servant

It is told in the Midrash:
The ministering angels once said to God: "You have permitted Moses to write whatever he wants to, so there is nothing to prevent him from saying to Israel: I have given you the Torah."

God replied: "This he would not do, but if he did, he would still be keeping faith with me."

Rabbi Yitzhak of Vorki's disciples once asked him to interpret this. He answered by telling them a parable:

A merchant wanted to go on a journey. He took on an assistant and let him work in his shop. He himself spent most of his time in the adjoining room from where he could hear what was going on next door. During the first year he sometimes heard his assistant tell a customer: "The master cannot let this go for so low a price." The merchant did not go on his journey. In the course of the second year he occasionally heard the voice next door say: "We cannot let it go for so low a price." He postponed his journey. But in the third year he heard his ⸱assistant say: "I can't let this go for so low a price." It was then that he started on his journey.

The Dwelling

Rabbi Yitzhak's disciples said to him: "Concerning the account in the Scriptures that 'the stuff' the people had brought for the building of the sanctuary was 'sufficient and too much,' so that there was something left over when the work was completed, the Midrash tells that Moses asked God what to do with it, and God replied: 'Make of it a dwelling for the tabernacle of the testimony,' and Moses did so. How are we to interpret this? Is it not the Ark which holds the tablets that is called the tabernacle of the testimony, and had it not already been completed?"

"You know," answered the rabbi, "that the sanctuary was holy because the Divine Presence had entered it. But over and over again people have asked how the splendor of Him about whom it is written: 'the heavens and the heaven of heavens cannot contain Thee,' could possibly be confined in the space between the staves of the Ark. But listen to the words in the Song of Songs: 'King Solomon made himself a palanquin of the wood of Lebanon. He made the pillars thereof of silver, the top thereof of gold, the seat thereof of purple.' And if you doubt that it was possible to rest on such a bed, here is the answer: 'The inside thereof being inlaid with love.' It was the love of the people who contributed to the building of the sanctuary that drew the Divine Presence down between the staves of the Ark. But because there was too much of their will to love, more than was needed for the work, Moses asked: 'What's to be done with all this will?' and God replied: 'Make of it,' and this means: make of the overflow of the innermost heart of Israel 'a dwelling for the tabernacle of the testimony' —the testimony that your love has drawn me into the world shall dwell within it."

On the Highest Rung

Rabbi Yitzhak was asked: "It is written: 'And this is the blessing, wherewith Moses the man of God blessed the children of Israel before his death.' Of the words 'before his death' Rashi says, 'just before his death,' and, in support of his interpretation, adds: 'If not now, when?'

"In what way does this mean more than what anyone can glean from the Scriptures?"

"Note," answered the rabbi, "that this is the only passage in which Moses is called 'a man of God.' Now this is how it was: Because of his great love for Israel, Moses wanted to bless them, time and again. But each time he felt he would reach a higher rung, and that his blessing would then have greater strength, and that was why he delayed giving it. But when he had reached the rung of 'a man of God,' and that is the rung of the angels who do not move from rung to rung like men, but remain fixed, he knew that he must be very close to death, and then he blessed Israel—for, 'If not now, when?' "

Faith

A hasid of Rabbi Yitzhak had no children. Time after time he begged his teacher to pray for him and time after time Rabbi Yitzhak referred him to Rabbi Baer of Radoshitz, the famous miracle-worker. But the hasid did not follow his suggestion. The other hasidim asked him why he did not go to Radoshitz. "If I go," he said, "and go without faith, I will not be helped. But if I scrape up some faith in the rabbi of Radoshitz, it means that I shall forfeit just that much of the faith I have in my rabbi. And if, God forbid, my faith in my rabbi became imperfect, then what would I want children for?"

MENAHEM MENDEL OF VORKI

The Test

Rabbi Yitzhak of Vorki once took his sons to see his teacher
Rabbi Bunam, who gave each of them a glass of bock beer and
asked them what it was. The elder boy said: "I don't know."
Menahem Mendel, the younger, who was three years old at
the time, said: "Bitter and good."

"This one will become the leader of a great congregation,"
said Rabbi Bunam.

The Driver

When Rabbi Yitzhak of Vorki and Mendel, his young son,
were visiting Rabbi Israel of Rizhyn, their host invited his
friend to go driving with him. Mendel begged to be allowed to
accompany them. "One who does not yet know the mystery of
the Divine Chariot may not come," said the rabbi of Rizhyn.
"But I know how to drive," said Mendel. The rabbi of Rizhyn
gave him a long look. "Then do it," he said. Mendel mounted
the coachman's box and took the reins in his hands.

In the course of their drive the rabbi of Rizhyn asked: "Rav
of Vorki, how did you deserve such a son?" Rabbi Yitzhak
replied: "He is an undeserved gift."

The Gang in the Wine Cellar

The group of contemporaries with whom young Mendel gadded
about consisted of youths on a high rung, but like himself all
of them were well versed in hiding their true character.

Rabbi Berish, later the rabbi of Biala, who was at the time a
disciple of the rabbi of Vorki and known as a learned man,
could not get over his surprise at not seeing them engage in
study. Once on the first night of the Feast of Weeks, when
everyone had left the table and day was already breaking, he
noticed the group with Mendel in the van going down into the
cellar. He stole after them, hid, and saw them put on their
prayer shawls, rattle off the Morning Prayer, and then sit

down together and drink. This displeased Rabbi Berish mightily. But then he noticed that the moment all of them had finished the second glass Mendel spoke to them in a low tone—he could not catch the words from his hiding place—and instantly they all bowed their heads over the table and wept. It looked to Rabbi Berish as though all the small glasses filled up with their tears. Later he asked them to accept him as a member of their group, but a period of waiting was imposed on him.

One Thing Is Needful

At Rabbi Mendel's wedding the *badhan* in the midst of his half-jesting, half-serious harangues uttered this singsong: "Pray and learn and serve your God." Rabbi Mendel took up the very same tune: "Don't pray and don't learn and don't anger your God."

Swift Obedience

When Rabbi Yitzhak of Vorki was in Warsaw on an errand concerning his congregation, he became ill, and his elder son Rabbi David of Omshinov implored him to go home. After holding out for a considerable time his father at last consented. Rabbi David summoned the coachman and told him to harness the horses. In the meantime Rabbi Mendel, the younger son, who had not been present during the discussion, arrived and heard from the coachman that his father was preparing to drive back to Vorki. "You can go home," said Mendel, "the rabbi is not leaving." When Rabbi David learned of the incident he complained to his father.

"What do you want of him?" said the rabbi of Vorki. "He obeys even before I give him an order."

You Have Done Too Little

When Rabbi Yitzhak of Vorki was seriously ill, his elder son fasted and recited psalms, but Rabbi Mendel, the younger, went about with a group of hasidim of his own age who had been devoted to him from boyhood on and called themselves his bodyguard. They toasted each other's health in schnapps. But there were times when he walked in the woods unaccompanied. When Rabbi Yitzhak recovered, a banquet was prepared to celebrate the event. Mendel said to his brother: "You have done too little to rejoice in good earnest—you did nothing but fast and pray."

The Voice

After Rabbi Yitzhak's death many hasidim came to Vorki for the Feast of Weeks. Among them was Rabbi Benjamin of Lublin, who had been a disciple of the Seer but had gone over to the much-maligned Yehudi, the Seer's disciple, while his first teacher was still alive. Since Rabbi Benjamin was very old and sickly, he had to lie down soon after his arrival. After prayers Rabbi Yitzhak's two sons went to see him. "Children," he said to them, "I wish you'd tell me how we are to interpret the words in the Scriptures: 'And all the people saw the voice.'" Rabbi Yaakov David, the elder son, gave a most perspicacious interpretation, but Rabbi Menahem Mendel, the younger, was silent as usual. "And what have you to say?" asked Rabbi Benjamin.

"I say," answered Menahem Mendel, "that we must take it to mean: they saw and realized that one must take the voice into oneself and make it one's own."

No Speech and No Words

Some time after Rabbi Yitzhak's death, when each of his sons already had his own congregation, they once met in a town far from the home of either and a banquet was held in their honor. Rabbi David delivered a lengthy sermon but Rabbi Mendel said nothing. "Why don't you also 'say Torah'?" asked his brother.

"Concerning the Heavens we read in the psalms," Mendel replied, "'There is no speech, there are no words, neither is their voice heard. Their line is gone out through all the earth.'"

* * *

But on another occasion, when a great zaddik asked him why he did not "say Torah," he replied: "The Talmud says that Simeon of Emmaus interpreted all the passages in the Scriptures in which the word *et* [which indicates the accusative] is used. But when he came to the verse where this word introduces the command: 'Thou shalt fear the Lord thy God,' he refrained from interpretation."

A Night of Silence

Once Rabbi Menahem Mendel spent an entire night in the company of his hasidim. No one spoke, but all were filled with great reverence and experienced great elation. Finally the rabbi said: "Well for the Jew who knows that the meaning of 'One' is one!"

Speech in Silence

Rabbi Mendel's hasidim once sat at his table in silence. The silence was so profound that one could hear the fly on the wall. After grace the rabbi of Biala said to his neighbor: "What a table we had today! I was probed so deeply that I thought my veins would burst, but I managed to hold out and answer every question I was asked."

The Way of Silence

The first time Rabbi Mendel, the son of the zaddik of Vorki, met Rabbi Eleazar, the grandson of the maggid of Koznitz, the two retired to a room. They seated themselves opposite each other and sat in silence for a whole hour. Then they admitted the others. "Now we are ready," said Rabbi Mendel.

* * *

When Mendel was in Kotzk, the rabbi of that town asked him: "Where did you learn the art of silence?" He was on the verge of answering the question, but then he changed his mind, and practiced his art.

Soundless Cry and Soundless Weeping

Rabbi Mendel once commented on the verse in the Scriptures: "For God hath heard the voice of the lad." He explained it in this way: "Nothing in the preceding verses indicates that Ishmael cried out. No, it was a soundless cry, and God heard it."

* * *

On another occasion he discussed the verse in the Scriptures which tells about Pharaoh's daughter in these words: "And she opened it, and *saw* . . . a boy that wept."

301

"What we should expect to be told," said he, "is that she *heard* the child Moses weeping. But the child was weeping inside himself. That is why later on we find the words: 'and (she) said: This is one of the Hebrews' children.' It was the Jewish kind of weeping."

Basic Attitudes

Rabbi Menahem Mendel of Vorki was asked what constitutes a true Jew. He said: "Three things are fitting for us: upright kneeling, silent screaming, motionless dance."

The Honest Sleep

It was the day before the New Year and people from all over had come to Vorki and gathered in the House of Study. Some were seated at the tables studying, others who had not been able to find a place for the night were lying on the floor with their heads on their knapsacks, for many of them had come on foot. Just then Rabbi Mendel entered, but the noise those at the tables made was so great that no one noticed him. First he looked at those who were studying, and then at those lying on the floor. "The way these folk sleep," he said, "pleases me more than the way those others are studying."

A Beautiful Death

Soon after the death of a zaddik who was a friend of the rabbi of Vorki, one of his hasidim, who had been present at the death, came to Rabbi Mendel and told him about it.

"How was it?" asked Rabbi Mendel.

"Very beautiful," said the hasid. "It was as though he went from one room into the next."

"From one room into the next?" said Rabbi Mendel. "No, from one corner of the room into another corner."

YITZHAK MEIR OF GER

Where Does God Live?

When Rabbi Yitzhak Meir was a little boy his mother once took him to see the maggid of Koznitz. There someone said to him: "Yitzhak Meir, I'll give you a gulden if you tell me where God lives!" He replied: "And I'll give you two gulden if you tell me where he doesn't!"

In Praise of Grammar

The rabbi of Ger told this story:

"As a child I did not want to study grammar, for I thought it was just a subject like many others. But later I devoted myself to it because I realized that the secrets of the Torah depend upon it."

The Malcontent

When Rabbi Yitzhak Meir was quite young he became a disciple of Rabbi Moshe of Koznitz, the son of the maggid of Koznitz. One day his teacher kissed him on the forehead because he had helped him solve a difficult problem with astonishing acumen. "What I need," said Yitzhak Meir to himself, "is a rabbi who rends the flesh from my bones—not one who kisses me."

Soon after he left Koznitz.

A Quick Sleep

Rabbi Yitzhak Meir's wife once asked him why he slept so little, and she worried that this might be bad for his health. He laughed and answered: "Why did your father choose me as a husband for you? Because I was a gifted student. And what does it mean to be a gifted student? It means that one person learns in two hours what it takes another a whole day to learn. Well, I sleep as much in two hours as another sleeps a whole night."

Like the Ox

A hasid complained to the rabbi of Ger: "I have worked and toiled and yet I have not the satisfaction of a master-craftsman who, after twenty years of effort, finds some result of his labors in his work: either it is better than it was at first, or he can do it more quickly. I see nothing at all. Just as I prayed twenty years ago, so I pray today."

The zaddik answered: "It is taught in Elijah's name: 'Man should take the Torah upon himself, as the ox takes the yoke and the ass his burden.' You see, the ox leaves his stall in the morning, goes to the field, plows, and is led home, and this happens day after day, and nothing changes with regard to the ox, but the ploughed field bears the harvest."

Coming Tests

The rabbi of Ger said:

"There will be many and grave temptations and he who has not prepared himself for them will be lost. For it is too late to prepare when temptation is actually at hand. Temptation is only a test; it shows what within you is dross and what is true metal."

Danger

The rabbi of Ger was on a journey with one of his favorite hasidim. The way led down a steep hill, and the startled horses ran for all they were worth and could not be reined in. The hasid looked out of the carriage and shuddered; but when he glanced at the zaddik, he saw that his face had lost nothing of its usual composure. "How is it that you are not afraid of the danger we are in?" he asked.

"Whoever is aware of the real danger at every instant," the zaddik replied, "is not terrified by any danger of the moment."

The Fortress

When the large House of Study the rabbi of Ger was having built was completed, the rav of Warsaw came to inspect it, and said: "Most likely you have a very good reason for moving away from us and building your house outside the town." The rabbi of Ger said nothing, so the rav continued: "I understand your reason. You wanted to put up a fortress for the protection of Warsaw, and such a fortress must of course be outside the town. And sometimes one must even use it as a point of vantage from which to fire into the town." Still the rabbi of Ger did not utter a word, but he laughed like one who agrees with the speaker.

About Eating

The rabbi of Ger once asked a hasid what he had learned from the lips of the rabbi of Kotzk. "I heard him say," said the hasid, "that he was surprised that merely saying grace is not enough to make man God-fearing and good."

"I think differently," said the rabbi of Ger. "I am surprised that merely eating is not enough to make man God-fearing and good. For it is written: 'The ox knoweth his owner and the ass his master's crib.'"

* * *

When the rabbi of Ger was asked the difference between ordinary fathers of families and hasidim, he laughed and replied: "Ordinary fathers of families pray and then study, but the hasidim pray and then eat. For when the hasid discovers that neither in his solitary reflection before prayer nor in prayer itself has he experienced the greatness of God, he goes to his meal and thinks: 'Though I am not yet like the ox who knows his owner, I can at least emulate the ass and stand at my master's crib.'"

"Throw Up the World"

The rabbi of Ger said: "I often hear men say: 'I want to throw up the world.' But I ask you: Is the world yours to throw up?"

The Sins of the People

Some time after the Feast of Weeks the rabbi of Radzimin came to visit the rabbi of Ger, who thought that his friend's face looked thin and tired. "What's the matter with you?" the rabbi of Ger asked. "Is it only the great heat we are having or is something troubling you?"

"I am like this every year," said the other, "in the summer months, when those chapters in the Scriptures which deal with Israel's wanderings through the wilderness are read. For there we hear of sin after sin; terrible sins, like those of the spies and those when 'Israel joined himself unto the Baal of Peor.' That such sins are reported as having been committed by a generation of knowledge—that is what keeps tormenting me!" The rabbi of Ger replied: "When they committed what is called their sin they must have had a great purpose in mind, for it is out of their sins that the Torah was made. Do you think that a Torah could have been made out of our good deeds?"

A Sermon

Before the Day of Atonement the rabbi of Ger said to the hasidim gathered around his table:

"Hillel, our teacher, says: 'If I am not for myself, who will be for me?' If I do not perform my service, who will perform it for me? Everyone must perform his own service. And further along, he says: 'And if not now, when?' When will this Now be? The Now that is now, this instant in which we are speaking, did not exist at any time since the world was created, and it will never exist again. Formerly there was another Now, and later there will be another Now, and every Now has its own service; as we read in the Book of Splendor: 'The garments of morning are not the garments of evening.'

"Strive for the Torah with all your strength and you will be linked to the Torah—but the sixty myriad letters in the Torah correspond to the sixty myriad souls in Israel, of whom the Torah is speaking: in this way you will become related to the whole. And if you proffer yourself to the whole, you receive from the whole; you receive even more than you put into it. And so to your own Now you can add something of your neighbor's Now, of the good he accomplishes in that Now. Furthermore Hillel, our teacher, says: 'And if I am only for myself, what am I?' If—God forbid—I should be separated from the community, when could I catch up on my Now? No other Now can make up for this Now, for every moment is concentrated in its particular light.

"He who has done ill and talks about it and thinks about it all the time does not cast the base thing he did out of his thoughts, and whatever one thinks, therein one is; one's soul is wholly and utterly in what one thinks, and so much a man dwells in baseness. He will certainly not be able to turn, for his spirit will grow coarse and his heart stubborn, and in addition to this he may be overcome by gloom. What would you? Rake the muck this way, rack the muck that way—it will always be muck. Have I sinned, or have I not sinned—what does Heaven get out of it? In the time I am brooding over it I could be stringing pearls for the delight of Heaven. That is why it is written: 'Depart from evil and do good'—turn wholly away from evil, do not dwell upon it, and do good. You have done wrong? Then counteract it by doing right.

"And so on this day before the Day of Atonement let us feel a withdrawal from sin and a strengthening of the spirit, feel it in our innermost heart and not through forced ecstasy, receive it in our hearts for all future time, and be merry. Let us recite the list of our sins as quickly as possible, and not dwell upon it, but rather dwell upon the words of the prayer: 'And thou, O Lord, shalt reign, thou alone . . .' "

Shame

While the rabbi of Ger was in the midst of "saying Torah," he heaved a deep sigh and said:

"Something our sages said touches me to the marrow, and devours at my vitals. They said: 'He who has no shame, his fathers did not stand at Mount Sinai.' Well then, and where is shame?"

Emphasis

The rabbi of Ger taught his disciples:

"Merely by emphasizing a word ever so slightly a man can cool his neighbor's fervor in the service of God. So for instance the serpent said to Eve: 'And though God did say'—as if someone said to you: Well, and suppose God did say that—what of it? A slight emphasis and Eve's faith was cooled and she ate of the forbidden fruit."

The Motive

The rabbi of Ger was asked: "What is the meaning of God's asking Cain why his countenance had fallen? How could his face not 'fall' since God had not accepted his gift?"

He replied: "God asked Cain: 'Why is thy countenance fallen?' Because I did not accept your gift, or because I accepted that of your brother?"

The Three Questions

When in expounding the Torah the rabbi of Ger came to the words Jacob says to his servant: "When Esau my brother meeteth thee, and asketh thee, saying: Whose art thou, and whither goest thou? and whose are these before thee?"—he said to his disciples: "Note how much Esau's questions resemble the saying of our sages: 'Reflect upon three things: know whence you have come, where you are going, and to whom you will some time have to give account and reckoning.' Note it well, for whoever reflects on these three things needs much self-examination, lest Esau ask within him. For Esau too can ask about these, and bring heaviness into the heart of man."

The Darkness of the Soul

Concerning the passage in the Scriptures which deals with the thick darkness in the land of Egypt, where "they saw not every man his brother, neither rose any from his place," the rabbi of Ger said: "He who does not want to look at his brother soon gets to the point where he cleaves to his place and is not able to move from it."

Seeing and Believing

The rabbi of Ger was asked:
"It is written: 'And Israel saw the great hand,' and further on it is written: 'And they believed in the Lord and in his servant Moses.' Why is this said? The question as to whether or not one believes can only be put while one does not as yet see." He answered: "You are mistaken. It is only then that the true question can be put. Seeing the great hand does not mean that faith can be dispensed with. It is only after seeing that we feel how much we are in need of it. Seeing the great hand is the beginning of belief in that which we cannot see."

The Real Exodus

The rabbi of Ger was asked: "Why is it that the Feast of Weeks, which was instituted to commemorate revelation, is referred to with the words 'a commemoration of the departure from Egypt'?"

He expounded: "Did not God speak to Moses out of the midst of the burning bush, saying: 'And this shall be the token unto thee, that I have sent thee: when thou hast brought forth the people out of Egypt, ye shall serve God upon this mountain.' Their receiving the Torah at Sinai was the sign that they were now out of Egypt. Up to that time they were still caught in the bondage of Egypt."

The Eternal Voice

The rabbi of Ger said:

"Concerning the voice over Sinai, the Scriptures say that 'it went on no more,' and the Targumim take this to mean that it went on uninterruptedly. And the voice does indeed speak today as it did long ago. But now as then it requires preparation to hear it. As it is written: 'Now therefore, if ye will hearken unto My voice.' Whenever we hear it, that 'Now' has arrived."

The Wheel and the Innermost Point

On an evening in late summer, Rabbi Yitzhak Meir was walking back and forth in the court of the House of Study in the company of his grandson. It was the first day of the month of Elul and the new moon was in the sky. The zaddik asked whether they had blown the ram's horn, for this should be done a month before the New Year. Then he said: "When a man becomes a leader, all the necessary things must be at hand: a House of Study and tables and chairs, and one man is made the manager, one the servant, and so on. And then Satan comes and wrests out the innermost point, but everything remains just as it was and the wheel keeps on turning, only that the innermost point is missing." The rabbi raised his voice: "But, so help us God, we must not let it happen!"

Forgive Me

When Rabbi Yitzhak Meir's mother died he followed the bier weeping and begged her to forgive him. And before they closed the grave, he cried: "In this world I am a man who is much honored and many call me rabbi. But now you will enter the world of truth and see that it is not as they think. So forgive me and do not bear me a grudge. What can I do, if people are mistaken in me!"

Who Is to Come?

On a certain Passover many people were gathered in the house of the rabbi of Ger. Suddenly he raised his voice and said to them: "You should know that I'm not just like any rabbi. I do not crave money and I am not out for honors. All I care about is turning the hearts of Jews to Heaven in the few years still allotted to me. And I beg anyone who has no longing in that direction to stop coming to me. Those who seek me out because they want to gain a livelihood or have children or be cured would do better to go to someone else. But he who feels that something is lacking in the service he gives God, and is troubled because sickness or worry about his livelihood or the desire for children are obstacles in the way of his service—I can help a man such as this both on the one score and the other."

Two Points of View

The rabbi of Ger once asked one of his disciples who was a guest in his house what thoughts he had had on the way to him. The man replied: "Hasidim come to the rabbi with all manner of requests, some because they have business troubles, other because they are sick or the like. 'What has all this to do with the rabbi?' I asked myself."

"And what did you answer yourself?" asked the zaddik.

"I told myself," said the disciple, "that the rabbi helps those who come to him to make the turning and thus raises them to a higher rung, from which their prayers will more readily be heard."

"I see it differently," said the zaddik. "The rabbi reflects: 'What am I and what is my life that these people should come to me and ask me to pray for them! Why I am nothing but a drop in the bucket!' And in this way he makes the turning and is uplifted and since he has linked his being to those who sought him out, salvation flows from him into them."

This was the last journey this disciple made to his teacher, for soon after this the rabbi died.

In the Dust

Someone asked the rabbi of Ger: "Why do people always weep when they say the words in the prayer: 'Man, his origin is of the dust and his end is in the dust'? If man sprang from gold and turned to dust, it would be proper to weep, but not if he returns whence he has come."

The zaddik replied: "The origin of the world is dust, and man has been placed in it that he may raise the dust to spirit. But man always fails in the end and everything crumbles into dust."

The Heart Remains

In his old age the rabbi of Ger told this story:

"When I was still a student, Rabbi Shelomo Leib came up to me in the House of Study and said: 'Young man, you are known as the gifted Jew from Poland, so tell me why our sages commented on the verse in the Scripture: "Thou shalt love the Lord thy God with all thy heart and with all thy soul," with the words: "Even if He takes your soul"; but failed to comment: "Even if He takes your heart," concerning the other part of the verse which says we should love Him with all our heart.'

"I did not know what to say, for I did not consider his question a question at all. For to take one's soul simply means to take one's life. But what was the matter with me that I did not even wish to know what he meant? The older I get, the larger his question looms before me. If God so desires, let him take our life, but he must leave us that with which we love him—he must leave us our heart."

The Fear of Death

The rabbi of Ger once said:

"Why is man afraid of dying? For does he not then go to his Father! What man fears is the moment he will survey from the other world everything he has experienced on this earth."

HANOKH OF ALEXANDER

Before God

In his youth when Rabbi Hanokh of Alexander was living in Pzhysha as Rabbi Bunam's disciple, it was his duty to act as congregational reader of the Morning Prayer in a house adjoining that of his teacher. Now he was in the habit of praying with vehement gestures and loud cries, quite differently from Rabbi Bunam, who spoke with his characteristic composure even when he conducted the services for the congregation. Once young Hanokh was praying when the rabbi entered the room, and he immediately lowered his voice and stopped gesturing. But hardly had he done this, when he reflected and said in his soul: "I am after all not concerned with the rabbi; I am standing before God!" And instantly he resumed his stormy manner of praying.

After the service Rabbi Bunam had him summoned. "Hanokh," he said to him, "today I took great pleasure in your praying."

Revelation

In his youth, Rabbi Yehiel Meir of Gostynin once attended a wedding in Pzhysha. At the inn they put him up in the same room with young Rabbi Hanokh of Alexander, whom he had never met, and he was forced to share the bed with him. On the eve of the wedding Rabbi Hanokh played the wag both in his actions and words, and this did not exactly serve to give his roommate a better opinion of him. But that night he noticed Hanokh leave the bed very softly and—thinking himself unobserved—go into the anteroom. Yehiel Meir listened intently. He heard a whispering that touched him to his very marrow. Whispered verses of psalms came to his ears and moved him as though he had never heard them before. When Hanokh returned, Yehiel Meir pretended to be asleep. During one of the evenings when the "Seven Benedictions" were recited, Rabbi Hanokh again clowned for all he was worth. He told of the merry pranks of a woman known as Hannele the thief, and his account was so vivid that the wedding guests were convulsed with laughter. Yehiel Meir stared at him in bewilderment. Was this the same man on whose fervent words he had eavesdropped that other night? Then suddenly in the midst of his wildest jest Hanokh turned his head and looked straight into his eyes. And now Yehiel Meir saw before him what he had heard that night, and it was addressed to him. He trembled from head to foot.

Secret

Rabbi Bunam used to say: "A secret is something you say in such a way that everyone can hear it, and yet no one who is not supposed to know can know it."

But Rabbi Hanokh, his disciple, added: "The secrets of the Torah are so well hidden that they cannot be communicated at all. As it is written: 'The secret counsel of the Lord is with them that fear him.' They can be grasped only through the fear of God, and save through the fear of God they cannot be grasped at all."

Look into the Book

A hasid came to Rabbi Hanokh and wept and complained about some misfortune which had overtaken him.

"When I was in the elementary school," the rabbi replied, "and a certain boy began to cry in class, the teacher said to him: 'He who looks into his book stops crying.'"

The Threat

A prominent man threatened to thrust Rabbi Hanokh down from all the spiritual rungs he had attained at a single blow. He replied: "You could not thrust me down to a lowlier place than the one I am already in."

The Butcher's Sigh

Shortly after he had become a rabbi, Rabbi Hanokh said: "A butcher was plying his chopping knife for all he was worth and chopped right on into the sabbath. Suddenly it dawned on him that the sabbath had come. He ran off to the House of Prayer, and just as he rushed in he heard them singing the hymn: 'Come, my friends, to meet the bride.' Then he heaved a deep sigh, and it was not the butcher who was sighing, it was the Jew who sighed out of him. For it is written: 'The children of Israel sighed out of their bondage.' It was Israel, it was the Jew that sighed out of them."

The House of Weddings

Rabbi Hanokh told this parable:

A man from a small town moved to Warsaw. From a house near the one in which he had rented a room he heard the sound of music and dancing. "They must be celebrating a wedding there," he thought to himself. But the next day he again heard festive music, and the same thing happened on the day after that. "I wonder who the owner of that house can be," he said to friends he had in the city. "He seems to have a lot of sons he is marrying off!" They laughed at him. "That house," they said, "is rented out every day for the purpose of celebrating weddings. Then the musicians play and the guests dance. Because of this we call it the house of weddings."

And then Rabbi Hanokh added: "That is why our sages compare this world to a house of weddings."

A Vain Search

Rabbi Hanokh told this story:

There was once a man who was very stupid. When he got up in the morning it was so hard for him to find his clothes that at night he almost hesitated to go to bed for thinking of the trouble he would have on waking. One evening he finally made a great effort, took paper and pencil and as he undressed noted down exactly where he put everything he had on. The next morning, very well pleased with himself, he took the slip of paper in hand and read: 'cap'—there it was, he set it on his head; 'pants'—there they lay, he got into them; and so it went until he was fully dressed.

"That's all very well, but now where am I myself?" he asked in great consternation. "Where in the world am I?" He looked and looked, but it was a vain search; he could not find himself. "And that is how it is with us," said the rabbi.

"Scaring Off"

Rabbi Hanokh told this story:

A servant girl from Poland hired herself out to work in Germany. In that country they use the term "to scare off" in their cookery. By this they mean pouring cold water into a pot in which meat is boiling, to make it easier to take off the scum. Once when the lady of the house in which the girl was working had to go off to market while the dinner was cooking, she said to her: "Watch the soup and don't forget 'to scare off.' " The girl did not understand the term, but she was ashamed to admit it. When she saw the scum rise to overflowing, she took a broom and threatened the pot on all sides, until it upset and the soup spilled all over the stove.

"Now if you try to scare off the Evil Urge when it rises up within you," the rabbi added, "you will upset everything. You must learn to skim off the scum."

The Real Exile

Rabbi Hanokh said:

"The real exile of Israel in Egypt was that they had learned to endure it."

Baseness

Rabbi Hanokh was asked: "It is written: 'The children of Israel lifted up their eyes and, behold, the Egyptians were marching after them; and they were much afraid; and the children of Israel cried out unto the Lord.' Why were they so afraid, since they knew that God himself was aiding them?"

Rabbi Hanokh answered: "When they were in Egypt, when they were in baseness up to their ears, they did not see it. But now they lifted their eyes and saw baseness coming after them. They had thought that since God had led them out of Egypt, all that was over and done with. Now suddenly they realized that baseness was still with them—and they cried out to God. 'And Moses said unto the people: Fear ye not, stand still, and see the salvation of the Lord, which He will work for you today; for whereas you have seen Egypt today, ye shall see them again no more for ever.' That means that now you see the baseness which is with you—that in itself is aid and succor. 'The

Lord will fight for you.' Now that you yourselves see that you are base, the Lord will help you out of your baseness. 'And ye shall hold your peace.' Hold your peace, for help has already been granted you."

Beyond the Pale of Nature

Rabbi Hanokh was asked: "Why does one speak of the 'rending asunder' of the Red Sea and not of its 'splitting asunder,' since it is written: 'He split the sea and caused them to pass through.' "

Rabbi Hanokh gave this explanation: " 'Split' indicates only a slight crack, but 'rend asunder' points to a great opening. In the Midrash we are told that when Moses bade the sea split, it replied that it did not intend to obey flesh and blood and go beyond the pale of nature; not until it saw Joseph's coffin did it do as it was bidden. That is why the verse in the psalm reads: 'The sea saw it and fled.' It saw and it realized that Joseph, whose bones the people were taking with them to the Promised Land, had once gone beyond the pale of nature in that he resisted temptation. Then the sea too went beyond the pale of nature and rent itself asunder. That is why we say 'rending asunder of the Red Sea.' "

Seeing and Hearing

Rabbi Hanokh was asked: "It is written: 'Lo, I come unto thee in a thick cloud, that the people may hear when I speak with thee.' Why should hearing be helped by the fact that He comes in a thick cloud?"

Rabbi Hanokh interpreted the words in this way: "The sense of seeing takes precedence over the sense of hearing. But the thick cloud makes it impossible to utilize the sense of seeing, and so hearing is everything."

Unto the Heart of Heaven

This is how Rabbi Hanokh interpreted the words in the Scriptures: ". . . and the mountain burned with fire unto the heart of heaven": The fire of Sinai burned into the core of men until it made them a heavenly heart.

Their Desire

Rabbi Hanokh was asked: "In the Book of Psalms, it is written: 'He will do the desire of them that fear Him.' How can one claim that God will do everything that those who fear Him desire? Do not the God-fearing, above all, have to suffer much that they do not desire, and do without much they do desire?" He said: "You must take it to mean that it is He who makes the desire of those who fear him. God created the desire itself. All that is necessary for man is to desire this desire."

To the Children of Men

When Rabbi Hanokh had said the verse in the psalms: "The heavens are the heavens of the Lord, but the earth hath He given to the children of men," he paused and then went on to say: " 'The heavens are the heavens of the Lord'—you see they are already of a heavenly character. 'But the earth hath He given to the children of men'—so that they might make of it something heavenly."

Two Worlds

Rabbi Hanokh said: "The other nations too believe that there are two worlds. They too say: 'In the other world.' The difference is this: They think that the two are separate and severed, but Israel professes that the two worlds are essentially one and shall, indeed, become one."

The Fight

Rabbi Hanokh was asked why the hasidim did not begin to pray at the set time.

"While soldiers are going through their training," he replied, "there is a certain set time for everything they have to do, and they must follow their schedule. But when they are in the thick of battle they forget what was prescribed and fight as the hour demands.

"The hasidim," the rabbi concluded, "are fighters."

At the Meal

Once when Rabbi Hanokh was eating the meal with his hasidim on one of the nine days which precede the Ninth Day of Av, the day of lamenting the destruction of the Temple, he said to them:

"Formerly when these days came around, everyone was shaken with anguish because the Temple was burned, and we have no sanctuary in which to make our offerings. But now the hasidim eat their meal as if they were making an offering, and say: 'The Lord was, is, and will be; the sanctuary was, is, and will be.'"

Once he said: "When the Messiah comes, we shall see what the tables at which we eat have effected."

On Growing Old

A fiddler once played Rabbi Hanokh a tune. He said: "Even melodies that grow old lose their savor. When we heard this one at Rabbi Bunam's long ago, it made our hearts leap. Now it has lost its savor. And that is how it really is. We must be very well prepared and ready for old age. We pray: 'Cast me not off in the time of old age!' For then we lose our savor. But sometimes this is a good thing. For when I see that after all I have done I am nothing at all, I must start my work over again. And it is said of God: 'Who reneweth the creation every day continually.'"

NOTES · GLOSSARY · GENEALOGY

INDEX TO THE TALES

NOTES

Numerals to the left of each note indicate the page
on which the expression occurs.

[19] *Love thy neighbor:* Lev. 19:18.
[28] *God will not despise:* Ps. 51:19.
[29] *Thou shalt be whole-hearted:* Deut. 18:13.
[36] *Justice:* Deut. 16:20.
[40] *The Torah was given:* Mekhilta on Exod. 16:4.
[40] *God is close:* Ps. 145:18.
[42] *There is no judgment:* Leviticus Rabbah XXVIII.1.
[42] *The tablets:* Berakhot 8b.
[50] *A wise man:* Samuel: Babylonia, 3rd cent.; Talmud Berakhot 58b.
[51] *A Psalm of David:* Ps. 51:1.
[53] *The heavens are the heavens of the Lord:* Ps. 115:16.
[55] *And when ye go to war:* Num. 10:9.
[56] *Hew thee:* Exod. 34:1.
[56] *Thou shalt not make:* Exod. 20:4.
[58] *For instruction:* Isa. 51:4.
[58] *What hath God wrought:* Num. 23:23.
[59] *When any man of you:* Lev. 1:2.
[59] *An altar of earth:* Exod. 20:21.
[59] *And there was evening:* Gen. 1:5.
[62] *And it shall be:* Deut. 8:19.
[62] *Strength and gladness:* I Chron. 16:27.
[62] *And the people saw it:* Exod. 20:18.
[63] *Which controversy:* Sayings of the Fathers, V,19.
[66] *Return, O Israel:* Hos. 14:2.
[66] *Between the sections of the sacrifice:* see Gen. 14:17.
[66] *Return unto me:* Zech. 1:3; Mal. 3:7.
[66] *Turn Thou us unto Thee:* Lam. 5:21.
[70] *When any man of you:* Lev. 1:2.
[71] *And they believed:* Exod. 14:31.
[71] *And the heaven and the earth:* Gen. 2:1.
[72] *There is not a thing:* Sayings of the Fathers, IV, 3.
[72] *Birth-pangs that herald:* a talmudic tradition (Sanhedrin 98b).
[72] *All the calculated dates:* Sanhedrin 97a.
[76] *Lo, I come unto thee:* Exod. 19:9.
[76] *Moses drew near:* Exod. 20:18.

[76] *Meek above all men:* Num. 12:3.

[77] *Nahshon:* a talmudic legend (Sotah 37a).

[77] *Even unto the soul:* Ps. 69:2.

[78] *A serving-maid saw more:* a midrashic teaching (Mekhilta on 15:12).

[87] *My beloved knocketh:* Cant. 5:2.

[88] *Awake and rise:* Isa. 52:2.

[88] *You will have pity on Zion:* Pss. 102:14; 51:20.

[96] *Wherefore did the son of Jesse:* I Sam. 20:27.

[96] *Lay not thy hand:* Gen. 22:12.

[97] *Uphold him:* Lev. 25:35.

[103] *And the fire abated:* Num. 11:2

[107] *For a gift doth blind:* Deut. 16:20.

[110] *Also unto Thee:* Ps. 62:13.

[112] *I and he cannot:* Talmud (Sotah 5a).

[112] *That dwelleth with them:* Lev. 16:16.

[114] *At the mouth of two witnesses:* Deut. 17:6.

[115] *For the Lord regardeth:* Ps. 1:6.

[116] *Go:* Gen. 12:1; 22:2.

[116] *And Jacob served:* Gen. 29:20.

[117] *Know what is above you:* Sayings of the Fathers, II,1.

[117] *And upon the likeness:* Ezek. 1:26.

[117] *To whom then:* Isa. 40:25.

[119] *So Moses:* Deut. 34:5.

[119] *After the death:* Josh. 1:1.

[120] *This is the land:* Deut. 34:4.

[121] *We have thought:* Ps. 48:10.

[128] *Welcoming guests:* Talmud (Shabbat 127a).

[128] *Divine Presence rests:* Talmud (Sotah 17a)

[130] *When the mount:* a talmudic tradition (Shabbat 88a).

[130] *And as for me:* Ps. 69:14.

[131] *And the people shall go out:* Exod. 16:4.

[131] *That I may prove them:* Exod. 16:4.

[131] *I will cause to rain bread:* Exod. 16:4.

[135] *Abraham fulfilled:* Yoma 28b.

[135] *Moses was told:* Exod. 36:5-6.

[137] *The Ark . . . carried its carriers:* a talmudic tradition (Sotah 35a) referring to the story of the crossing of the Jordan (Josh. 3).

[141] *The law of the Lord:* Ps. 19:8.

[141] *A God of faithfulness:* Deut. 32:4.

[145] *He also brought:* Gen. 4:4.

[146] *And to walk hidden:* Mic. 6:8.

[146] *If I ascend:* Ps. 139:8.

[146] *Open Thou mine eyes:* Ps. 119:18.

[146] *A great light:* this refers to the talmudic tradition (Hagigah 12a)

about the light created on the first day of creation which preceded the creation of the sun and the stars.

[148] *For man shall not see me:* Exod. 33:20.

[149] *Manna that enters . . .:* a talmudic legend (Yoma 75b).

[150] *Unto thee it was shown:* Deut. 4:35.

[150] *YHVH is Elohim:* I Kings 18:39.

[152] *There is no unity:* Ps. 38:4.

[153] *From Moses to Joshua:* Sayings of the Fathers, I,1.

[155] *Rejoice the soul:* Ps. 86:4.

[155] *And the Lord set:* Gen. 4:15.

[155] *Called him an old king:* Eccles. 4:13.

[157] *But I was brutish:* Ps. 73:22.

[158] *Let there be light:* Gen. 1:13.

[161] *The end of the matter:* Eccles. 12:13.

[163] *If thou wilt take the left hand:* Gen. 13:9.

[163] *Man doth not live:* Deut. 8:3.

[165] *The people saw:* Exod. 20:15.

[165] *My soul thirsteth:* Pss. 42:3; 63:3.

[167] *You will give truth:* Mic. 7:20.

[167] *Ye shall be holy:* Lev. 19:2.

[167] *Thou knowest:* Ps. 69:6.

[169] *Blessed art thou, O Lord our God:* introductory words in a benediction.

[169] *But they that wait:* Isa. 40:31.

[170] *The sage:* Judah ha-Levi, medieval Hebrew liturgical poet.

[170] *The whole earth:* Isa. 6:3.

[170] *And he dreamed:* Gen. 28:12.

[170] *Put off thy shoes:* Exod. 3:5.

[170] *How can we be delivered:* see Yalkut Shimeoni on Exodus, No. 190.

[170] *Hark! my beloved:* Cant. 2:8.

[171] *And Moses reported the words:* Exod. 19:6.

[171] *Speak thou with us:* Exod. 20:19.

[171] *Dathan and Abiram:* Num. 16:13.

[173] *Praise the Lord:* Ps. 146:1.

[173] *I will praise the Lord:* Ps. 146:2.

[177] *Pure olive oil:* Exod. 27:20.

[178] *Give forth its water:* see Num. 20:8.

[181] *In thy love:* Prov. 5:19.

[181] *Words of the living God:* talmudic tradition (Erubin 13b).

[182] *I will betroth thee:* Hos. 2:21.

[188] *We are upright men:* Gen. 42:11.

[188] *We are verily guilty:* Gen. 42:21.

[190] *If a man comes:* a talmudic teaching (Yoma 38b).

[191] *I am the man:* Lam. 3:1.

[194] *The radiance of Moses' face:* a talmudic tradition (Baba Batra 75a).

[195] *Arise, cry out:* Lam. 2:19.

[196] *Thine iniquity:* Isa. 6:7.

[198] *The Yehudi:* Yaakov Yitzhak of Pzhysha (see pp. 224-233).

[199] *And everyone that was in distress:* I Sam. 22:2.

[205] *My son, I and you:* Talmud (Shabbat 33b).

[205] *God himself prays:* Talmud (Berakhot 7a).

[205] *And I shall bring them:* Isa. 56:7; the translation follows the talmudic interpretation. The correct translation is: ". . . in My house of prayer."

[209] *My soul failed me:* Cant. 5:6.

[209] *And Moses went down:* Exod. 19:14.

[216] *A king is not saved:* Ps. 33:16.

[218] *The righteous . . .:* Prov. 10:25 (the usual translation is: "The righteous is an everlasting foundation").

[218] *He hangeth the world:* Job 26:7.

[218] *The world rests:* Talmud (Hullin 89a).

[219] *Whoever occupies himself:* Talmud (Hagigah 12b).

[221] *Darkness, cloud:* Deut. 4:11.

[222] *The air of the land of Israel:* a talmudic saying (Baba Batra 158b).

[230] *How long shall I take counsel:* Ps. 13:3.

[230] *And Moses spoke:* Deut. 31:30.

[231] *And he stood over them:* Gen. 18:8.

[235] *Pardon, I pray:* Num. 14:19-20.

[235] *Love thy neighbor:* Lev. 19:18.

[240] *Pharaoh:* Exod. 5:2.

[242] *Bright-colored dress:* they reminded Rabbi Bunam of the white shrouds.

[242] *Thou shalt surely give him:* Deut. 15:10.

[245] *Elijah found Elisha:* I Kings 19:19-20.

[248] *All joys:* see Tales of the Hasidim: The Early Masters, p. 135.

[249] *Taste and see:* Ps. 34:9.

[249] *All my bones:* Ps. 35:10.

[250] *I am earth:* Gen. 18:27.

[252] *Be not like servants:* Sayings of the Fathers, I,3.

[253] *And I am prayer:* Ps. 109:4.

[257] *The Lord has put away:* II Sam. 12:13.

[259] *Curse upon the serpent:* see Gen. 3:14, 16, 17.

[259] *And now, lest he put:* Gen. 3:22.

[260] *Both of them together:* Gen. 22:6.

[260] *And the children of Israel:* Exod. 2:23.

[260] *And I will bring you out:* Exod. 6:6.

[261] *And ye shall be unto me:* Exod. 19:6.

[261] *And he set before them:* Exod. 19:7.

[261] *I am the Lord:* Exod. 20:2.

[261] *We will do:* Exod. 24:7.

[262] *And Korah took:* Num. 16:1.

[262] *Golden calf:* see Exod. 32.

[262] *Sin of the spies:* see Num. 13.

[262] *I saw all Israel:* I Kings 22:17.

[263] *Who healeth the broken:* Ps. 147:3.

[263] *The sacrifices of God:* Ps. 51:19.

[263] *As in water:* Prov. 27:19.

[263] *Open to me:* Ps. 118:19.

[264] *And they two made a covenant:* Gen. 21:27.

[264] *Seek peace:* a talmudic saying (Palestinian Talmud, Peah 15d).

[264] *There is no peace:* Ps. 38:4.

[265] *Return, O backsliding children:* Jer. 3:14; to this quotation the "Voice from Heaven" added: all except Aher. A talmudic story (Hagigah 15a).

[270] *This is my God:* Exod. 15:2.

[271] *It is good for a man:* Lam. 3:27.

[272] *If a disciple is banished:* a talmudic statement (Makkot 10a).

[274] *But a trustworthy man:* Prov. 20:6.

[274] *And in His temple:* Ps. 29:9.

[275] *Thou shalt not steal:* Exod. 20:15.

[275] *Passed by a castle:* Genesis Rabbah XXXIX.1.

[275] *And thou shalt see My back:* Exod. 33:23.

[276] *The ordinances of the Lord:* Ps. 19:10.

[276] *This is the law:* Lev. 6:2.

[277] *The waters of immersion of Israel:* Mishnah Yoma VIII. 9, in interpreting Jer. 17:13.

[278] *We do, we hear:* Exod. 24:7.

[278] *And these words which I command:* Deut. 6:6.

[278] *There shall no strange God:* Ps. 81:10.

[278] *Thou shalt have no other gods:* Exod. 20:3.

[278] *Thou shalt make thee:* Exod. 34:17.

[279] *Take heed unto yourselves:* Deut. 4:23.

[279] *Speak thou with us:* Exod. 20:19.

[281] *And ye shall be holy men:* Exod. 22:30.

[281] *Am I a God:* Jer. 23:23.

[281] *Let the wicked forsake:* Isa. 55:7.

[282] *Ye shall serve the Lord:* Exod. 23:25.

[283] *How the angels formed:* Genesis Rabbah VIII.5.

[283] *Controversy:* Sayings of the Fathers, V,20.

[284] *He that increaseth knowledge:* Eccles. 1:18.

[284] *Only take heed:* Deut. 4:9.

[286] *Thou shalt not steal:* Exod. 20:15.

[287] *And the fear of thy master:* Sayings of the Fathers, IV, 15.

[287] *Wherefore criest thou:* Exod. 14:15.

[287] *Three pillars:* Sayings of the Fathers, I,2.

[287] *Zion shall be redeemed:* Isa. 1:27.

[288] *He setteth an end:* Job 28:3.

[291] *I shall not die:* Ps. 118:17.

[292] *That they take for Me:* Exod. 25:2.

[292] *About Rabbi Zera:* Megillah 28a.

[293] *You shall do all your host:* Talmud (Pesahim 86b).

[293] *He that is banished:* II Sam. 14:14.

[293] *Return, O backsliding children:* Jer. 3:14; see the story "The Test" in the chapter "Simha Bunam of Pzhysha."

[294] *Can any hide himself:* Jer. 23:24.

[296] *Sufficient and too much:* Exod. 36:7.

[296] *Heaven and the heaven of heavens:* I Kings 8:27.

[296] *King Solomon made himself:* Cant. 3:9.

[296] *The inside thereof:* Cant. 3:10.

[297] *This is the blessing:* Deut. 33:1.

[300] *And all the people saw:* Exod. 20:18.

[300] *There is no speech:* Ps. 19:4.

[300] *Simeon of Emmaus:* Pesahim 22b.

[301] *Thou shalt fear the Lord:* Deut. 6:13.

[301] *For God hath heard:* Gen. 21:17.

[301] *And she opened:* Exod. 2:6.

[304] *Man should take the Torah:* Talmud (Abodah Zarah 5b).

[305] *The ox knoweth:* Isa. 1:3.

[306] *Israel joined himself:* Num. 25:3.

[306] *If I am not for myself:* Sayings of the Fathers, I,14.

[307] *Depart from evil:* Ps. 34:15.

[307] *He who has no shame:* Talmud (Nedarim 20a).

[307] *And though God did say:* Gen. 3:1.

[308] *Why is thy countenance:* Gen. 4:6.

[308] *When Esau my brother:* Gen. 32:18.

[308] *Reflect upon three things:* Sayings of the Fathers, III, 1.

[308] *They saw not:* Exod. 10:23.

[308] *And Israel saw the great hand:* Exod. 14:31.

[309] *And this shall be the token:* Exod. 3:12.

[309] *It went on no more:* Deut. 5:19.

[309] *If ye will hearken:* Exod. 19:5.

[311] *Thou shalt love:* Deut. 6:5.

[311] *Even if He takes:* a talmudic teaching (Berakhot 61b).

[313] *The secret counsel of the Lord:* Ps. 25:14.

[314] *The children of Israel sighed:* Exod. 2:23.

[314] *Our sages compare this world:* Talmud (Erubin 54a).

[315] *The children of Israel lifted their eyes:* Exod. 14:10.

[315] *And Moses said:* Exod. 14:13.
[316] *The Lord will fight:* Exod. 14:14.
[316] *He split the sea:* Ps. 78:13.
[316] *Moses bade the sea split:* Exodus Rabbah XXI
[316] *The sea saw it and fled:* Ps. 114:3.
[316] *I come unto thee:* Exod. 19:9.
[316] *The mountain burned:* Deut. 4:11.
[317] *He will do the desire:* Ps. 145:19.
[317] *The heavens are the heavens:* Ps. 115:16.
[318] *Cast me not off:* Ps. 71:9.
[318] *Who reneweth the creation:* Morning Prayer.

GLOSSARY

ABAYYI: talmudic sage of Babylonia, third, fourth centuries. He was born an orphan.

ADDITIONAL PRAYER: Hebrew, *Musaf*. *Musaf* was originally an additional sacrifice on the Sabbath and holidays; later as its substitute, an additional prayer service recited after the general Morning Prayer.

AḤER: *see* ELISHA BEN ABUYA.

AKIBA: leading Palestinian teacher of the second century C.E.

ALL VOWS: *see* KOL NIDRE.

AMORA, *pl.*, AMORAIM: talmudic sage quoted in the Gemara.

BADHAN: master of ceremonies and merry-maker at a wedding.

BAR MITZVAH ("son of commandment"): upon the completion of his thirteenth year a boy accepts the responsibility of fulfilling the religious law. He becomes a *Bar Mitzvah*. This event is festively celebrated.

BENEDICTION OF SANCTIFICATION *(Kiddush)*: benediction pronounced over the wine at the commencement of the Sabbath and holidays.

BENEDICTION OF SEPARATION *(Havdalah)*: "separation" (of the holy and the profane); benediction pronounced over the wine, spices, and the light at the conclusion of the Sabbath and holidays.

BLESSING OF THE NEW MOON: outdoor benediction service on the appearance of the new moon, which marks the beginning of a month according to the Hebrew calendar.

BOOK OF THE ANGEL RAZIEL: a kabbalistic work.

BOOK OF SPLENDOR: the book *Zohar*, the foremost work of Jewish mysticism, composed, in Aramaic, as a commentary on the Pentateuch (thirteenth century).

BREAKING OF THE VESSELS: *see* SPARKS.

BREASTPLATE OF JUDGMENT *(Hoshen Mishpat)*: one of the four parts of the Shulhan Arukh, the authoritative code of Jewish law.

COUNTING OF THE FIFTY DAYS: *see* Lev. 23:15.

CURTAIN: the Talmud (Hagigah 12b) speaks of seven heavens and their names and functions; the curtain is the lowest heaven.

DAY OF ATONEMENT *(Yom Kippur)*: the last of the "Ten Days of Turning" (and repentance) which commence with the New Year. It is a day of fasting and uninterrupted prayer for atonement.

DAYS OF AWE: the New Year's days and the Day of Atonement.

DIVINE CHARIOT *(Merkavah)*: a mystical interpretation of Ezekiel's vision (Ezek. 1), the basis of kabbalistic theosophy.

DIVINE PRESENCE: *see* SHEKHINAH.

EIGHTEEN BENEDICTIONS: one of the oldest parts of liturgy, occurring in the regular prayer service. After silent recitation by the worshippers it is repeated aloud by the reader.

ELIJAH: after his ascent to heaven, the prophet Elijah, according to legend, continued to help and instruct the world of man in his function as a messenger of God. Especially, he appears at every feast of circumcision and at every Seder celebration. To behold him and to receive instruction from him are considered an initiation into the mysteries of the Torah.

ELISHA: the disciple and successor of Elijah the prophet.

ELISHA BEN ABUYA: talmudic sage, teacher of Rabbi Meir. Under the influence of foreign, probably Gnostic teachings, he deserted pharisaic Judaism, hence is called *Aher* ("the other").

ELOHIM: name of God, in rabbinical literature interpreted as referring to the divine attribute of rigor. *See* MERCY-RIGOR.

ELUL: the month preceding the Days of Awe and the days of heavenly judgment. It is devoted to inner preparation and self-examination.

EMDEN, JACOB: rabbi in Germany (Emden and Altona); eighteenth century.

ESCORT OF THE SABBATH QUEEN: the meal taken after the departure of the Sabbath. This meal is understood as bidding farewell to the Sabbath Queen. It "escorts" her away. It is also called "the feast of King David." According to the legend, David was told by God that he would die on a Sabbath; he therefore feasted after every Sabbath in celebration of his continued living.

EVIL URGE: the inclination to evil, which is opposed to "the inclination to good." It is not considered as evil *per se*, but as a power abused by men. It is rather the "passion" in which all human action originates. Man is called upon to serve God "with both inclinations," directing his passion toward the good and the holy.

EXILARCH *(Resh Galuta)*: title of the head of the autonomous Jewish community in the Babylonian diaspora; an especially active office in the period between the seventh and the eleventh centuries.

EXILE FESTIVAL: the three festivals of Passover, Feast of Weeks and Feast of Booths are observed in the countries of the Diaspora one day longer than in Palestine. The additional day of observance is called Exile Festival.

EZRA THE SCRIBE: leader of Palestinian Jewry in the fifth century B.C.E. His institutions and ordinances greatly influenced the development of traditional Judaism.

FEAST OF BOOTHS *(Sukkot)*: tabernacles; an eight-day holiday beginning on the fifth day after the Day of Atonement. It commemorates the wandering in the desert. During this period the houses are abandoned and the people live in booths covered with leaves.

FEAST OF WEEKS *(Shavuot)*: a two-day holiday (in Palestine, one day), seven weeks after Passover. It is the feast of the first fruits and a season dedicated to the memory of the revelation on Mount Sinai. Pious Jews stay awake at night to read and study holy writings.

FIRST GATE *(Baba Kamma)*: a talmudic tractate.

GALUT: the dispersion of Israel; according to Jewish tradition, the Divine Presence takes part in the sufferings of exile and also waits for redemption.

GEMARA ("completion") : part of the Talmud which consists of discussions of the Mishnah.

GLORY AND FAITHFULNESS: ancient mystical hymn recited by many hasidim among the prayers on Sabbath morning.

GREAT ASSEMBLY *(Keneset ha-Gedolah)*: legislative body in Palestine at the time of the Second Temple.

GREAT PRAYER OF SALVATION: chanted on *Hoshana Rabba* ("The Great Salvation") observed on the seventh day of the Feast of Booths.

GREAT SABBATH: the Sabbath which precedes Passover.

HAGGADAH ("narrative") : usually, *Haggadah shel Pesah*, the collection of sayings, scriptural interpretations, and hymns pertaining to the exodus from Egypt, as recited in the home service on Passover night (*see* SEDER).

HALLEL ("praise") : a group of psalms recited in the prayer service at certain festivals.

HANUKKAH ("dedication") : an eight-day holiday beginning on the twenty-fifth day of *Kislev* (November or December) and commemorating the rededication of the Temple by the Maccabees (167 B.C.E.) and their victory over the Syrian Greeks who had desecrated it. In remembrance of the Maccabean Feast of Lights, candles are lighted in Jewish homes on each of the eight evenings, one candle the first evening, two the second, etc.

HIDDEN ZADDIK: *see* THIRTY-SIX HIDDEN ZADDIKIM.

HILLEL AND SHAMMAI: Palestinian teachers and founders of schools in the first century B.C.E.

HOLY BROTHERHOOD (*Hevra Kaddisha*, "holy society") : its members devote themselves to the burial of the dead.

HOSHANOT: prayers for help and salvation during the Feast of Booths.

HOUSE OF LIFE: cemetery.

HOUSE OF STUDY *(Bet ha-Midrash)*: identical, usually, with the House of Prayer. It is a place of learning and worship. Travelers without lodgings are put up in the House of Study.

IMMERSION: the ancient bath which, in the Kabbalah and especially among the hasidim, became an important ceremony with mystical meanings of its own. Immersion in a river or stream is higher in value than the ordinary ritual bath.

JOURNEY (to the zaddik) : see TRAVEL.

KAVVANAH, pl., KAVVANOT: mystical meaning of scriptural phrases, prayers, or religious acts; also, the concentration on this meaning. Direction of the heart towards God while performing a religious deed. In Jewish mysticism, *kavvanot* denote also the permutations of the divine name that aim at overcoming the separation of the forces in the Upper World.

KOL NIDRE ("All Vows") : the initial words in the solemn formula of absolution from unfulfilled and unfulfillable vows, pronounced on the eve of the Day of Atonement.

LAMENTATIONS AT MIDNIGHT: the pious are accustomed to rise at midnight from their beds, sit down on the floor, without shoes, put ashes on their forehead, and read lamentations on the fall of Zion and prayers for redemption.

LURIA, ISAAC: Safed, Palestine, sixteenth century. The outstanding representative of later Kabbalah.

MEIR: talmudic sage of Palestine, second century; post-talmudic legend describes him as a "miracle-worker."

MERCY-RIGOR: the chief attributes of God.

MESSIAH SON OF JOSEPH: a Messiah who will prepare the way, gathering Israel together and re-establishing the kingdom, and who will then fall in a war against the Romans led by Armilus. Another tradition holds that he reappears "from generation to generation."

METATRON: name of an angel, mentioned in talmudic and kabbalistic literature; among other functions he mediates between God and the material world. He is referred to as "Prince of the Divine Face," or "Prince of the Innermost Chamber."

MIDRASH, pl., MIDRASHIM ("exposition, interpretation") : books of the talmudic and post-talmudic times devoted to the homiletic exegesis of the Scriptures. They are rich in legends, parables, similes, and sayings.

MIRIAM'S WELL: due to the merits of Miriam, sister of Moses and Aaron, a well, according to a talmudic legend, accompanied the children of Israel through the desert (*see* Taanit 9a).

MISHNAH ("repetition, teaching") : the earliest and basic part of the Talmud.

MITNAGED, *pl.*, MITNACDIM ("opponent, antagonist") : the avowed opponents of hasidism.

MOSES BEN MAIMON: Maimonides, born 1135, Cordova; died 1204, Cairo. Foremost Jewish thinker of Middle Ages.

NEW MOON: *see* BLESSING OF THE NEW MOON.

NEW YEAR'S DAY *(Rosh ha-Shanah)*: observed on the first and second day of *Tishri* (September or October), the days of judgment.

NEW YEAR OF THE TREES: observed on the fifteenth day of *Shevat* (January or February) ; arbor day.

NINTH DAY OF AV *(Tishah be-Av)*: *Av*: July or August. A day of fasting and mourning in memory of the destruction of the first Temple by Nebuchadnezzar and the second Temple by Titus. The worshippers sit, like mourners of the dead, without shoes, on the floor of the darkened House of Prayer and recite the Book of Lamentations. According to tradition, the Messiah was born on the Ninth Day of Av and will reappear on that day.

NOTES OF REQUEST (in Yiddish, *kvittel*) : addressed to the zaddik, written on slips of paper containing the name of the supplicant, the name of his mother, and his request.

PASSOVER *(Pesah*, "passing over," i.e., the sparing of the houses of the children of Israel) : eight-day holiday (in Palestine seven days) beginning on the fifteenth day of *Nisan* (March or April) and commemorating the exodus from Egypt.

PATH OF LIFE *(Orah Hayyim)*: one of the four parts of the Shulhan Arukh, the authoritative code of Jewish law.

PENITENTIAL PRAYERS *(Selihot)*: prayers recited especially on the days preceding the New Year's days, in the period between these and the Day of Atonement, and on the latter day itself.

PHYLACTERIES *(tefillin)*: leather cubicles containing scriptural texts inscribed on parchment. Following the commandment in Deut. 11:18, *tefillin* are attached to the left arm and the head during the weekday morning service. They are a sign of the covenant between God and Israel. An error in

333

the written text disqualifies the phylacteries. There is a talmudic conception (Berakhot 6a) of the "phylacteries of God," which are said to contain the verse II Sam. 7:23.

PRAYER OF BENEDICTIONS: central prayer in the synagogue service. *See also* EIGHTEEN BENEDICTIONS.

PRAYER SHAWL *(tallit)*: a rectangular shawl worn at prayers; its four corners have fringes *(tzitzit)* attached.

PRESENCE OF GOD: *see* SHEKHINAH.

PRINCIPLES OF FAITH: a section of the Morning Prayer arranged according to the formulation of the articles of Jewish creed by Moses ben Maimon (Maimonides) in the twelfth century.

QUORUM *(minyan)*: the minimum of ten males (all past thirteen years of age) required for community prayer.

RABBI: *see* RAV.

RAM'S HORN *(shofar)*: sounded in the synagogue, principally on the New Year. A blast on the ram's horn will announce the coming of the Messiah.

RASHI: abbreviation for Rabbi Solomon (ben) Isaac (of Troyes), the classical commentator on the Bible and the Babylonian Talmud (died 1105).

RAV ("master, teacher"): the leader of the religious community. He teaches the law and, as the "head of the law court," supervises its fulfilment; whereas *rabbi*, in most cases, denotes the leader of the local hasidic group. In some instances the rabbi, also called zaddik, was, in addition, the rav of his town.

READER OF PRAYERS *(Hazan, Baal Tefillah)*: the man who, "standing in front of the Ark," or the Reader's desk, leads the congregation in the synagogue worship; cantor.

REJOICING IN THE LAW *(Simhat Torah)*: feast on the day following the Feast of Booths. The Torah scrolls are taken out of the Ark and are carried through the House of Prayer by a festive procession.

RIGOR: *see* MERCY-RIGOR.

RITUAL BATH: *see* IMMERSION.

SABBATAI ZEVI: born in Smyrna, Turkey, in 1626. He proclaimed himself Messiah; central figure of the greatest messianic movement in the history of the Diaspora. The movement broke down and its founder embraced Islam.

SABBATH OF SONG *(Shabbat Shirah)*: the Sabbath on which the song of the Israelites at the Red Sea is sung (Exod. 15).

SABBATH OF TURNING *(Shabbat Shuvah)*: the Sabbath within the Ten Days of Turning between the New Year's Day and the Day of Atonement.

SABBATIANS: followers of Sabbatai Zevi.

SAMMAEL: post-biblical name for Satan, the prince of demons.

SANCTIFICATION OF THE NAME (of God): designates every sacrificial act of man; by it man participates in the establishment of the kingdom of God on earth. The death of a martyr is the highest instance of Sanctification of the Name.

SAYING TORAH: At the communal meal with the hasidim, the zaddik delivers a discourse on a topic of hasidic teachings usually based on a scriptural passage.

SECTION OF SONGS *(Perek Shirah)*: a compilation of scriptural verses which, it is said, are recited by all kinds of living creatures in praise of God, each one speaking a particular verse.

SEDER ("order"): the festival meal and home service on the first and second (in Palestine, only the first) night of Passover. In this celebration, each succeeding generation identifies itself anew with the generation that went out of Egypt (*see* HAGGADAH).

SEFIROT: the mystical and organically related hierarchy of the ten creative powers emanating from God, constituting, according to the kabbalistic system, the foundation of the existence of the worlds.

SEVEN BENEDICTIONS: recited at weddings, and after Grace on the seven days following, if new guests are present.

SEVEN DAYS OF THE FEAST: observed after the wedding day.

SEVEN SHEPHERDS: the three patriarchs, together with Joseph, Moses, Aaron and David, who are greeted by the pious as guests in the holiday booths during the Feast of Booths.

SHAMMAI: *see* HILLEL AND SHAMMAI.

SHEKHINAH ("indwelling"): divine hypostasis indwelling in

the world and sharing the exile of Israel; Divine Presence among men.

SON OF COMMANDMENT: *see* BAR MITZVAH.

SPARKS: according to the Kabbalah, in the primeval creation preceding the creation of our world, the divine light-substance burst and the "sparks" fell into the lower depths, filling the "shells" of the things and creatures of our world.

TANNA, *pl.*, TANNAIM ("repeater, teacher") : the masters of the Mishnah.

TENT OF MEETING *(Ohel Moed; Mishkan)*: the portable sanctuary (Tabernacle) built by Bezalel for the Israelites when they were in the desert. *See* Exod. 26, 27; and 35-38.

THIRD MEAL: the principal meal of the Sabbath, eaten after the Afternoon Prayer, and accompanied by community singing and an address by the zaddik.

THIRTY-SIX HIDDEN ZADDIKIM: the Talmud (Sukkah 45b) speaks of the thirty-six pious men who welcome the presence of God every day; in later legends they are described as humble, unrecognized saints. Disguised as peasants, artisans, or porters, they go around doing good deeds. They constitute the true "foundation of the world."

TORAH: teaching, law, both the written (biblical) and the oral (traditional) law.

TOSEFTA ("addition") : a collection of laws closely related to the Mishnah and supplementing it.

TRAVEL (to the zaddik) : to become a follower of a zaddik, to receive his teachings, and to visit him from time to time.

TURNING *(Teshuvah,* usually "repentance") : man's turning from his aberrations to the "way of God." It is interpreted as the fundamental act by which man contributes to his redemption.

UNIFICATION: the overcoming of the separation of forces and principles in the Divine Realm, the accomplishment of which is attempted by man through religious action and sacred ceremonies.

UNLEAVENED BREAD *(matzah)*: eaten during the week of Passover.

WORLD OF CONFUSION *(Olam ha-Tohu)*: the realm in which the souls exist after death before they achieve their redemption.

WORLD OF EMANATION: according to the kabbalistic doctrine the World of Emanation and of Divinity is the highest among the four "Worlds" which are placed between the Infinite and our earthly cosmos.

WORLD OF ILLUSION *(Olam ha-Dimyon)*: a realm "in which the souls of all those who died deluded by their vanity stray."

YHVH: the tetragram for the name of God which, according to tradition, was not to be pronounced; usually *Adonai* (the Lord) is substituted. In rabbinical literature YHVH is interpreted as referring to the divine attribute of mercy. *See* MERCY-RIGOR.

ZADDIK: the leader of the hasidic community (*see* RAV).

GENEALOGY OF THE HASIDIC MASTERS*

THE FOUNDER:

1. Israel ben Eliezer, the Baal Shem Tov (abbrev. the Baal Shem), 1700-1760 [I. 35-86]

GRANDSONS OF THE BAAL SHEM (NOS. 2.3):

2. Moshe Hayyim Efraim of Sadylkov [I. 53, 65, 167]
3. Barukh of Mezbizh, d.1811 [I. 87-97, 167]

GREAT-GRANDSON OF THE BAAL SHEM:

4. Nahman of Bratzlav, d.1810 [I. 74-77]

DISCIPLES OF THE BAAL SHEM (NOS. 5.6.8.10.15.17.18.19.20.21):

5. Dov Baer of Mezritch, "the Great Maggid," d.1772 [I. 98-112]
6. Yaakov Joseph of Polnoye, d.1782 [I. 50-51, 56-59, 100, 167-168]

HIS DISCIPLE:

7. Arye Leib of Spola, "the Spola grandfather," d.1811 [I. 170-172]

8. Pinhas of Koretz, d.1791 [I. 118-137]

HIS DISCIPLE:

9. Rafael of Bershad, d.1816 [I. 122-137]

10. Yehiel Mikhal of Zlotchov, "the Maggid of Zlotchov," d. about 1786 [I. 138-157]

HIS SONS (NOS. 11.12):

11. Mordecai of Kremnitz
12. Zev Wolf of Zbarazh, d.1800 [I. 158-162]

HIS DISCIPLES (NOS. 13.14):

13. Mordecai of Neskhizh, d.1800 [I. 163-166]
14. Aaron Leib of Primishlan

15. Nahum of Tchernobil, d.1798 [I. 60, 85, 172-174]

*The numerals in square brackets refer to the main portions in *Tales of the Hasidim* dealing with the masters in question: I indicates *The Early Masters*; II, *The Later Masters.*

16. Mordecai (Motel) of Tchernobil, d.1837 [I. 55]

17. David Leikes [I. 55, 174]
18. Wolf Kitzes [I. 63-64, 72-73, 77]
19. Meir Margaliot [I. 42-43]
20. Zevi the Scribe [I. 77-78]
21. Leib, son of Sarah [I. 59, 86, 107, 169]

DESCENDANTS OF DOV BAER OF MEZRITCH,
"THE GREAT MAGGID," (NOS. 22-27):

22. Abraham "the Angel," d.1776 [I. 113-117]

HIS SON:

23. Shalom Shakhna of Probishtch, d.1803 [II. 49-51]

SON OF SHALOM:

24. Israel of Rizhyn, d.1850 [II. 52-69]

SONS OF ISRAEL:

25. Abraham Yaakov of Sadagora, d.1883 [II. 70-72]
26. Nahum of Stepinesht [II. 73-74]
27. David Moshe of Tchortkov, d.1903 [II. 74-78]

DISCIPLES OF DOV BAER OF MEZRITCH
(NOS. 28.29.30.37.38.39.43.44.52.57):

28. Menahem Mendel of Vitebsk, d.1788 [I. 175-181]
29. Aaron of Karlin, d.1772 [I. 195-202]
30. Shmelke of Nikolsburg, d.1778 [I. 182-194]

HIS DISCIPLES (NOS. 31.32.36):

31. Abraham Hayyim of Zlotchov
32. Moshe Leib of Sasov, d.1807 [II. 81-95]

SON OF MOSHE LEIB:

33. Shmelke of Sasov

DISCIPLE OF MOSHE LEIB:

34. Menahem Mendel of Kosov, d.1825 [II. 96-98]

SON OF MENAHEM MENDEL:

35. Hayyim of Kosov [II. 98-99]

36. Yitzhak Eisik of Kalev, d.1821 [II. 100-104]

37. Levi Yitzhak of Berditchev, d.1809 [I. 203-234]
38. Meshullam Zusya of Hanipol, d.1800 [I. 235-252]
39. Elimelekh of Lizhensk, Zusya's brother, d.1786 [I. 253-264]

ALPHABETICAL INDEX TO THE GENEALOGY

Peretz (82)
Pinhas of Kinsk (71)
Pinhas of Koretz (8)

Rafael of Bershad (9)

Seer of Lublin, Yaakov Yitzhak of Lublin (57)
Shalom of Belz (68)
Shalom Shakhna of Probishtch (23)
Shelomo Hayyim of Kaidanov (50)
Shelomo of Karlin (44)
Shelomo Leib of Lentshno (66)
Shmelke of Nikolsburg (30)
Shmelke of Sasov (33)
Shneur Zalman of Ladi, the Rav (43)
Simha Bunam of Pzhysha (76)

Uri of Strelisk (45)

Wolf Kitzes (18)

Yaakov Joseph of Polnoye (6)

Yaakov Yitzhak of Lublin, the Seer (57)
Yaakov Yitzhak of Pzhysha, the Yehudi (69)
Yaakov Zevi of Parysov (73)
Yehezkel of Shenyava (61)
Yehiel Mikhal of Zlotchov, the Maggid of Zlotchov (10)
Yehudah Zevi of Rozdol (63)
Yehudah Zevi of Stretyn (46)
Yehudi, the; Yaakov Yitzhak of Pzhysha (69)
Yehoshua Asher (72)
Yerahmiel of Pzhysha (70)
Yisakhar of Wolborz (56)
Yisakhar Baer of Radoshitz (67)
Yitzhak of Vorki (78)
Yitzhak Eisik of Kalev (36)
Yitzhak Eisik of Zhydatchov (64)
Yitzhak Meir of Ger (80)

Zev Wolf of Zbarazh (12)
Zevi Hirsh of Rymanov (41)
Zevi Hirsh of Zhydatchov (62)
Zevi the Scribe (20)
Zusya, Meshullam, of Hanipol (38)

Sephardic pronunciation has been followed in the spelling of the proper names in *Tales of the Hasidim*, exception being made for some names which here appear in their equivalents in the English Bible.

The names of geographical locations appear in a transliteration of their popular Jewish versions. Thus we say Alexander for Alexandrowo, Apt for Opatów, Hanipol for Annopol, Koretz for Korzec, Koznitz for Koziniec, Lizhensk for Leżajsk, Mezbizh for Miedzyborz, Mezritch for Miedzyrzecze, Polnoye for Polennoje, Primishlan for Przemyślany, Pzhysha for Przysucha, Rizhyn for Rużyn, Roptchitz for Ropczyce, Tchernobil for Czernobiel, Zlotchov for Zloczów.

INDEX TO THE TALES

The Descendants of the Great Maggid

344

From the School of Rabbi Shelomo of Karlin

From the House of the Maggid of Koznitz

From the School of the Rabbi of Lublin

Pzhysha And Its Daughter Schools

349